EGYPTIAN READINGBOOK

EGYPTIAN READINGBOOK

EXERCISES AND MIDDLE EGYPTIAN TEXTS

SELECTED AND EDITED

BY

Dr A. DE BUCK
LATE PROFESSOR OF EGYPTOLOGY IN THE UNIVERSITY OF LEIDEN

Fourth Edition

LEIDEN
NEDERLANDS INSTITUUT VOOR HET NABIJE OOSTEN
1977

ISBN 90 6258 107 2

PREFACE

This volume intends to provide students who wish to familiarize themselves with the hieroglyphs, the grammar, and the literature of Middle Egyptian with suitable exercises and texts.

According to my experience the lack of the former is a serious difficulty for beginners. As a rule grammars do not quote more than a few examples and short sentences to illustrate the facts and rules which they record, the number of these quotations being altogether insufficient to inculcate the more vital rules of grammar. Gardiner's Egyptian Grammar *with its wealth of examples and exercises is of course a conspicuous exception; his book, however, is too exhaustive and too ponderous a volume for most beginners. We hope that the abundance of illustrative examples corresponding to the various subjects of grammar, which are offered in the first part of this book will smooth the student's path and prove a useful supplement of the current Egyptian grammars and that the book will make the study of these grammars more attractive. The numbers of §§ mentioned in the headings of the sections refer to the §§ of my short elementary* Egyptische Grammatica *(in Dutch) of which a French translation is ready since long and will be published as soon as circumstances allow it. A transcription of pp. 7—37 has been added in order to help the beginning student in his rather tedious search for signs in the sign-list and to give him the means of controlling his finds. Afterwards he is supposed to be familiar with most signs and to be able to find his way in the sign-list with some ease. The references of the type (A 1) refer to section and number of Gardiner's Sign-list or other lists which follow his system.*

As to the second part of the book we hope that this selection of Middle Egyptian pieces may also fill up a void. At present Erman's delightful little Aegyptische Chrestomathie *of 1904 is a rare and nearly forgotten book and as Sethe's* Aegyptische Lesestücke *is also out of print and difficult to be found, no handy reading-book for students seems to exist for the time being. The present chrestomathy contains, as we hope, a fairly representative selection of historical, literary, and religious texts composed in the classical Middle Egyptian language. As to this collection little need be said. Although presumably others will have other predilections, an attempt has been made to offer texts of varying contents so that everybody may find something to his taste. We also intended to give both easier and more difficult pieces. We may remark here that the story of Sinuhe has been excluded intentionally from the literary texts, as this text is accessible to all students in Blackman's edition in the* Bibliotheca Aegyptiaca.

A second volume will provide the rest of the notes on purely textual matters of which a few pages have already been included in this book. That second volume will also contain a vocabulary and a series of philological explanations, rather detailed and complete in the initial pieces, more succinct and rare in the latter parts of the book.

TABLE OF CONTENTS

HISTORICAL TEXTS

LITERARY TEXTS

RELIGIOUS TEXTS

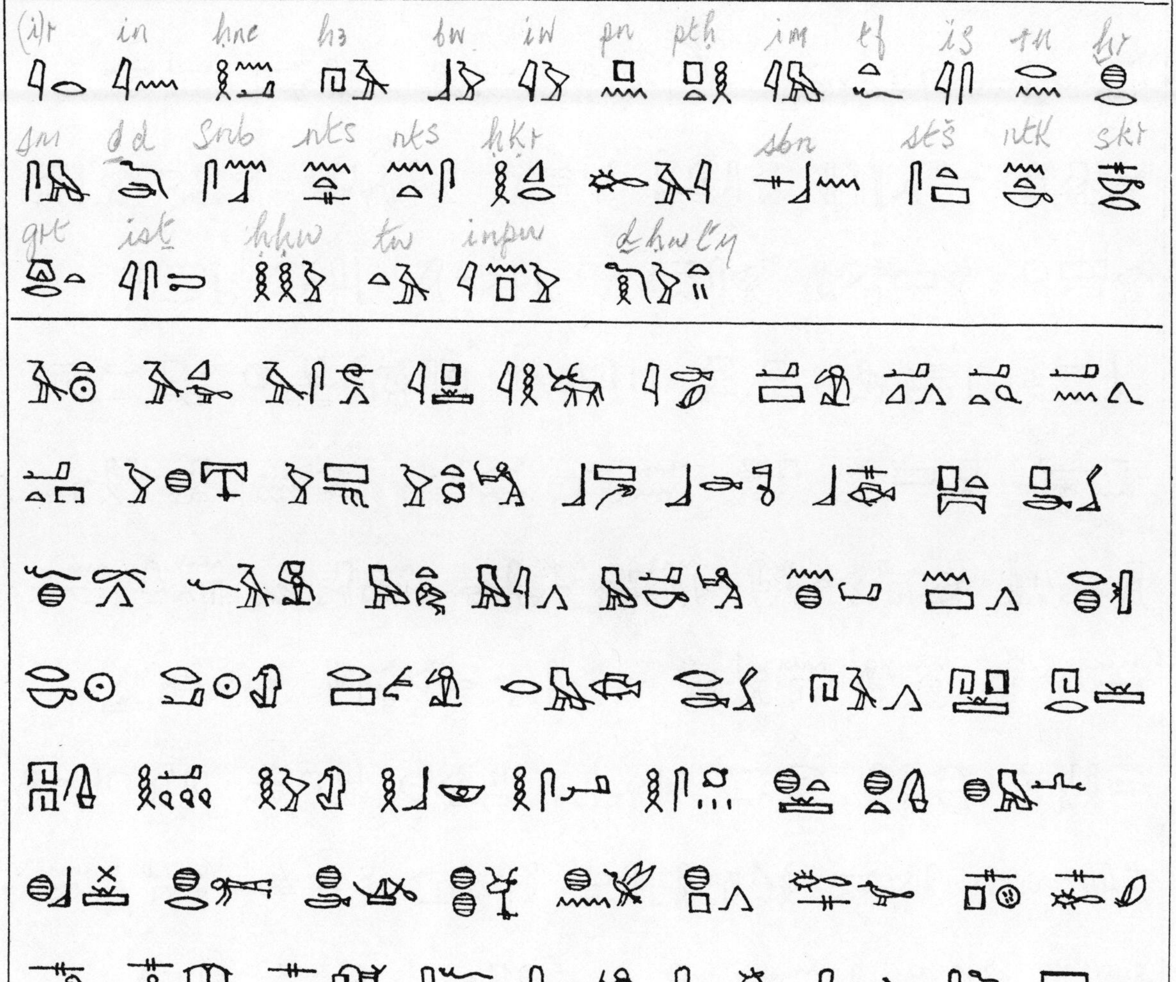
(i)r in ḥnc ḥ3 bw iw pn ptḥ im tf is sn ḥr
sm ḏd snb nts nts ḥkr sbn sts ntk skr
grt ist ḥḥw tw inpw ḏḥwty

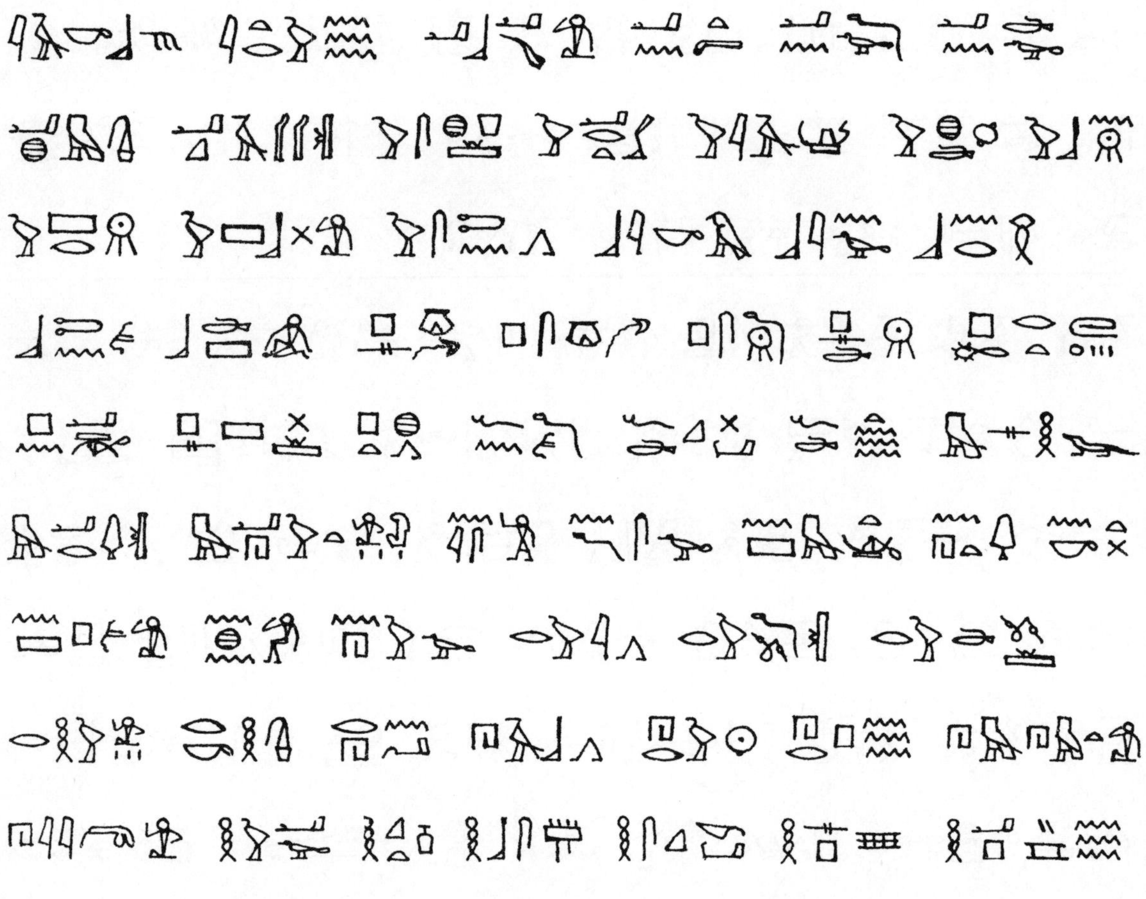

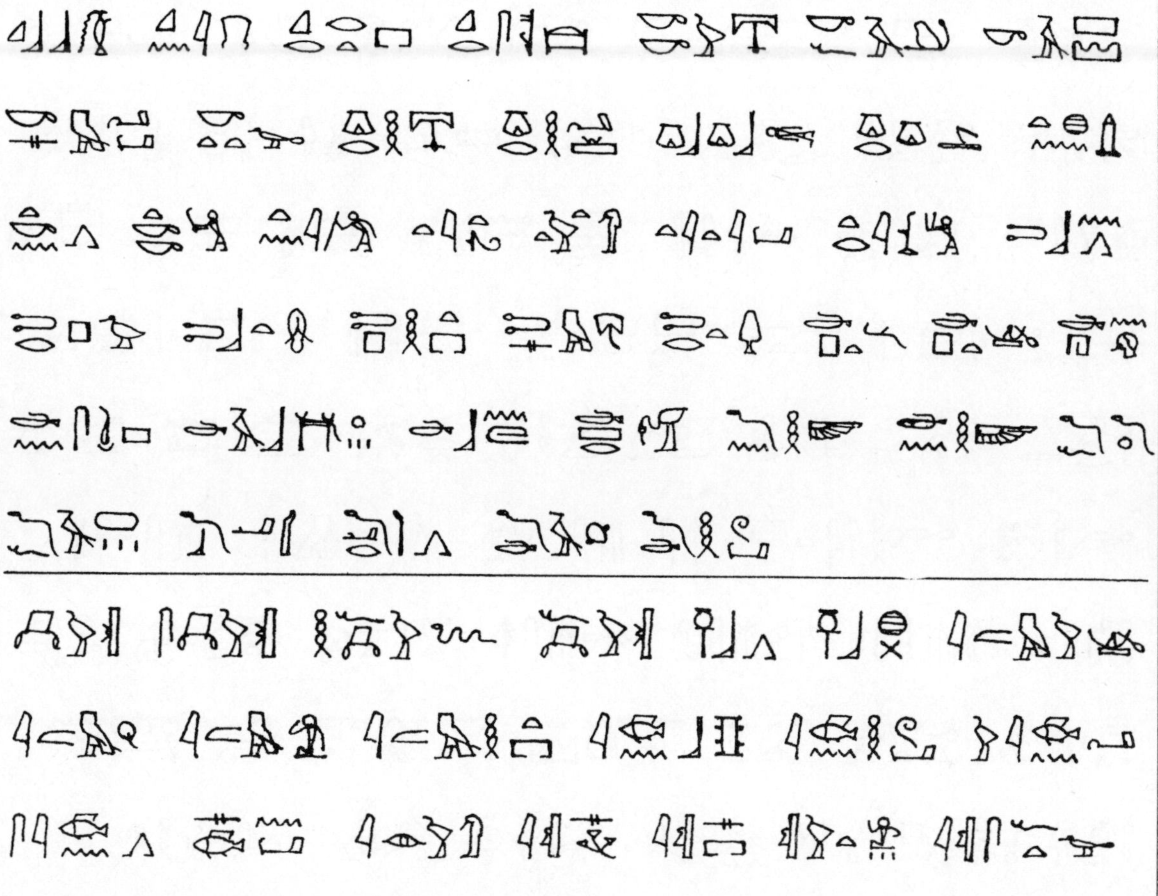

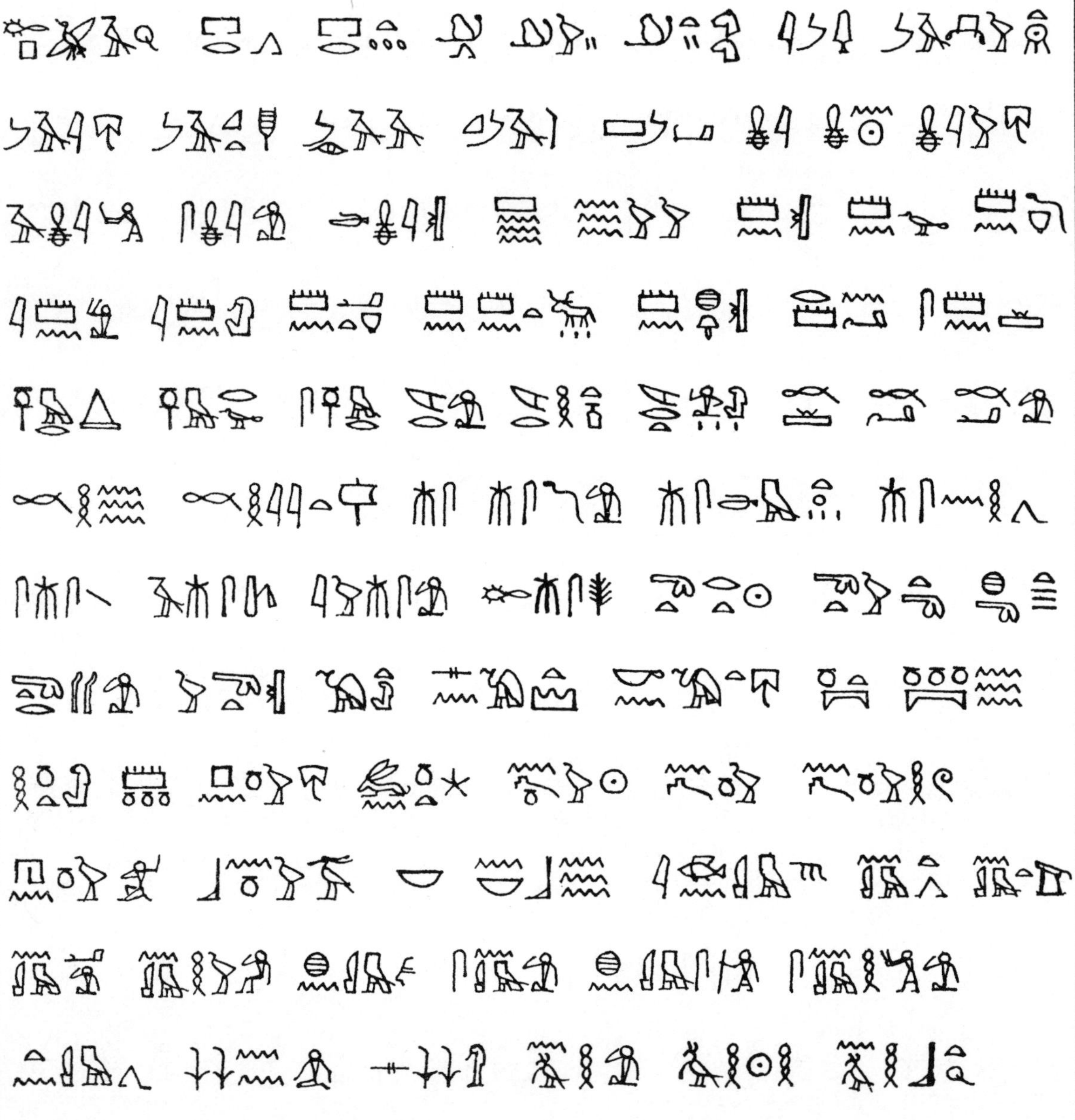

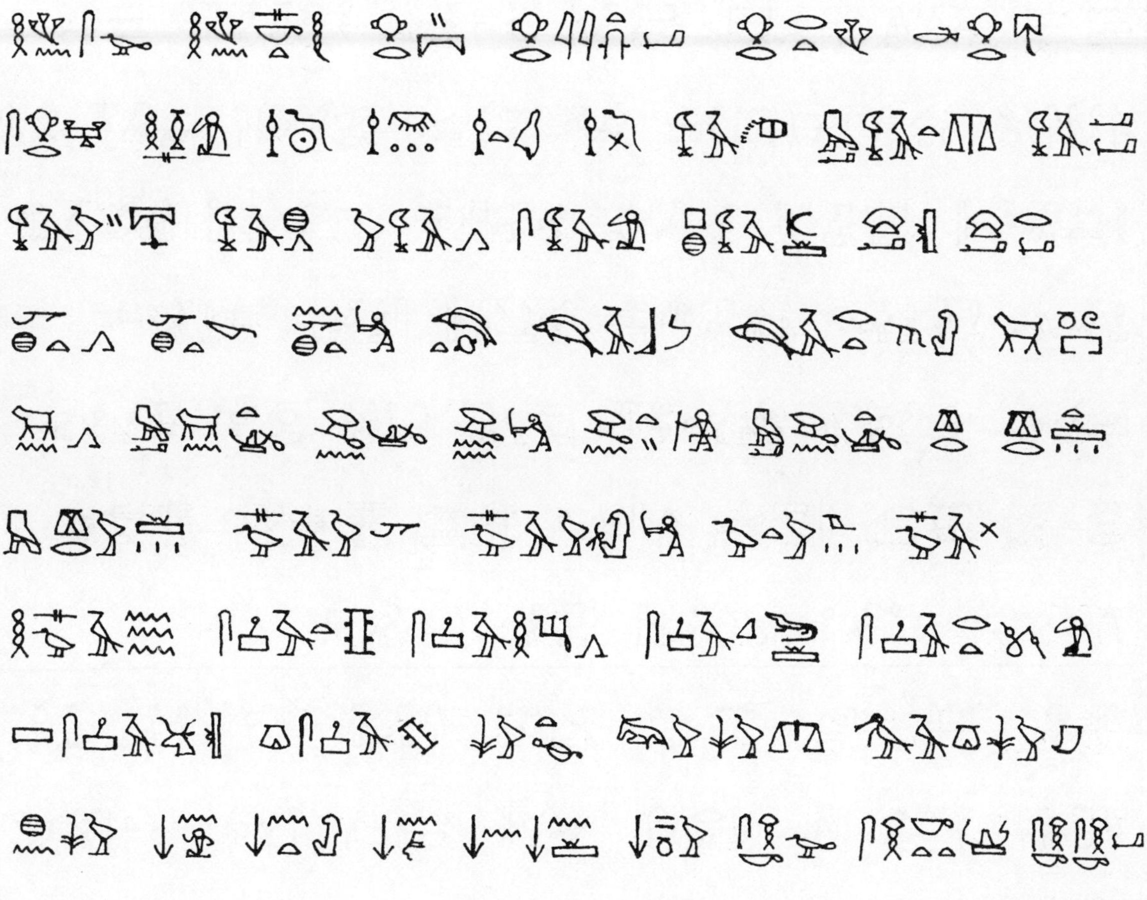

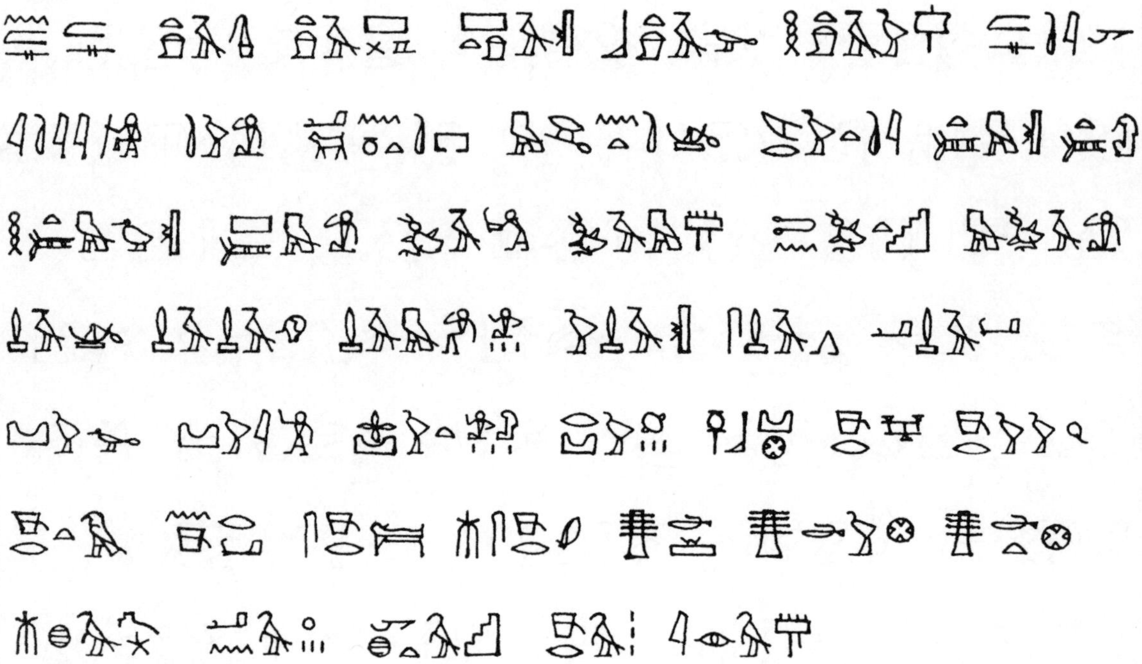

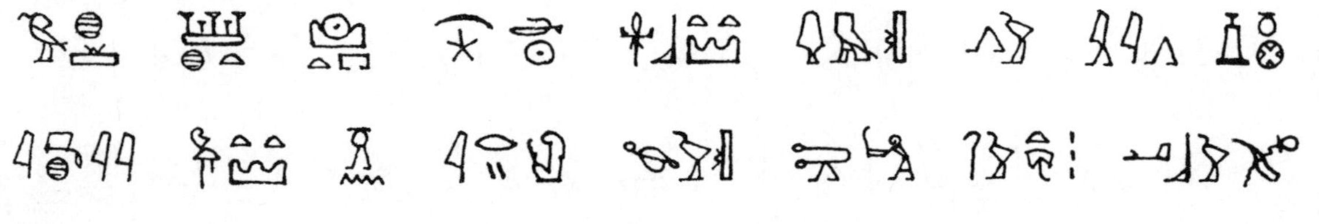

The commonest ideograms. The references in brackets of the type (G 25) refer to section and number of Gardiner's Sign-list.

ꜣḫ (G 25), ꜣḫ·t (M 8), ꜣḫ·t (N 27), ꜣbd (N 11, 14), ỉꜣbt·t (R 15), ỉꜣm (M 1), ỉw (D 54), ỉỉ (M 18), ỉwnw (O 28),

ỉmꜣḫj (F 39), ỉmnt·t (R 14), ỉnỉ (W 25), ỉrj (A 48), ỉśw (F 44), ỉṯỉ (V 15), ꜥw·t (S 38, 39), ꜥbw (F 17)

ꜥpr (Aa 20), ꜥnḫ (S 34), ꜥrḳ, ꜥrḳj (V 12), ꜥḥ (O 11), ꜥḥꜣ (D 34), ꜥḥꜥ (P 6),

ꜥšꜣ (I 1), wꜣḥ (V 29), wꜣś (S 40), wꜣś·t (R 19), wꜣḏ (M 13), wꜥb (D 60), wbꜣ (U 26), wḫm (F 25)

wḥꜥ (P 4), wśr (F 12), wḏꜥ (Aa 21), bꜣḥ (D 53), bỉtj (L 2), bỉꜣ (N 41), pẖr (F 46), pśḏ·t (N 9), mꜣꜥ (Aa 11),

mꜣꜥ (Aa 11), mšꜥ (A 12), mdw (S 43), mḏ (V 21), mḏḥ (S 10), mḏd (Aa 23), nbw (S 12), nfr (F 35),

nṯr (R 8), nḏm (M 29), rwḏ (T 12), rnp·t (M 4), rś (T 13), rśj (M 24), ḥ·t (O 6), ḥꜣtj (F 4), ḥp·t (Aa 5), ḥm (U 36), ḥm·t (U 24),

bỉꜣ (N 34), ḥnmm·t (N 8), ḥḳꜣ (S 38), ḥtp (R 4), ḫpr (L 1), ḫnr·t (U 31), ḫnt (W 17), ḫrw (P 8),

ḫśf (U 34, 35), ẖnm (W 9), sꜣw (A 47), sj (O 35), sỉnw (T 11), smꜣ (F 36), sš (Y 3), stỉ (Aa 32),

[§26] 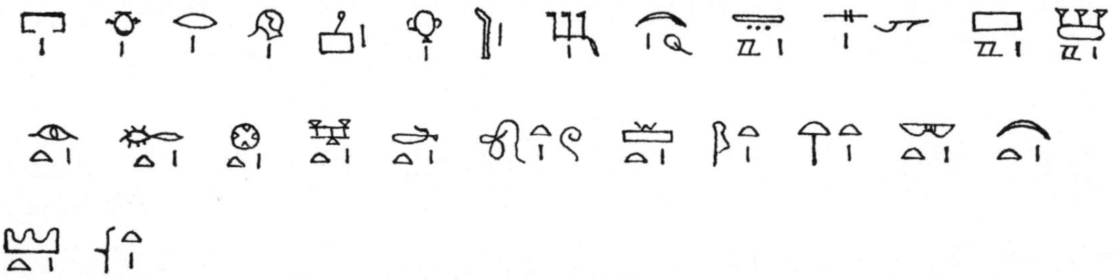

[§27] 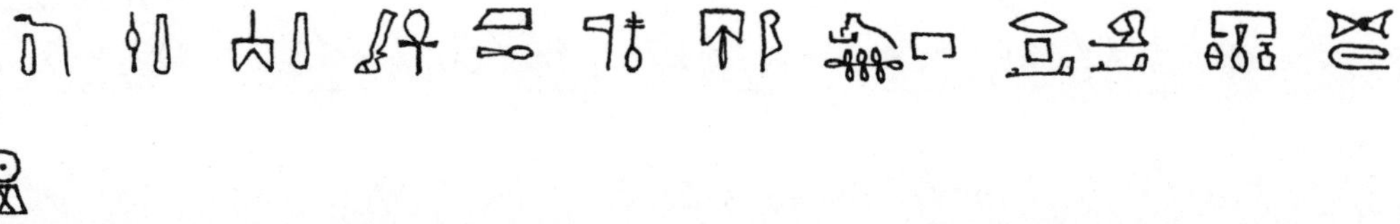

[§29] 

[§32] 

[§33] 

sbỉ(O35), ś·t(Q1), śỉꜣ(S32), śwꜣỉ(Z9), śbꜣ(N14), špr(F42), śpd·t(M44), śmśw, wr(A19), śnḏ(G54), śḫ·t(M20), śḫm(S42), śšm(T31,32), śṯꜣ(V2), śḏb(after U12), śḏm(F21), špśỉ(A50), šmꜥw(M26,27), šmś(T18), šnꜥ(U13), ššp(O42), ššꜣw(F5), kn(Aa8), kꜣp(R5), gb(G38), grg(U17), ṯ(X1,2), ṯꜣ-wr(O16), tpj(T8), ṯḥn·t(S15), ṯꜣw(P5), dwꜣw(N14), ḏbn(F46), dmḏ(S23), dšr·t(G27), ḏꜥm(S41), ḏb·t(G22), ḏbꜣ(T25), ḏbꜥ·t(D50), dšr(D45).

wśỉr(Q1), śḏꜣwtj(S19), ḏỉ, rḏỉ(X8,D37), ššr(V33), ỉt(4 spellings), nj-św·t(M23)

pr(O1), ỉb(F34), r(D21), tp(D1), śꜣ(Aa17,18), ḥr(D2), ḏbꜥ(D50), *špr(F42), tꜣ(N16), s(O34), š(N37), šꜣ(M8), wp·t(F13), ỉr·t(D4), ḥ·t(F32), nỉw·t(O49), wꜣ·t(N31), dr·t(D46), wꜣ·t(V4), mḏꜣ·t(Y1), św·t(H6), šw·t(S35), pḏ·t(T10), śp·t(D24), ḥꜣ·t(F4), ḥꜣś·t(N25), rnp·t(M4). *śꜣḥ(D61)

Abbreviations. ḏd mdw, wḏ mdw, wḏꜥ mdw, wḥm ꜥnḫ, mꜣꜥ ḫrw, nṯr nfr, śꜣb šw·t, śtp sꜣ, ỉrj-pꜥ·t ḥꜣtj-ꜥ, pr·t ḫrw, ṯs pḥr, ḥr·t nṯr, ḥr·t ḫrw.

Transpositions. ḥm nṯr, mdw nṯr, sḥ nṯr, ỉt nṯr mrj nṯr, pr nj-św·t, sꜣ nj-św·t, ḥtp ḏỉ nj-św·t, śnṯr.

Mixed spellings. ỉmꜣ > (i.e. gives rise to) ỉꜣm, ḳmꜣ > ḳꜣm, mꜣr > mꜣỉ, dꜣr > dꜣỉ, swr > swỉ, kꜣr > kꜣỉ, śmꜣ > śꜣm, fśỉ > pśỉ, npr > npỉ.

Group-writing. ḫrb, krkmš, ỉṯn, śrkš.

[§§ 34-45]

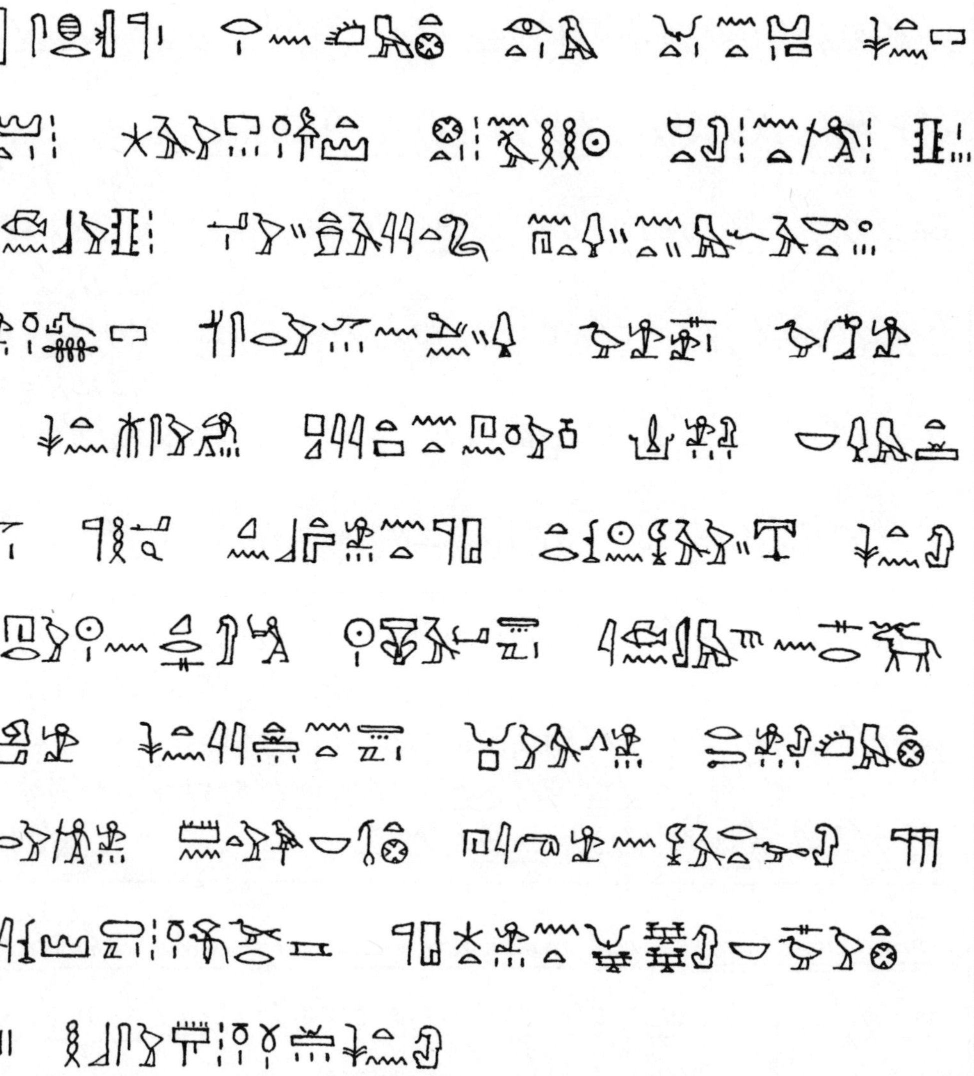

[§§ 46-59]

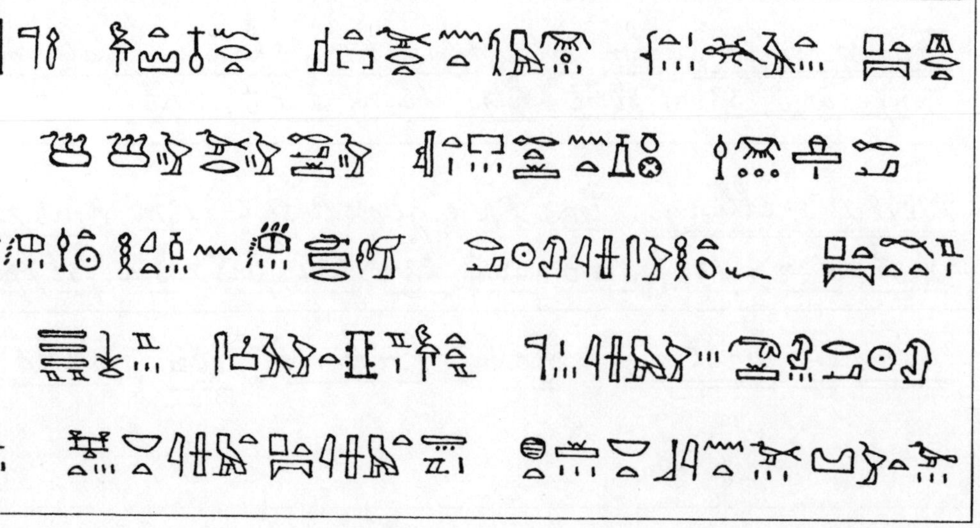

Nouns (gender, number). Genitive (direct, indirect). Apposition.

śḫr nṯr, r n(j) km·t, ir·t ḥr, wp·t n(j)·t ḏw, pr nj-św·t,

ḥḳꜣ·w ḫꜣś·wt, śbꜣ·w nj·w imn·t, niw·wt nḥḥ, ḥm·wt nj(·w)t wr·w,

inb·w ḥḳꜣ, ꜥ·wj tꜣj·t, nh·tj nj·tj mfkꜣ·t,

śmr·w nj·w śtp-sꜣ, wśr·w n hbnj, sꜣ s, sꜣ wꜥb,

sꜣ nj-św·t, mś·w nj-św·t, pkj·t n(j)·t hnw, ḥm·w kꜣ, nb iꜣm·t,

mrḥ·t n ḫt, ḥꜥ nṯr, ḳnb·t n(j)·t ḥ·t nṯr, tr n(j) ḫꜣwj, nj-św·t

n(j) km·t, hrw n(j) ḳrś, hrw smꜣ-tꜣ, inm n(j) sr, ḥ·(w)t pr ḥꜣtj-ꜥ,

nśj·t(?) n(j)·t tꜣ, wpwtj·w, rmṯ km·t, sḥ n(j) śr·w, mnṯw

nb wꜣś·t, ḥi n(j) ḫꜣr·t, nṯr·w nb·w (§51) tꜣ-mri iw·w nj·w wꜣḏ-wr,

wnw·t ḥ·t nṯr n(j)·t wp-wꜣ·wt nb sꜣwtj, ḥḳ·t dś 2, ḥbś·w nj·w śšr-nj-św·t.

Adjectives; used as epithets or nouns; qualified by a noun; degrees of comparison.

nṯr ꜥꜣ, imn·t nfr·t, ś·t wr·t n(j)·t ḏꜥm, rnp·(w)t ꜥšꜣ·(w)t, p·t hrj·t,

p·t ẖrj·t, sś·wj wr·wj ꜥꜣ·wj, is·t ꜥꜣ·t n(j)·t iwnw, ḥḏ ḥtp ꜥꜣ,

ṯ n(j) bd·t ḥḏ·t ḥḳ·t n it dšr, rꜥ imj śwḥ·t·f (his egg), p·t mḥtj·t,

ḫꜣś·(w)t mḥtj(·w)t, tꜣ·w rśj·w, sꜣw·t imntj·t, nṯr·w imj·w-bꜣḥ rꜥ,

nṯr·w iꜣbtj·w, wꜣ·wt nb·(w)t imj·(w)t p·t imj·(w)t tꜣ, ḫ·t nb·t bin·t ḏw·t,

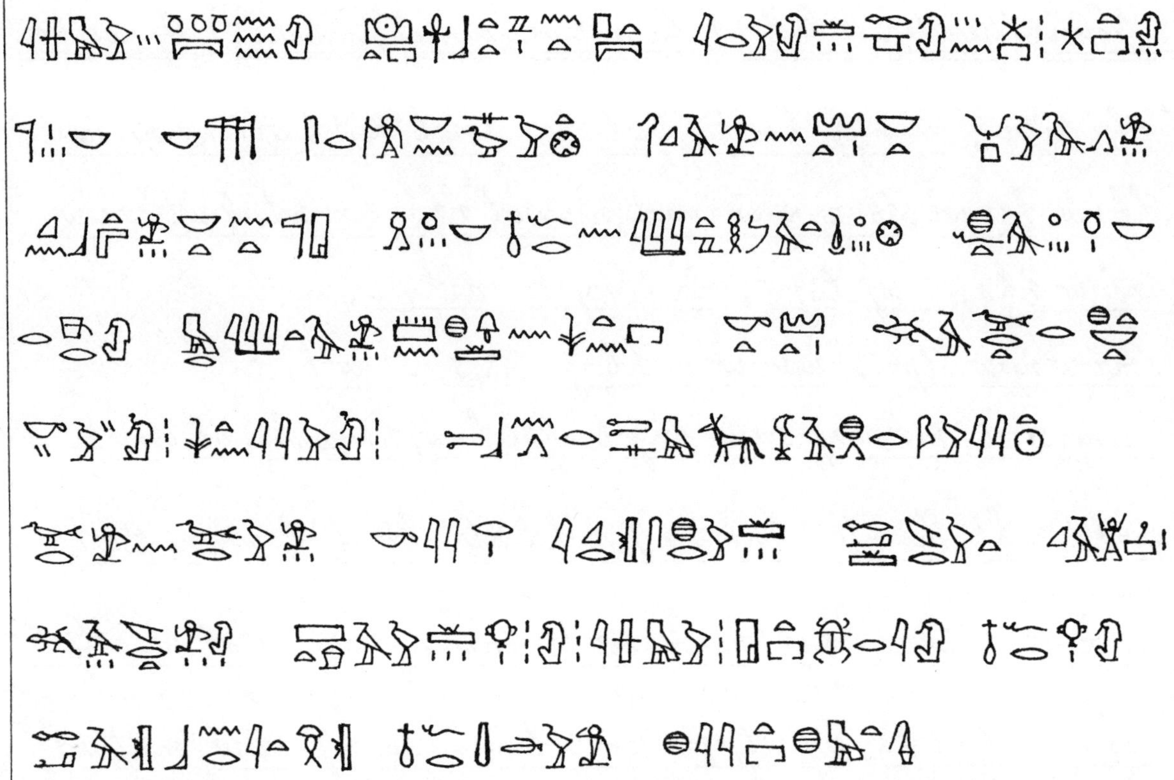

[§ 63]

[§§ 70-73]

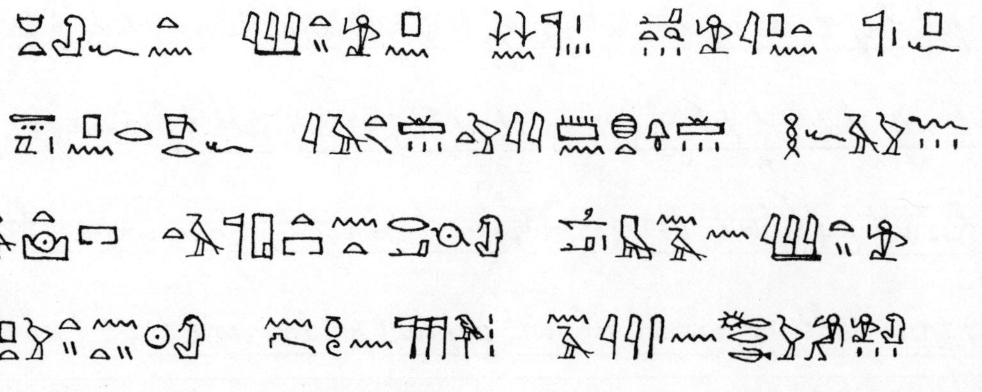

ỉmj·w nww, ꜣḫ·t ỉꜣbt(j)·t n(j)·t p·t, ỉrj·w-ꜥꜣ n śbꜣ·w dꜣ·t, nṯr·w nb(w), nb nṯr·w, śr nb n(j) sꜣwtj, ḥḳꜣ n(j) ḫꜣś·t nb·t, wpwtj·w, ḳnb·t nb·t n(j)·t ḥ·t nṯr, ỉnw nb nfr n(j) sḫ·t ḥmꜣ·t, ḫftj·w nj·w nb-r-ḏr, ỉmj-r sḫtj·w mnḫ n(j) pr nj-św·t, k·t ḫꜣś·t, ꜥšꜣ wr·t r ḫt nb·t, kj·wj njw-św·t(?), ṯbn r ṯsm ḫꜣḫ r šw·t(>šj·t), wr n(j) wr·w, kj r, ỉḳr sḫr·w, ꜥꜣ mrw·t, kꜣ(i) sꜣ, ꜥšꜣ mr·t, štꜣ·w-ḫr ỉmj·w ḥ·t ḫpri, nfr ḥr, ꜥꜣ bnr·t(>bni·t), nfr mdw, ḫj·t ḥm·t.

The Suffix-pronouns.

ib·śn, rd·wj·i, ꜥ·wj·kj, ib n(j) ḥm·k, nṯr·tn niwtj, ib·n, iwꜥ·t n(j)·t it·f, pr nj-św·t ꜥnḫ wḏꜣ śnb mi ḳi·f, ḏw·t ỉrj·t·i, ḫpri ḫrj-ib wiꜣ·f, ỉmj·w ꜣbd·śn, wꜥ im·ṯn nb, s·t-ḥm(w)t nfr·(w)t n(j)·(w)t ḥꜥ·w·śn.

The Demonstratives.

ḥm·t·f tn, sḫtj pn, nn nṯr·w, ꜥ·wt·i iptn, nṯr pf mnḫ, tꜣ pn r ḏr·f, iꜣ·t twj mnḫ·t, ḥfꜣ·w ipw n(j)·w ꜣḫ·t, tꜣ ḥ·t-nṯr n(j)·t rꜥ, wꜥ m nꜣ n sḫtj, mrw·tj iptw·tj n(j)·tj rꜥ, nw n nṯr·w, nꜣj·ś n ḫrd·w.

[§60; §220]

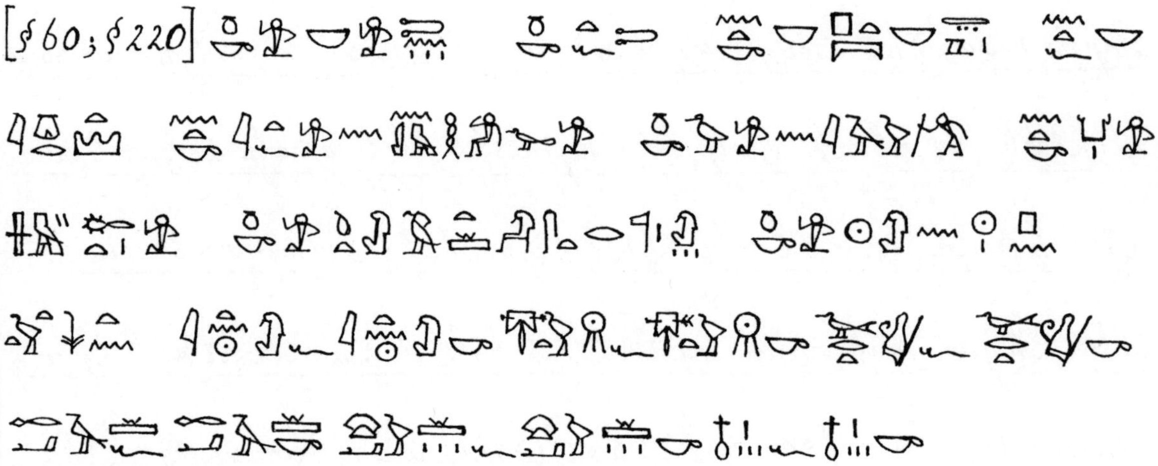

[§61; §232; §233; §236; §241]

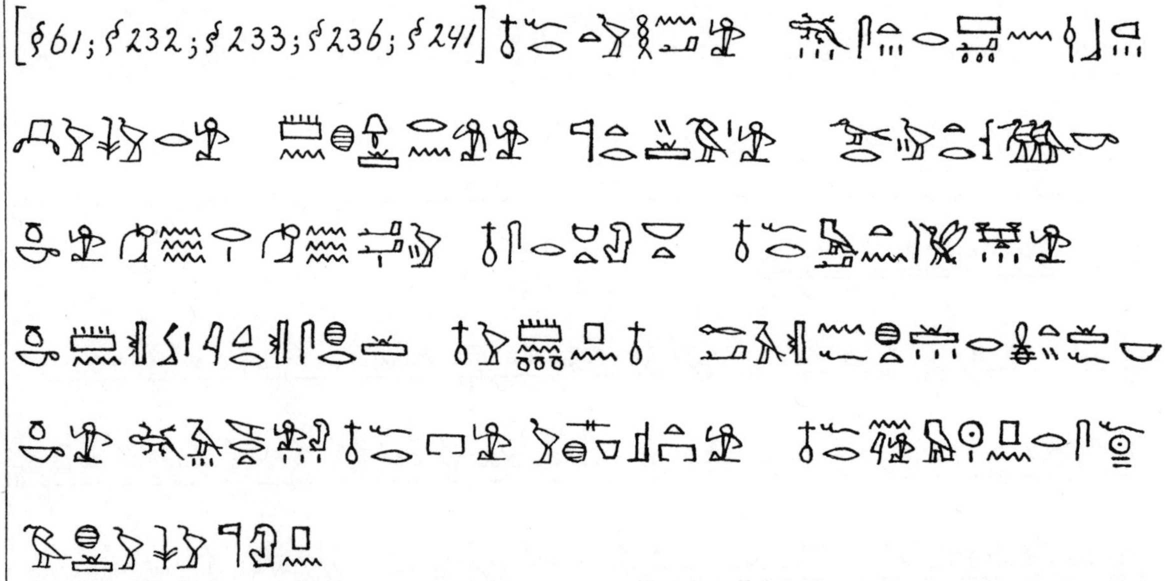

[§61; §203; §205; §207]

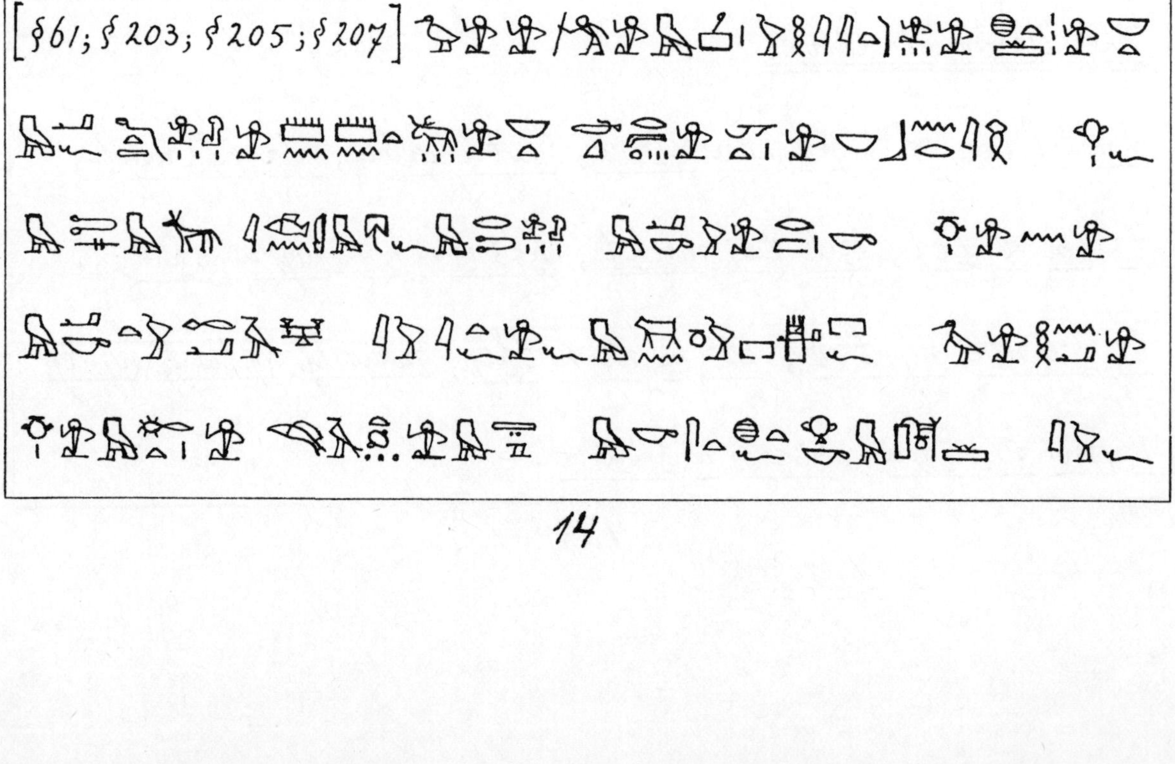

The independent pronouns. Syntax of non-verbal sentences with substantival predicate.

ink nb·tn; ink it·ṯ; ntk nb p·t nb tꜣ; ntf nb igr·t; ntk it n(j) nmḥ; ink sꜣ n(j) iꜣw; ntk kꜣ·i imj ẖ·t·i; ink ꜣs·t ꜣḫ·t špsi·t r nṯrw, ink rꜥ n(j) ḥrw pn; ṯwt nj-św·t; itn·f itn·k, śtw·t·f śtw·t·k, wr·t·f wr·t·k, ꜥꜣ·f ꜥꜣ·k, ḫꜥw·f ḫꜥw·k, nfrw·f nfrw·k.

The dependent pronouns. Syntax of non-verbal sentences with adjectival predicate.

nfr ṯw ḥnꜥ·i; ꜥšꜣ śt r śꜥ n(j) wḏb/w; ꜣw św r·i; mnḫ rn·i; nṯrj ꜣḫ·i; wr wj tr bꜣ·w·k; ink wꜥb r wꜥb ꜥ·wj; nfr ś(j) r ḥm·t nb·t; nfr mṯn·w·i; ink mn rd iḳr sḫr; nfr w(j) mnw pn nfr; ꜥꜣ n·f ḫt r mitj·f nb; ink ꜥšꜣ mr·t, nfr pr·i, wśḫ ś·t·i; nfr n·i m ḥrw pn r śf; ꜣḫ wj św nṯr pn.

The dependent pronouns. Syntax of non-verbal sentences with adverbial predicate.

sꜣ·i śmśw·i m-sꜣ wḥj·t·i, ẖ·t·i nb·t m-ꜥ·f ḏ·t·i mnmn·t·i nb·t dḳr·w·i ẖt·i nb bnr; ḥr·f m ṯsm, inm·f m rmṯ; mk wi r gś·k; ib·i n·i; mk ṯw ꜥꜣ; iw it·f m-ẖnw ꜥḥ·f; bꜣ·i ḥnꜥ·i, ib·i m ẖ·t·i, ẖꜣ·t·i m tꜣ; mk śt ḫft ḥr·k m sš; iw·f

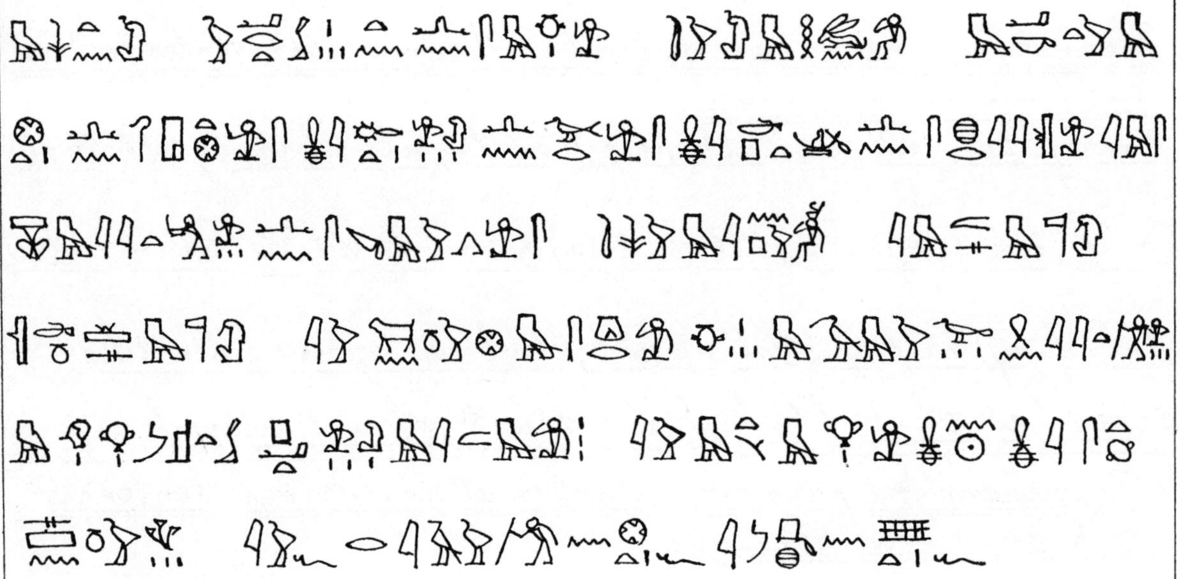

[§§ 222-224]

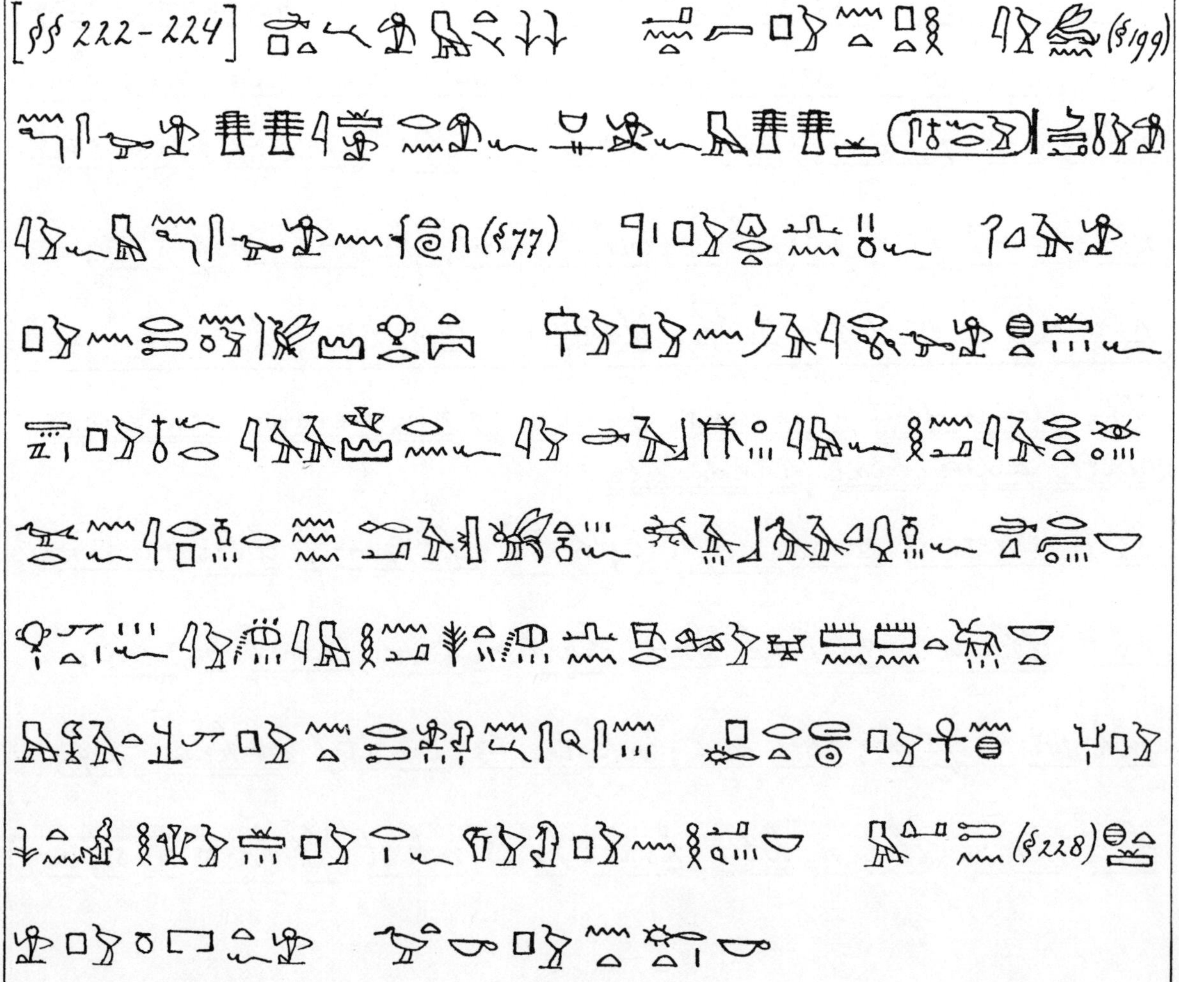
(§199)
(§77)
(§228)

m.nj-św·t; wꜥr·t tn nn ś(j) m ỉb·ỉ; tỉ wỉ m ḥwn; mk ṯw m nỉwt nn ḥḳꜣ-ḥ·t·ś, mỉ ẖ·t nn wr·ś, mỉ dp·t nn śḫrj ỉm·ś, smꜣj·t nn śšmw·ś; tỉ św m ỉnpw; ỉm·ś m nṯr, ḳd·ś m nṯr; ỉw ẖnw m śgr, ỉb·w m gmw, šnj·t m tp-ḥr-mꜣś·t, pꜥ·t m ỉm(w); ỉw mt m ḥr·ỉ mỉn mỉ śṯ(ỉ) sšn·w; ỉw·f r ỉꜣw n(j) nỉw·t·f, ỉmꜣḫ(w) n(j) śp·t·f.

Syntax of non-verbal sentences with substantival predicate.

dp·t mt nn; ꜥn·t pw n(j)·t ptḥ; ỉw wn nḏś ḏdỉ rn·f, ḥmś(w)·f m ḏd-snfrw mꜣꜥ-ḫrw, ỉw·f m nḏś n(j) rnp·t 110; nṯr pw grt nn śn·nw·f; ḥḳꜣ pw n(j) rṯnw ḥrj·t; ṯꜣw pw n(j) mꜣr ḫ(w)t·f; tꜣ pw nfr ỉꜣꜣ rn·f, ỉw dꜣb·w ỉm·f ḥnꜥ ỉꜣrr·(w)t, wr n·f ỉrp r mw, ꜥꜣ bỉ·t·f, ꜥšꜣ bꜣḳ·f, dḳr·w nb ḥr ḫt·w·f, ỉw ỉt ỉm ḥnꜥ bd·t, nn ḏrw mnmn·t nb·t; mḫꜣ·t pw n(j)·t rmṯ nś·śn; pẖr·t pw ꜥnḫ; kꜣ pw nj-św·t, ḥꜣw pw r·f, ẖnmw pw n(j) ḥꜥ nb; mṯn ḫ·t·ỉ pw nj·w pr ỉt·ỉ; sꜣ·t·k pw n(j)·t ẖ·t·k.

[§§84-96; §158; §155]

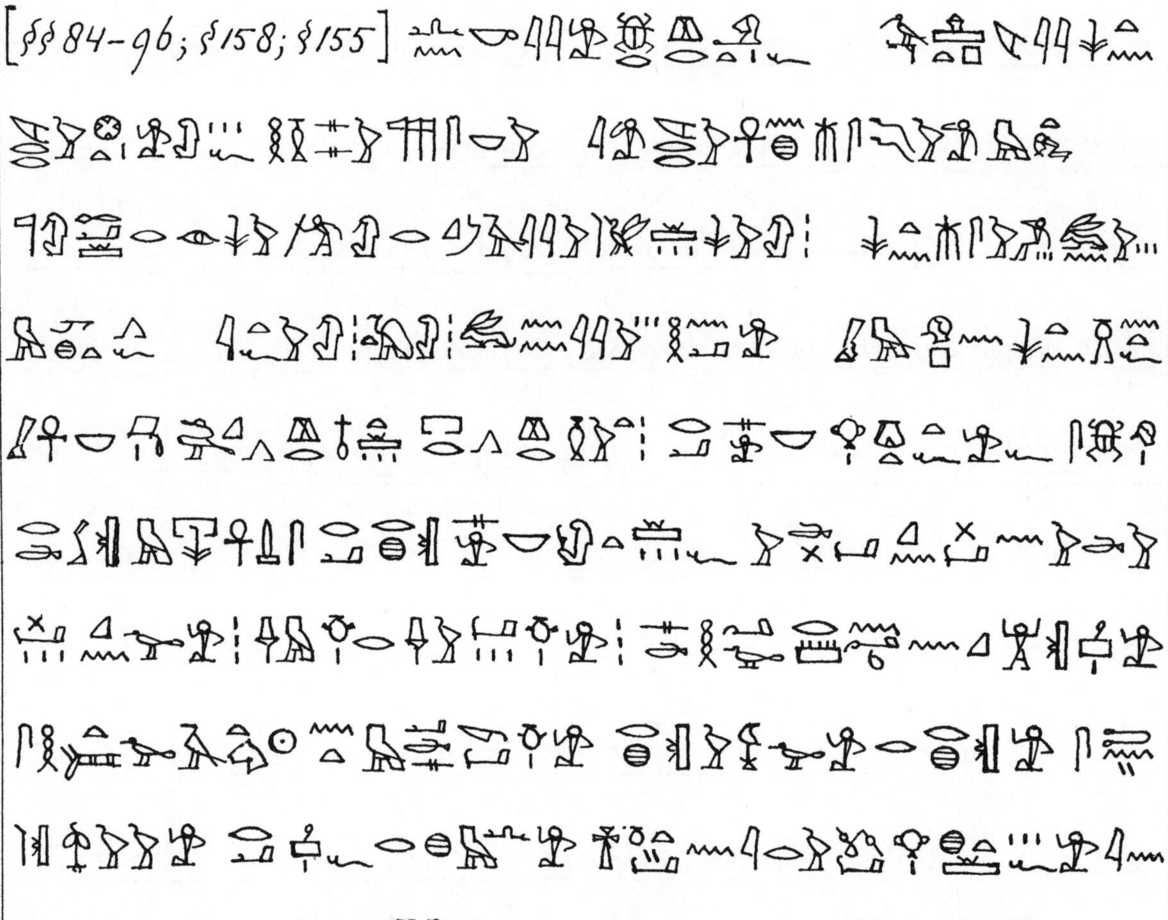

The Participles; used as epithets or nouns; expression of object and subject; negation of the participles.

nn kj ḫpr ḫr-ḥ3·t·f ; ḏḥwtj-ḥtp (name of person) mrj nj-św·t, mrr·w niw·t·f, ḥss·w nṯr·w·ś nb·w; i mrr·w ʿnḫ mśḏḏ·w mt; nṯr ʿ3 r iri św wr r ḳm3·jw św; mś·w nj-św·t wn·w m-ḫt·f; it·w mw·(w)t wnn·jw ḥnʿ·i; whm(w) tpj n(j) nj-św·t intf (personal name) whm ʿnḫ nb im3ḫ, ʿḳ ḫr nfr·t, pri ḫr ḥsw·t, rdi s nb ḥr nś·t it·f, śḫpr tp-rd m pr nj-św·t ʿnḫ wḏ3 śnb, rdi rḫ s (§126,2) nb irj·t·f, wd(i) ḳn(i) n wd(i)·w ḳn(i), śḫm ib r śḫm·w ib, śdḥ rmn n(j) ḳ3(i) ś3, śḫtm 3·t n(j)·t mdś ib, rḫ wḫ3 r rḫ, śtnj ḥmww, rdi ś3·f r ḫm, nḏtj n(j) ir·w ḥr ḥ(w)t·f in wśr r·f; rḫt inw inj n b3·w ḥm·f in wr·w nj·w rṯnw; pr·t nṯr 3ḫ·t pri·t ḫnt·f; imj-r pr wr krs (personal name) ḫrp rś tp n(j) mw·t nj-św·t, tm ṯni(·w) grḥ r hrw; i ʿʿn·w (the last ⌐□ is superfluous) ipw ḥmśj·w m-ḥ3·t wi3 n(j) rʿ, śʿr·jw m3ʿt n nb-r-ḏr, wpp·jw m3r ḥnʿ wśr, śḥtp·jw nṯr·w m ḫh n(j) r·śn, didj·w ḥtp(·w)-nṯr n nṯr·w pr·t-r-ḫrw n 3ḫ·w, ʿnḫ·jw m m3ʿ·t, śʿm·jw m m3ʿ·t ib; s3 rʿ ḏḥwtj-mś(w) ini ḏr·w t3 ḥr nḏb(w)·t·f, ḫnd pḥ·wj·fj m ḫpš·f;

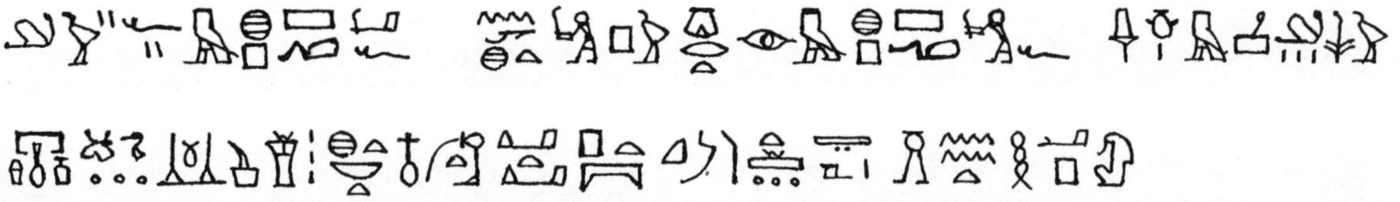

[§221]

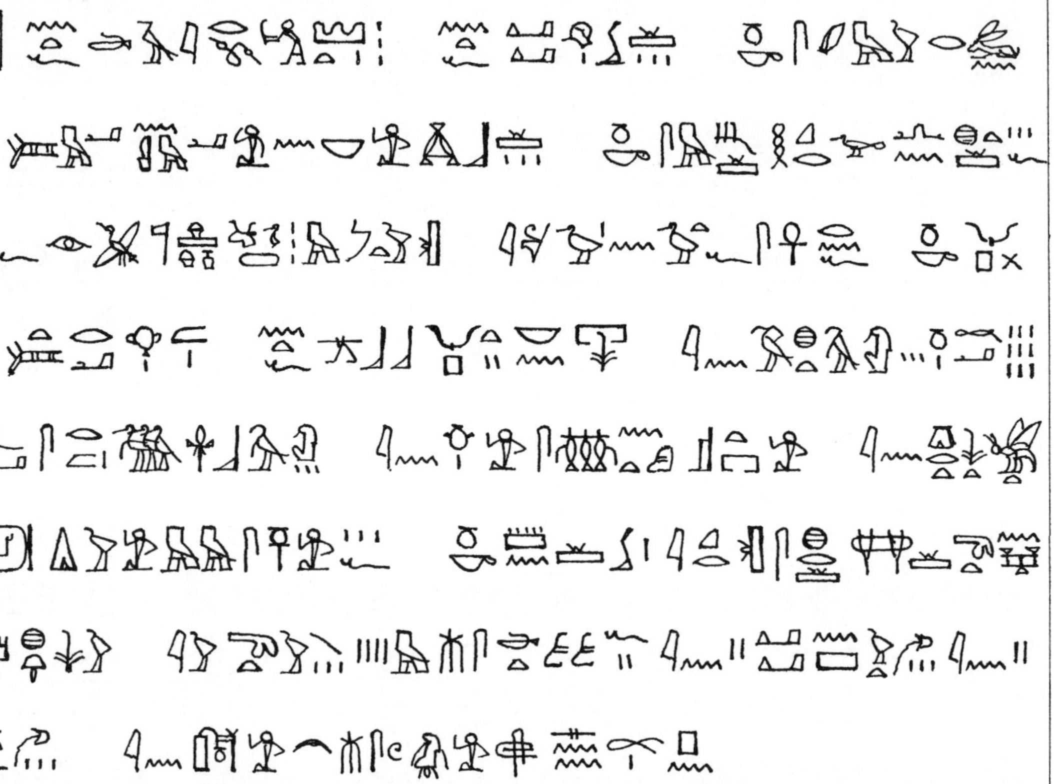

[§§97-107]

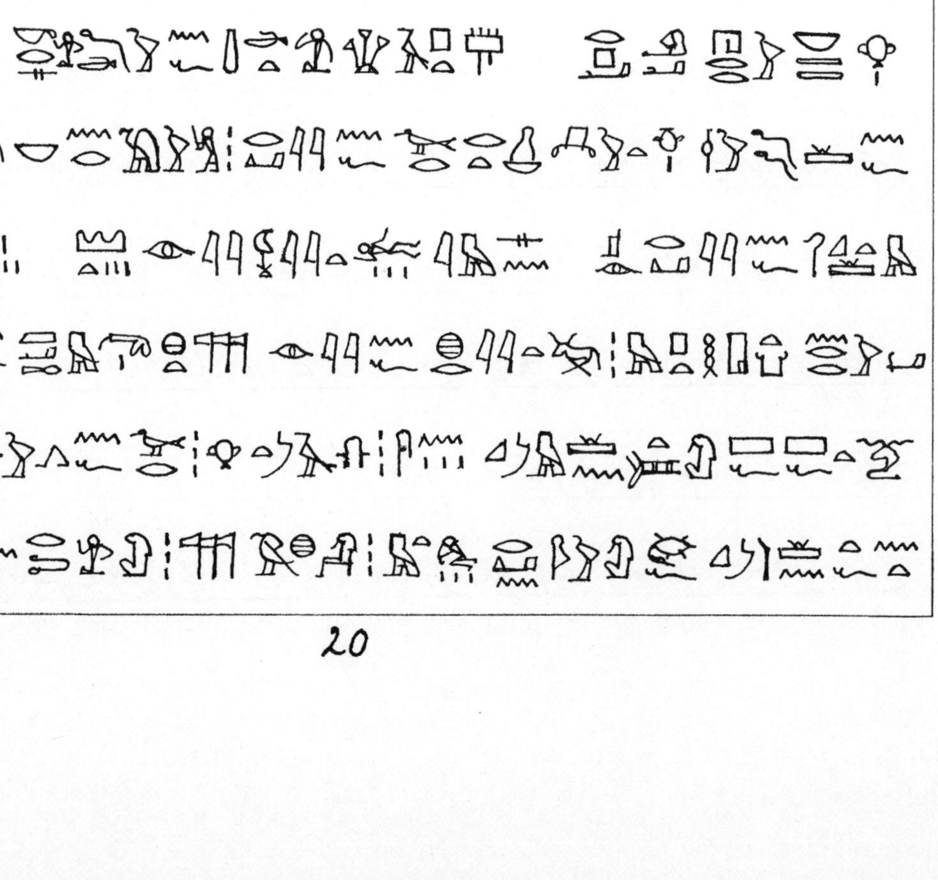

nḫt pw grt ỉri m ḫpš·f; śḫm ỉb m-sꜣ pḥ·w św; pr·t-ḫrw (m) t (m) ḥḳ·t (m) kꜣ·w (m) ꜣpd·w (m) šś (m) mnḫ·t (m) snṯr (m) mrḥ·t (m) ḫt nb·t nfr(·t) wꜥb·t, ḏỉḏỉ·t p·t, ḳmꜣ·t tꜣ, ỉnn·t ḥꜥpj.

The active participles as predicate in non-verbal sentences.

ntf ḏꜣr ḫꜣś·(w)t; ntf ḏỉḏỉ tp-rd; ỉnk śḏm·w r wn-mꜣꜥ, tm nmꜥ(·w)n nb ḏbꜣ·w; ỉnk śm ḥkr nn ḥ·t·f; ỉn ḥm·f ỉri pꜣ ḥtp-nṯr m mꜣw·t; ỉn sꜣ n(j) sꜣ·t·f śꜥnḫ rn·f; ỉnk wpỉ mꜣꜥ·t, tm rdỉ(·w) ḥr gś; ntf sbb wpwtj nb n(j) pr nj-św·t; ỉn ꜣḫtj·w nj·w mḥ 9 ꜣsḫ ś(j) r-gś bꜣ·w ỉꜣbtj·w; ỉn ỉb·ỉ śḫnt ś·t·ỉ; ỉn grt nj-św·t bỉtj ḫpr-kꜣ-rꜥ ḏỉ wỉ mm śmr·w·f; ỉnk mn rd, ỉḳr śḫr, mḏd mtn n(j) śmnḫ św; ỉw mt·w 4 m mśḏ·tj·fj, ỉn 2 ḏỉḏỉ nśw·t, ỉn 2 ḏỉḏỉ snf; ỉn sš ỉꜥḥ-mś(w) (personal name) śpḫr snn pn.

Complex constructions with the passive participle. The Relative Forms.

krs (personal name) ḏd·w n·f mḏ·t ḥꜣp·t; (ỉ)r(j)-pꜥ(·t) ḥꜣtj-ꜥ hrr·w nb tꜣ·wj ḥr tp(j)·t-r·f; ỉ nb nrw, rdj n·f wrr·t ꜣw·t-ỉb, wḏd n·f ḥḳꜣ·t m nṯr·w; ḫꜣś·(w)t ỉrj ḫꜣj·t ỉm·śn; wśỉr rdj n·f ḥḳꜣ·t m ỉwnw, rdj n·f mꜣꜥ-ḫrw m-bꜣḥ pśḏ·t, ỉrj n·f ḫrj·t m ḥ·t-kꜣ-ptḥ, nrr·w n·f śḫm·w ꜥꜣ·w, ꜥḥꜥ·w n·f wr·w ḥr tmꜣ·w·śn, ḳmꜣ(·w)·n ỉtm šfšf·t·f m ỉb n(j) rmṯ nṯr·w ꜣḫ·w mt·w, rdỉ(·w)·n św śnḏ·f, ḳmꜣ(·w)·n tfn·t šf·t·f,

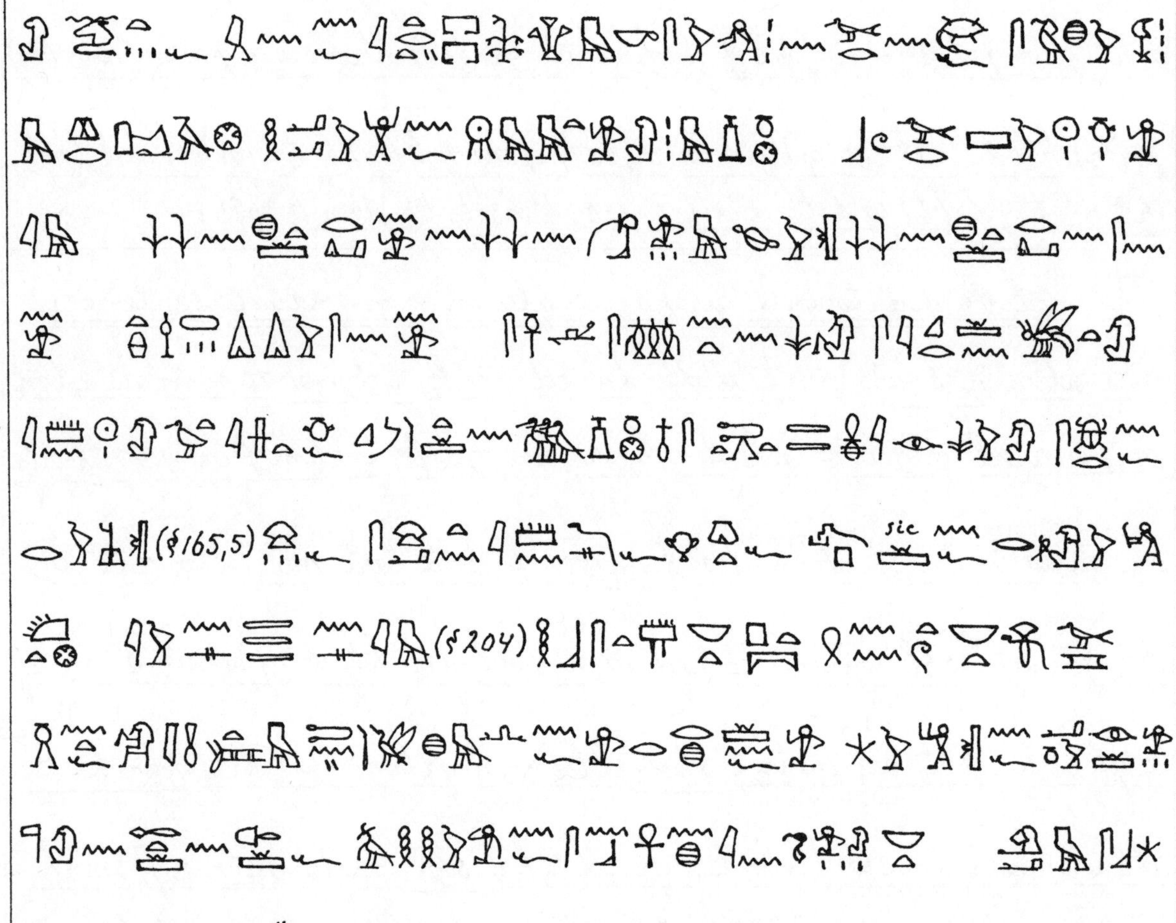
(§165,5)
sic
(§204)

ỉỉ(·w)·n n·f ỉtr·tj šmꜥw mḥw m kśw n-wr-n śnḏ·f, śꜣḫ·w ḫꜣ·w
m ḥr-ꜥḥꜣ, ḥꜥꜥ·w n·f ḥnmm·t m ỉwnw; bw wrš·w ỉb·ỉ ỉm;
nn n ḫ·t rdỉ(·w)·n·ỉ n nn n wꜥb(·w) m ỉśw nn n ḫ·t rdỉ(·w)·n·śn
n·ỉ; t-ḥḏ didi·w·śn n·ỉ; śmr wꜥ(tj) śḫnt(·w)·n nj-św·t, śỉḳr(·w)
·n bỉtj; sꜣ·t ỉmn-rꜥ ỉmj·t ỉb·f, ḳmꜣ·t·n bꜣ·w ỉwnw nfr(w)·ś, ỉṯỉ·t
tꜣ·wj mỉ ỉrỉ św, śḫpr⟨·t⟩·n·f r wṯs ḫꜥw·f, śḫꜥỉ·t·n ỉmn ḏś·f ḥr
nś·t·f, śtp⟨·t⟩·n·f r mnỉw km·t; ỉw n·ś tꜣ·wj, n·ś ỉmj ḥbś·t nb·t p·t
šnn·t nb·t wꜣḏ-wr; ỉntf (pers. name) mꜣꜥ-ḫrw tm ṯnj(·w) ḫm(·w)·n·f
r rḫ(·w)·n·f, dwꜣ·w n·f ꜥn·w nṯr n-ꜥꜣ·t-n mnḫ·f, nḥḥ·w n·f
śnb ꜥnḫ ỉn rmṯ nb·t; ḥꜣ·t-ꜥ m śbꜣj·t ỉrỉ·t·n s n sꜣ·f; nfr
wj śbꜣ(·w)·n ỉt·f, wr ỉrỉ·t·n·f r ḏdd·t n·f; ỉmj·t-pr ỉrỉ·t·n
mtj n(j) sꜣ mrj sꜣ ỉntf (personal name) ḏd·w n·f kbỉ (pers. name) n
sꜣ·f ỉntf sꜣ mrj ḏd·w n·f ỉw-śnb; nṯr wꜥ ꜥnḫ·w ḥr śšm·f;
s n(j) wꜥjw, wbꜣ·w n·f ỉb, didi wḏ·w n šmꜥw, ỉp r-ỉdr n(j) tꜣ-
mḥw, šm·w bw nb m šw·f, didi kꜣ·w, śḫnt ỉꜣw·(w)t; ỉnk śmr
mrj nb·f, ỉrr ḥss·t nṯr·f m ḫr·t hrw n·t rꜥ nb, śꜥnḫ rḫ(j)·t,
ỉj·w n·f wr·w m kśw r rw·tj pr nj-św·t.

[§§108,109]

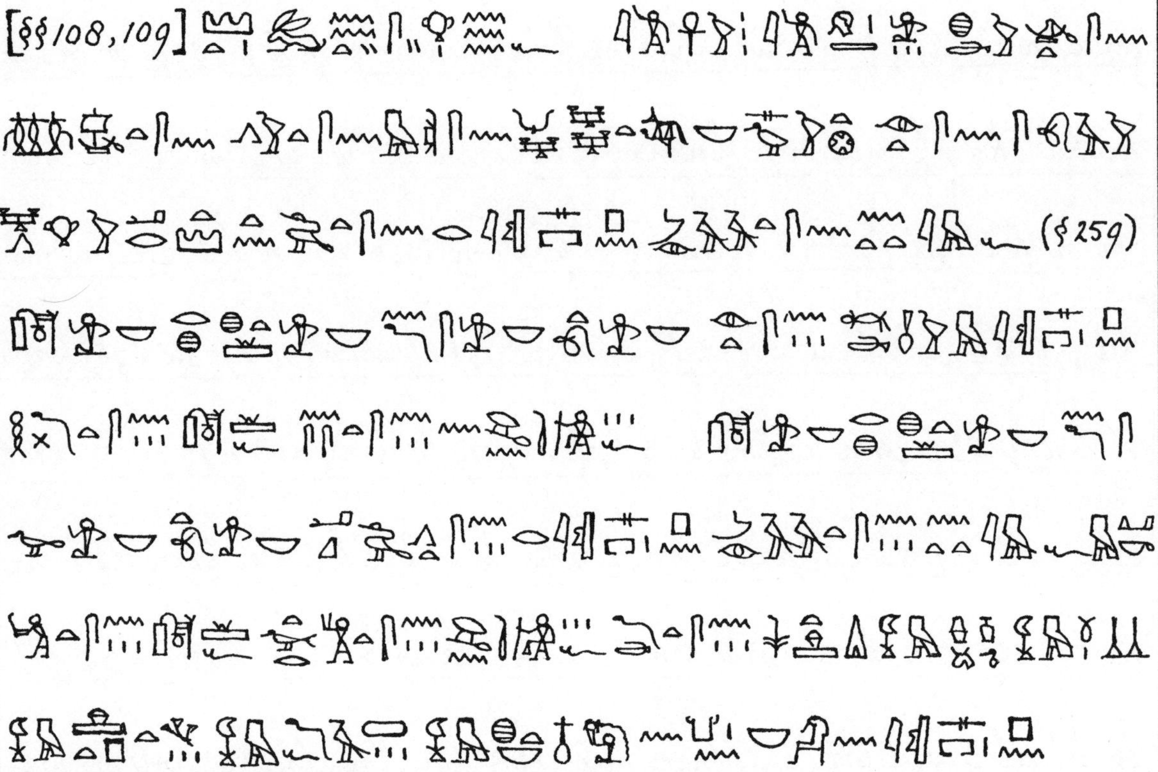

(§259)

§244
[§§110-130]

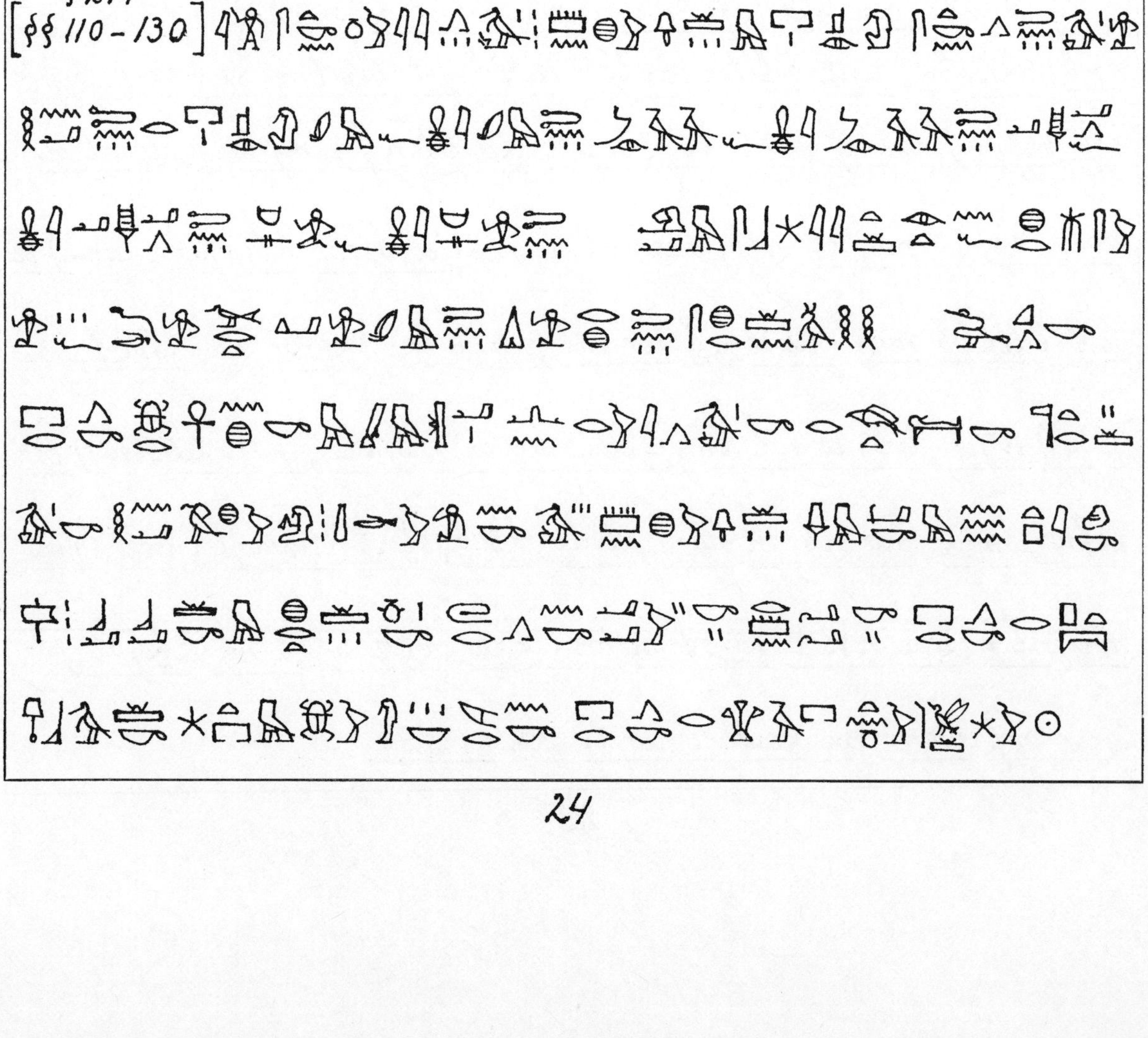

The śḏm·tj·fj form.

ḥꜣś·t wnn·tj·śj ḥr mw·f; i ꜥnḫ·w i tpj·w-tꜣ ḫdw·t(j)·śn ḫnt·t(j)·śn iw·t(j)·śn m šmś(w) n(j) wp-wꜣ·(w)t nb sꜣwtj iri·t(j)·śn św3w ḥr wꜥr·t tn ꜥḳ·t(j)·śn r is pn mꜣꜣ·t(j)·śn nt·t im·f; sš nb rḫ-ḫ·t nb nḏś nb ṯwꜣ nb iri·t(j)·śn śḏ-ḫrw m is pn ḥḏi·t(j)·śn sš·f nśś·t(j)·śn n(superfluous?) ḫntj·w·f; sš nb rḫ-ḫ·t nb nḏś nb ṯwꜣ nb ꜥḳ·t(j)·śn r is pn mꜣꜣ·t(j)·śn nt·t im·f mki·t(j)·śn sš·f twr·t(j)·śn ḫntj·w·f dd·t(j)·śn: ḥtp-di-nj-św·t ḫꜣ m t (m) ḥḳ·t (m) kꜣ·w (m) ꜣpd·w ḫꜣ m šs(m) mnḫ·t ḫꜣ m ḥtp·t ḫꜣ m dfꜣ·w ḫꜣ m ḫ·t nb(·t) nfr(·t) wꜥb(·t) n kꜣ n(j) nb n(j) is pn.

The śḏm·f forms. Syntax of the verbal sentence.

i śtkn·jw bꜣ·w mnḫ·w m pr wśir, śtkn·ṯn bꜣ·i ḥnꜥ·ṯn r pr wśir, śḏm·f mi śḏm·ṯn, mꜣꜣ·f mi mꜣꜣ·ṯn, ꜥḥꜥ·f mi ꜥḥꜥ·ṯn, ḥmśi·f mi ḥmśi·ṯn; ḥꜣ·t-ꜥ m sbꜣj·t iri·t·n·f ḫr ms·w·f: dd·i wr·t, di·i śḏm·ṯn, di·i rḫ·ṯn śḫr n(j) nḥḥ; ꜥḳ·k, pri·k, ḫpr ꜥnḫ·k m wḥm-ꜥ, nn rwi bꜣ·k r ḫꜣ·t·k, nṯrj bꜣ·k ḥnꜥ ꜣḫ·w, mdw n·k bꜣ·w mnḫ·w, śḫm·k m mw, tpi·k ṯꜣw, bꜥbꜥ·k m ḥr·t ib·k, pḥr n·k ꜥwj·kj rmn·wj·kj, pri·k r p·t, wbꜣ·k dꜣ·t m ḫprw nb mri(·w)·n·k, pri·k r ḫꜣ tnw dwꜣw,

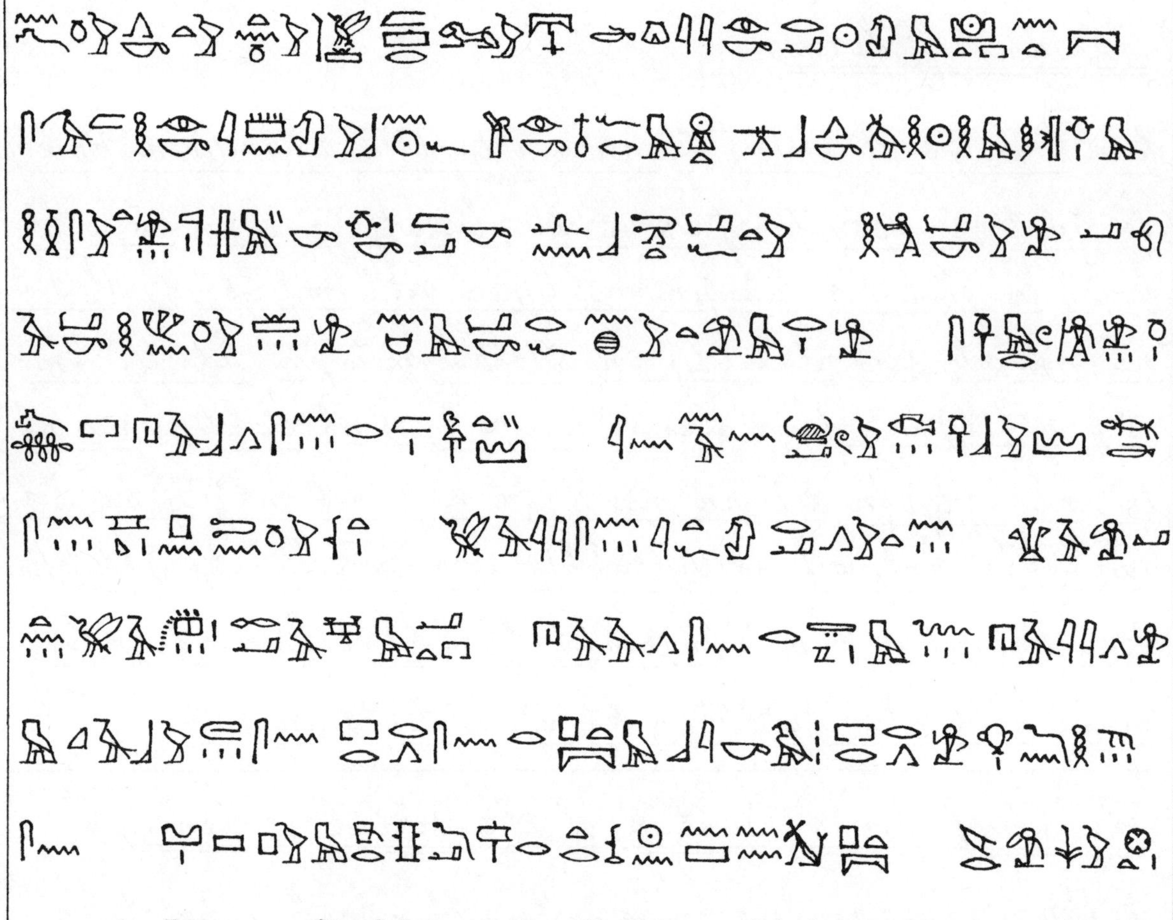
(§153)

nw·k ṯw ṯnw mšrw, dgj·k rꜥ m ꜣẖt n·t p·t, śgmḥ·k ỉmn wbn·f, rś·k nfr m ẖr·t hrw, sbi·k nḥḥ m nḏm-ỉb m ḥsw·t nṯr ỉmj·k, ỉb·k m-ꜥ·k, nn bṯ·f ṯw; ḥwi·k wi, ꜥwꜣ·k ḥnw·i, nḥm·k r·f nẖw·t m r·i; śmr·w nj·w śtp-sꜣ ḥꜣb·śn r gś ỉmntj; ỉn nꜣ n wḥꜥ·w ꜣbw śdi·śn mr pn ṯnw rnp·t; pꜣj·śn ỉt rdi ỉwt·n; ḥꜣ di·ṯn pꜣ ỉt ꜥꜣ m ꜥ·t; ḥꜣꜣ·śn r tꜣ m ḥfꜣ·w, ḥꜣj·i m ḳꜣb·w·śn, prr·śn r p·t m bik·w, prr·i ḥr ḏnḥ·w·śn; ḏw pw mḏr ḏꜥ(w) r tr n(j) nšnn p·t; mri św nỉw·t·f r ḥꜥ·śn; ỉw mi śšm rśw·t, mi mꜣꜣ św ỉdḥj m ꜣbw; nn ḏd śḏm·t(j)·fj nn, ꜥbꜥ pw ḏd·t·n·i; nn wn·i n·k, nn di·i ꜥḳ·k ḥr·i, in[1] ỉrj-ꜥꜣ n(j) śbꜣ pn, nn śmi·i ṯw, in ỉrj-ꜥꜣ n(j) wśẖt tn n·t mꜣꜥ·tj; n sp ỉrj·i ẖ·t nb·t ḏwi r rmṯ nb; n nmḥ·i nmḥ m ẖ(w)t·f, n ỉri·i bw·t nṯr·w, n śḏw·i ḥm n ḥrj-tp·f, n ẖbi·i šbw m r-pr·w, n ḥḏi·i pꜣw·t nṯr·w,

[1] says the door-keeper.

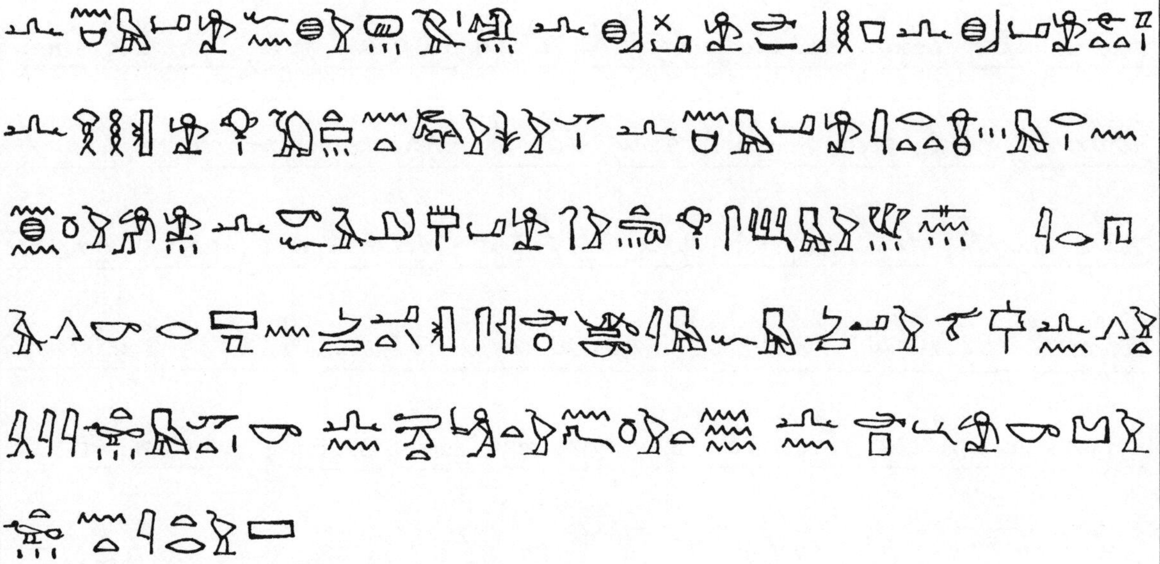

[§§ 131–139; § 244]

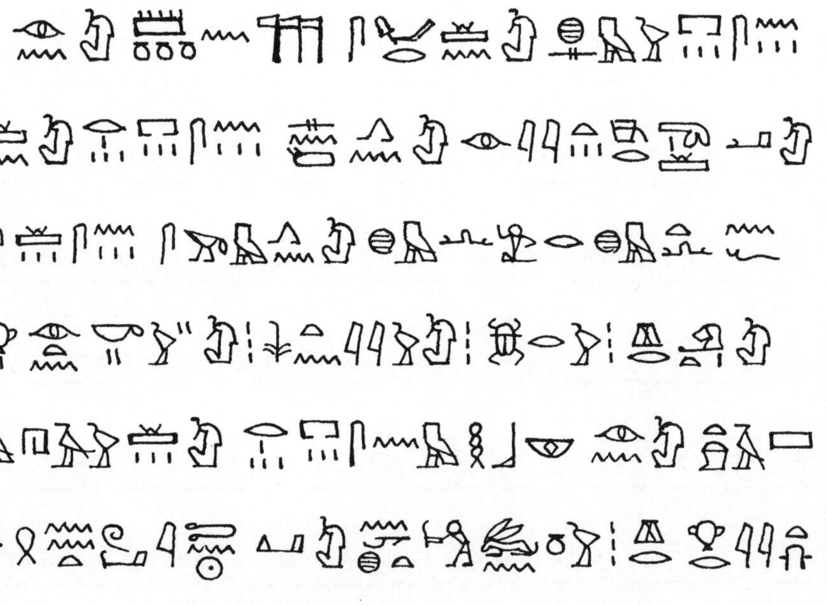

n nḥm·i fnḫ·w ꜣḫ·w, n ḫbi·i dbḥ, n ḫbi·i śṯꜣ·t, n wꜣḥ·i ḥr mw·(w)t n·t iwśw, n nḥm·i irṯ·t m r n(j) nḫn·w, n kfꜣ·i (for kfi·i) ꜥw·t ḥr śmw·śn; ir ḥꜣi·k r š n(j) mꜣꜥ·t, śḳdi·k im·f m mꜣꜥw, nn iwt ij·t m ḫt·k, nn iṯi ṯw nw·t, nn dp·k ḏw·t n·t itrw.

The śḏm·n·f, śḏm·in·f, śḏm·kꜣ·f, śḏm·ḫr·f forms.

iri·n·i mnw n nṯr·w, śḏśr·n·i ḥm·w·śn n m-ḫt, śmnḫ·n·i r-pr·w·śn, sni·n·i irj·t ḏr bꜣḥ, di·i rḫ wꜥb·w irj·t·śn, śšm·n·i ḥm r ḫm·t·n·f, di·i ḥꜣw ḥr iri·t·n kj·wj nj·w-św·t ḫpr·w ḥr ḥꜣ·t·i, nṯr·w ḥr rśw·t m hꜣw·i, r-pr·w·śn m ḥb, iri·n·i tꜣš·w tꜣ-mri r šnn·t itn, di·i nḫt wn·w ḥr ḥrj·t, dri ḏw·t ḥr·ś, di·i wn km·t m ḥrj·t-tp, tꜣ nb m mr·t·ś; ii·n·f n·n, smꜣ·n·f tꜣ·wj, ꜣbḫ·n·f św·t n bi·t, ii·n·f n·n, ḥkꜣ·n·f km·t, rdi·n·f dśr·t m ꜥb·f, ii·n·f n·n, mki·n·f tꜣ·wj, śgrḥ·n·f idb·wj, ii·n·f n·n, śꜥnḫ·n·f pꜥ·t, śrḳ·n·f ḫtj·t rḫ(j)·t;

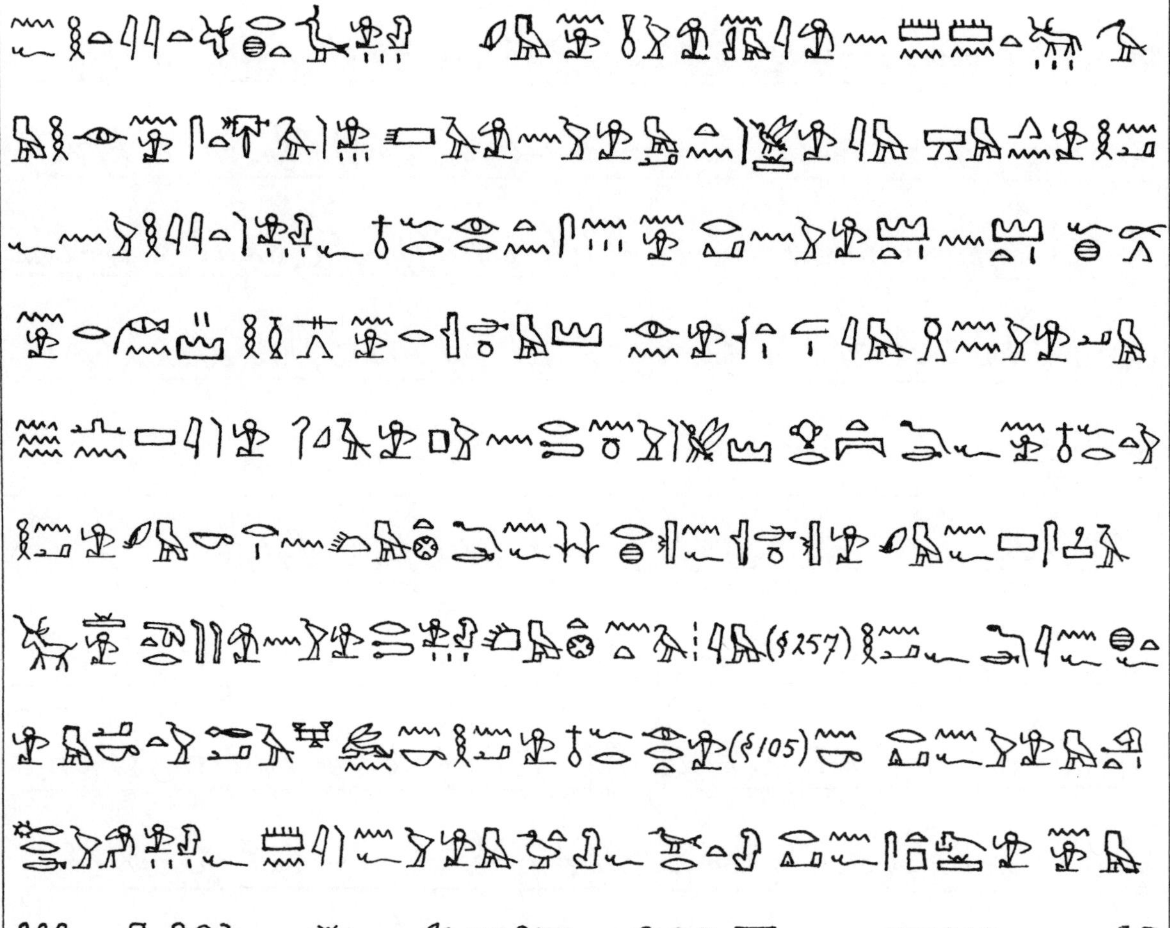
(§257)
(§105)
(§247)
(§246)
(§196)
(§159,5)

śḏm·n·i ḫrw nmi n(j) mnmn·t, gmḥ·n·i śṯtj·w, śiꜣ·n wi mṯn im, šm·n·i ḥnʿ·f n wḥj·t·f, nfr iri·t·n·śn n·i, rdi·n wi ḫꜣś·t n ḫꜣś·t, fḫ·n·i r kpnj, ḥsi·n·i r ḳdm, iri·n·i rnp·t gś (a year and a half) im, ini·n wi ʿmwnnši, ḥḳꜣ pw n(j) rṯnw ḥrj·t, ḏd·f n·i: nfr ṯw ḥnʿ·i, śḏm·k r n(j) km·t, ḏd·n·f nn, rḫ·n·f ḳd·i, śḏm·n·f šśꜣ·i, mtr·n wi rmṯ km·t ntj·w im ḥnʿ·f, ḏd·in·f ḫft·i: mk ṯw ʿꜣ, wnn·k ḥnʿ·i, nfr ir(i)·t·i (or: irr·t·i §103) n·k, rdi·n·f wi m-ḥꜣ·t ẖrd·w·f, mni·n·f wi m sꜣ·t·f wr·t, rdi·n·f śtp·i n·i m ḫꜣś·t·f m śtpw n(j) wn·t ḥnʿ·f ḥr tꜣš·f n(j) k·t ḫꜣś·t; ʿnw pw, n rdi·n·f śꜣ·f; ir ꜣḫ nb irr·w n·f nn, iw·f mm ʿnḫ·w, n śki·n·f, wnn·f m nṯr ḏśr, n ḫmi·n św ḫ·t nb·t ḏw·t, wnn·f m ꜣḫ mnḫ m imn·t, n mt·n·f m whm; wr·w nj·w pwn·t, ḏd·ḫr·śn dbḥ·śn ḥtpw ḫr ḥm·t·ś; i mr irr nn r·i, di·k pri·i r ḫftj·i, di·k mꜣʿ ḫrw·i r·f m ḏꜣḏꜣ·t n·t nṯr ʿꜣ m-bꜣḥ psḏ·t ʿꜣ·t, ir ḥm tm·k rdi(·w) prj·i r ḫftj pf, pri·kꜣ ḥʿpj r p·t, ʿnḫ·f m mꜣʿ·t,

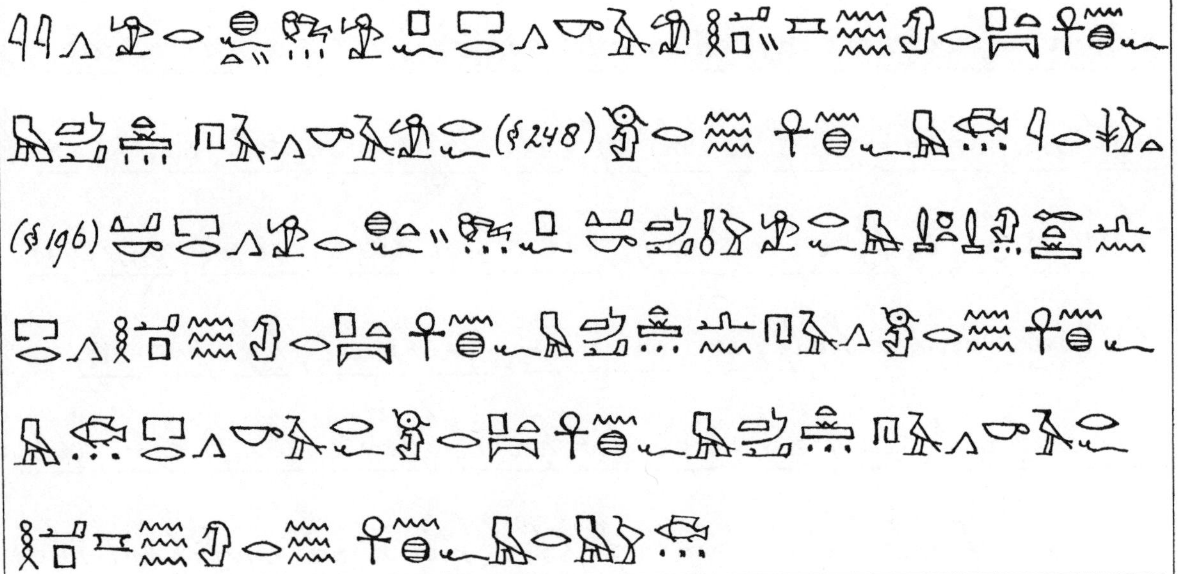
(§248)
(§196)

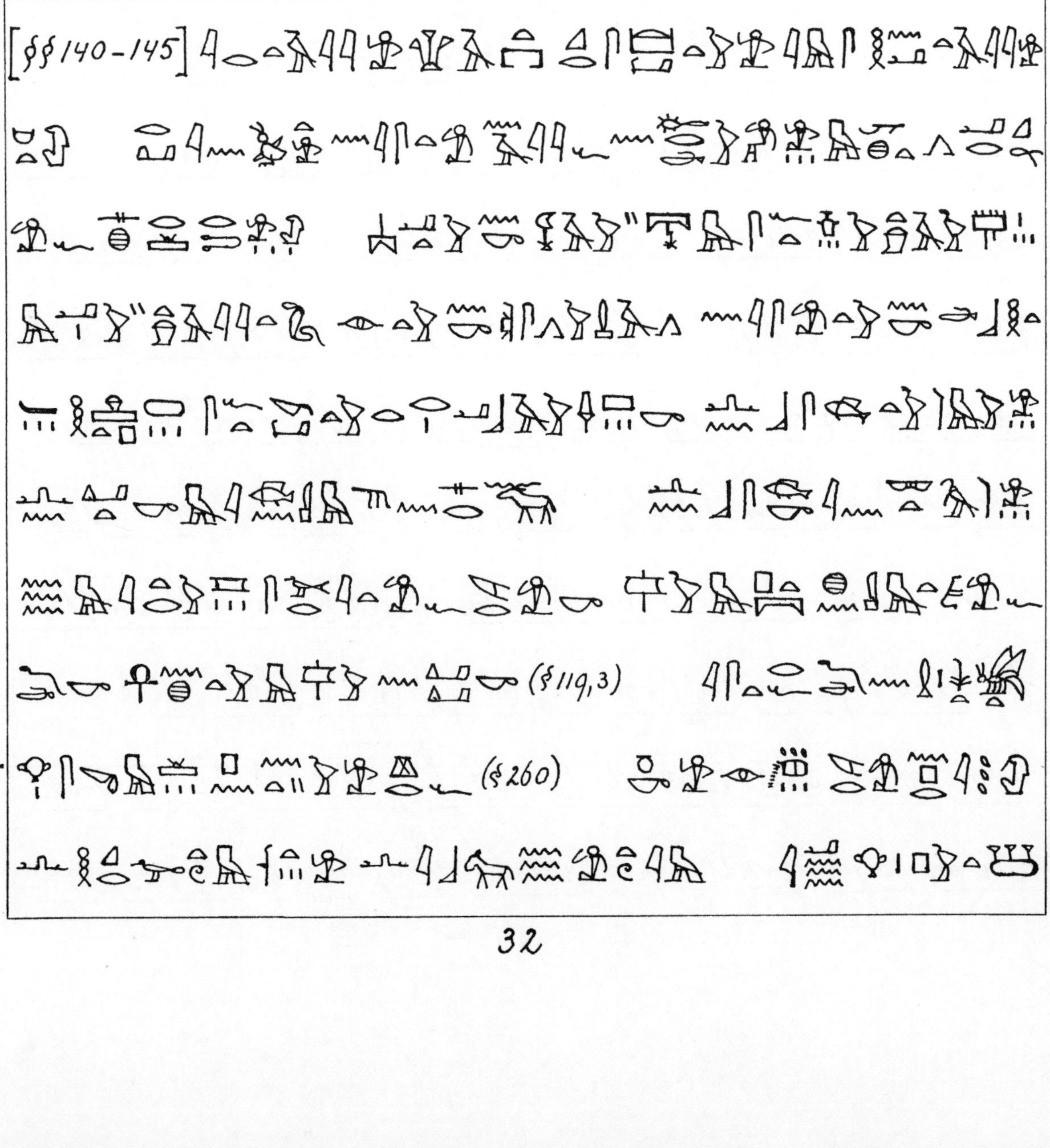
[§§140-145]
(§119,3)
(§260)

hȝi·kȝ r·f rꜥ r mw, ꜥnḫ·f m rm·w, ir św·t di·k pri·i r ḫftj pf, di·k mȝꜥ ẖrw·i r·f m ḏȝḏȝ·t ꜥȝ·t, nn pri ḥꜥpj r p·t, ꜥnḫ·f m mȝꜥ·t, nn hȝi rꜥ r mw, ꜥnḫ·f m rm·w, pri·kȝ r·f rꜥ r p·t, ꜥnḫ·f m mȝꜥ·t, hȝi·kȝ r·f ḥꜥpj r mw, ꜥnḫ·f m rm·w.

The passive śḏm·w·f and passives created by means of ·tw.

ir tȝj·i ḥȝ·t, ḳrś·tw·i im·ś ḥnꜥ tȝj·i ḥm·t; rdi·in tȝtj niś·t(w) nȝj·f n ẖrd·w, m-ḫt ꜥrḳ·f śḫr rmṯ; wḏꜥ·tw n·k ḫȝwj m śfṯ wtȝ·w m ꜥ·wj tȝj·t, iri·tw n·k šmś wḏȝ, niś·tw n·k dbḥ·t-ḥtp, sfṯ·tw r r ꜥbȝ·w·k, nn bs ṯw ꜥȝm·w, nn di·t(w)·k m inm n(j) sr; nn bs·(w)·k in pḏtj·w; mw m itrw swr·t(w)·f, mri·k, ṯȝw m p·t ḫnm·t(w)·f, dd·k, ꜥnḫ·tw m ṯȝw n(j) didi·k; iśṯ r·f dd(·w) n ḥm nj-św·t bitj ḥr śšm pn ntj wi ḥr·f; ink iri it mri npr, n ḥkr·tw m rnp·(w)t·i, n ibi·tw im; iꜥi ḥr pw tšȝ wp·(w)t, n ꜥḥꜥ·n·tw m hȝw·f;

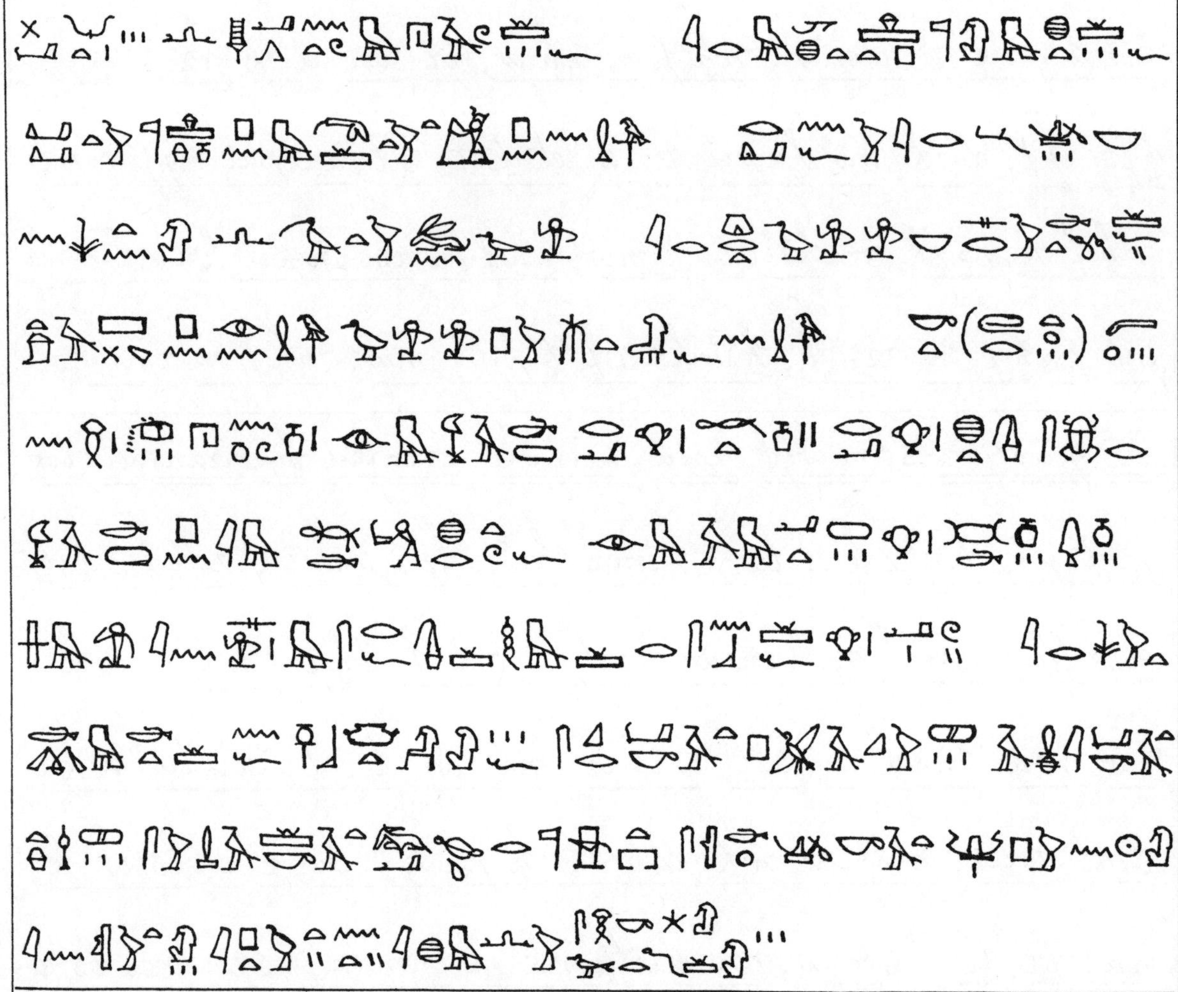

[§§146-153]

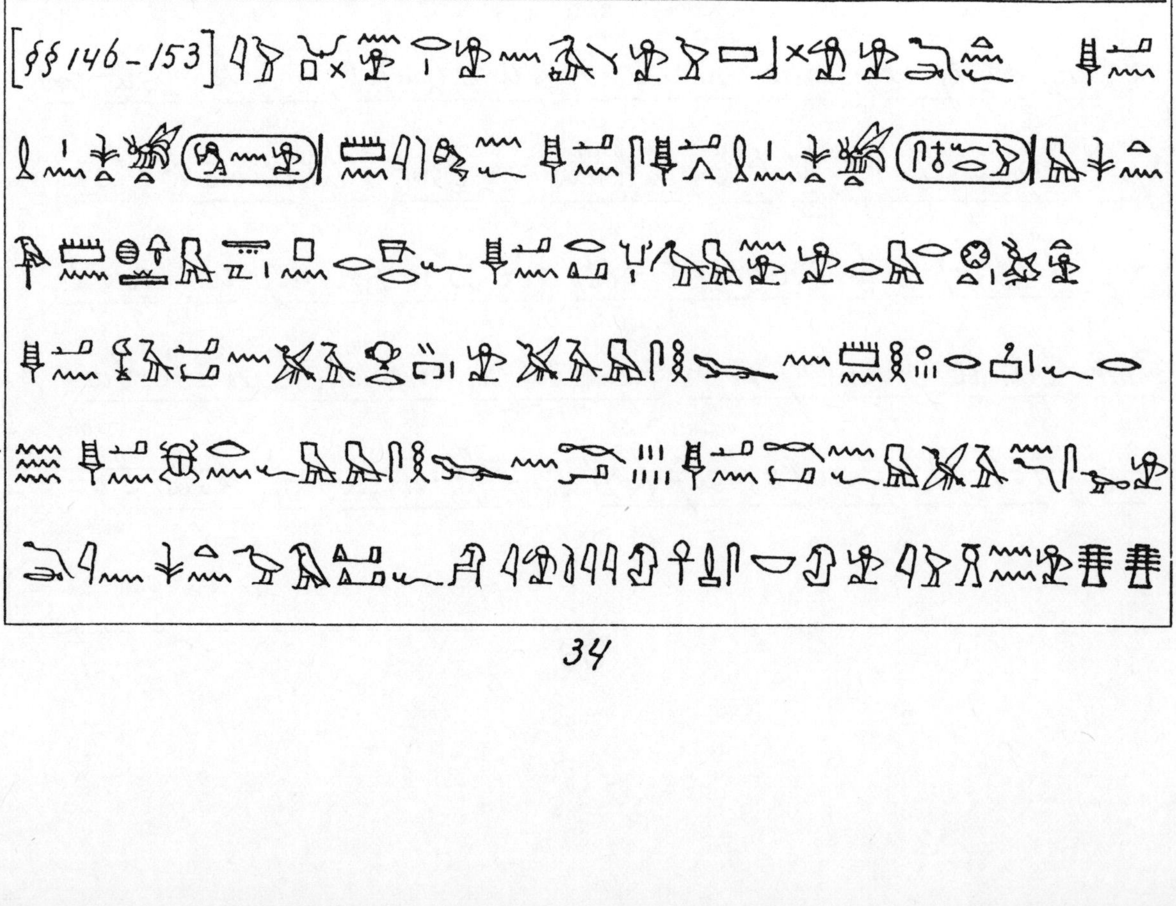

ir m-ẖt ḥtp nṯr m ḥ·(w)t·f, ḏiḏi·tw ḥtp-nṯr pn m-b3ḥ twt pn n(j) ḥm·i; rdi·n·f wi r imj-r ḥᶜw nb n(j) nj-św·t, n gmi·tw wn·i; ir grt s3·i nb śrwḏ·t(j)·fj t3š pn iri(w)·n ḥm·i, s3·i pw, mśi·t(w)·f n ḥm·i; ḳ·t (pẖr·t): dḳr·w n bnr hnw 1, iri(·w) m ẖ3d(w), rdi(·w) ḥr mḥ·t 2, rdi(w) ḥr ẖ·t, śẖpr(·w) ẖ3d(w) pn im, śdi·ẖr·tw·f, iri(·w) m 3mᶜ·t ḥr ᶜḏ b3ḳ, wnm(·w) in s m śrf nḏm r śnb.f ḥr ᶜ-wj; ir śwt dmḏi·t(w) n·f 3b·t·f, śḳr·k3·t(w) p3ḳ·w, 3mi·k3·t(w) t-ḥḏ(·w), śwḏ3·k3·t(w) iwᶜ r nm·t nṯr, śḳdi·k3·t(w) wi3 pw n(j) rᶜ in isw·t(j) iptw·tj n(j)·tj iẖm·w {śki / wrd}.

Compound verb-forms introduced by iw, ᶜḥᶜ; the auxiliary p3w; the verbs i(n), k3, ḫr contained in the forms śḏm·in·f, etc.

iw wpi·n·i r·i n b3·i, wšb·i ḏd·t·n·f; ᶜḥᶜ·n ḥm n(j) nj-św·t biti ḫwni mni·n·f, ᶜḥᶜ·n śᶜḥᶜ(·w) ḥm n(j) nj-św·t biti śnfrw m nj-św·t mnḫ m t3 pn r ḏr·f, ᶜḥᶜ·n rdi(·w) k3gmni (pers. name) r imj-r niw·t t3tj; ᶜḥᶜ·n ẖ3ᶜ·n p3 ḥrj-pr p3 msḥ n(j) mnḥ r-s3·f r mw, ᶜḥᶜ·n ḫpr·n·f m msḥ n(j) mḥ 7, ᶜḥᶜ·n mḥ·n·f m p3 nḏś; ḏd·in s3 nj-św·t ḏdi·f-ḥr: itj ᶜ·w·ś· nb·i, iw ini·n·i ḏdi (pers. n.);

(§250)

(§250)

[§§160-169]

ꜥnḫ·k ìrf m ìśś·t, ḥr·śn nṯr·w r·i; nn dì·n ꜥḳ·k ḥr·n, ìn bnš·w n śbꜣ pn, n ìś dd·n·k rn·n, tḫ pw n(j) bw mꜣꜥ rn·w·ṯn; ìw ìrì·n·i dd·t rmṯ hrr·t nṯr·w ḥr·ś, ìw śḥtp·n·i nṯr m mrr·t·f, ìw rdì·n·i t n ḥḳr, mw n ìbì, ḥbś·w n ḥꜣw(>ḥꜣj), mḫn·t n ìw, ìw ìrì·n·i ḥtp-nṯr n nṯr·w prì·t-r-ḫrw n ꜣḫ·w; ìw rdì(w) n·i pr n(j) nb-š, ìw ḫws·w n·i mr m ìnr; ìrì(·w)n·i ꜥḳw m mìn·t ìrp m ḫr·t hrw ì(w)f pśì ꜣpd m ꜣšr ḥrw r ꜥw·t ḫꜣś·t, ìw grg·t(w) n·i, ìw wꜣḥ·t(w) n·i, ḥrw r ìnw n(j) ṯsm·w·i; ìw ìkn n(j) mw ḫm·f ìb·t, ìw mḥ·t[1] r m šww śmn·f ìb; ìw pꜣ(w)·n śdm mìt·t; ꜥḥꜥ·n fḳꜣ·n wì nb·i m nbw; ìn wnm dp, ìw wšd·w wšb·f, ìn śdrw mꜣꜣ rśw·t; ꜥnḫ·k ìrf m m, ḫrw·fj·śn nṯr·w ꜣḫ·w r·i.

[1] A masc. word was meant as śmn·f shows. Read mḥw, cf. Peas. B1,14  (i.e. my donkey) 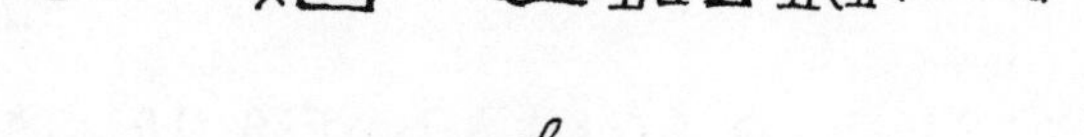 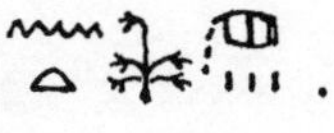. In hieratic △ and c are very similar.

Reading-book 38

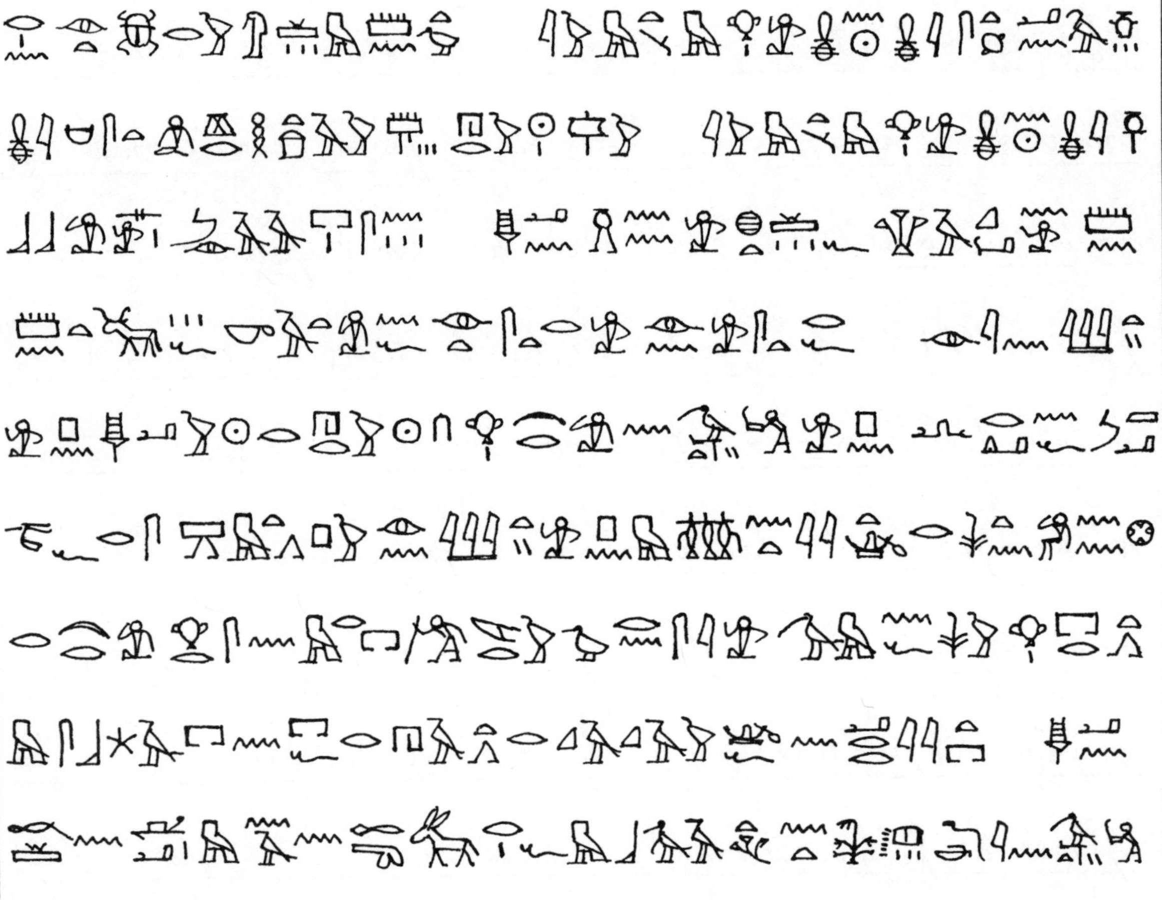

[§§ 177–184]

(§63,2)

(dbn·n·i)

(§226)

(§191)

(mi ḥ^c.t = m^c ḥ^c.t) (§141)

(§69)

(§134)

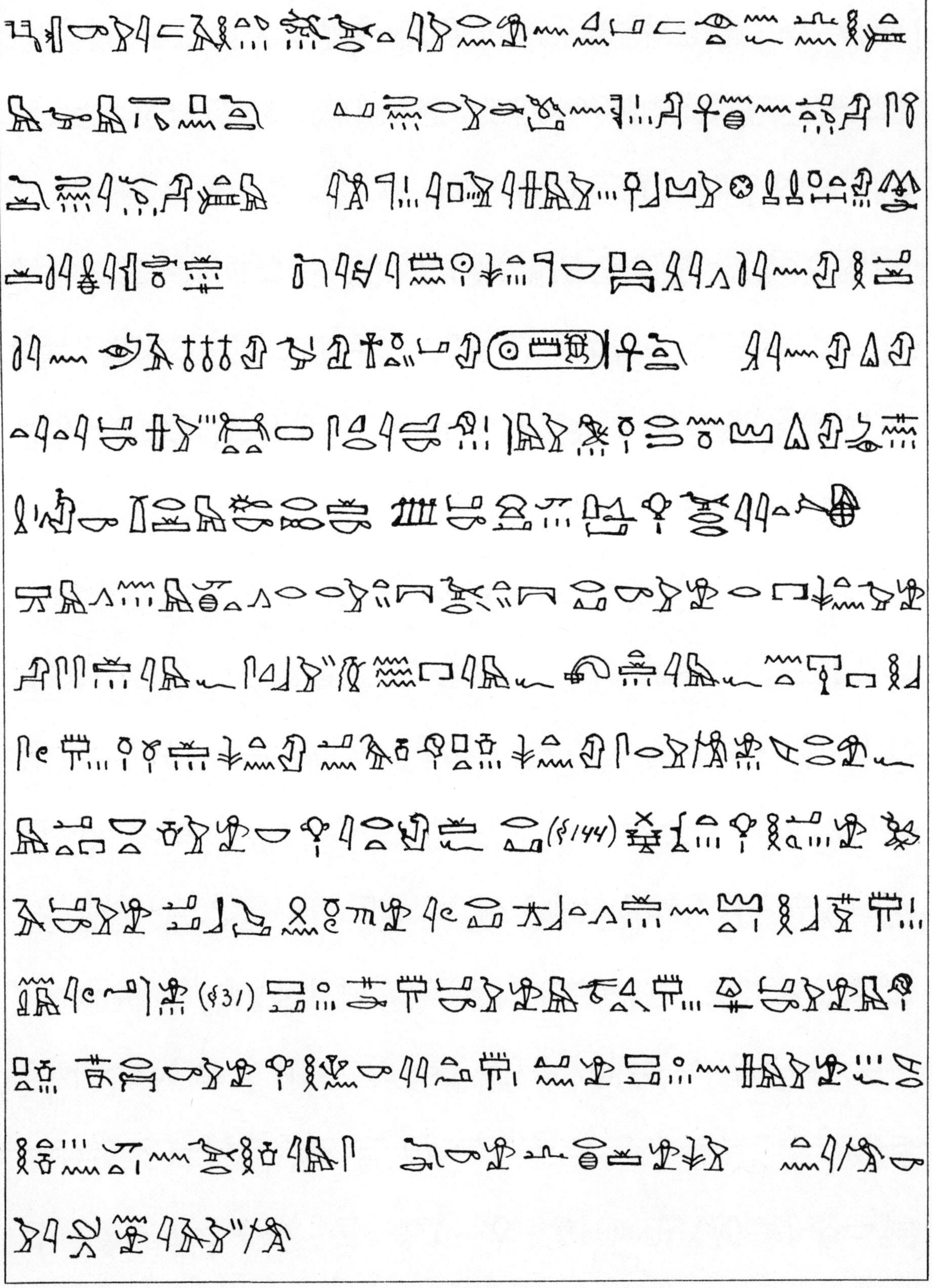
(§144)
(§31)

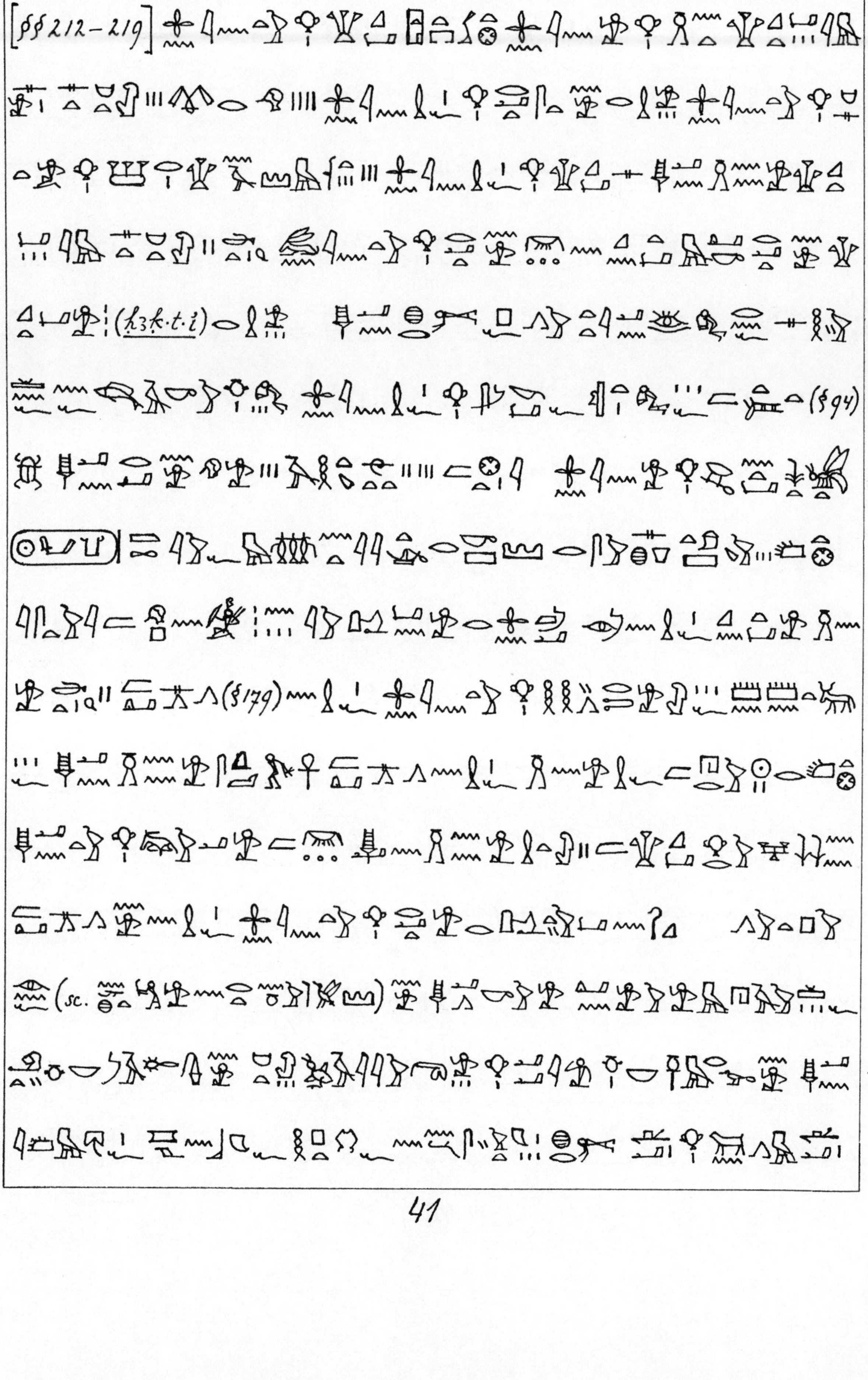
[§§ 212–219]
(ḫ3k·t·i)
(§ 94)
(§ 179)
(sc.

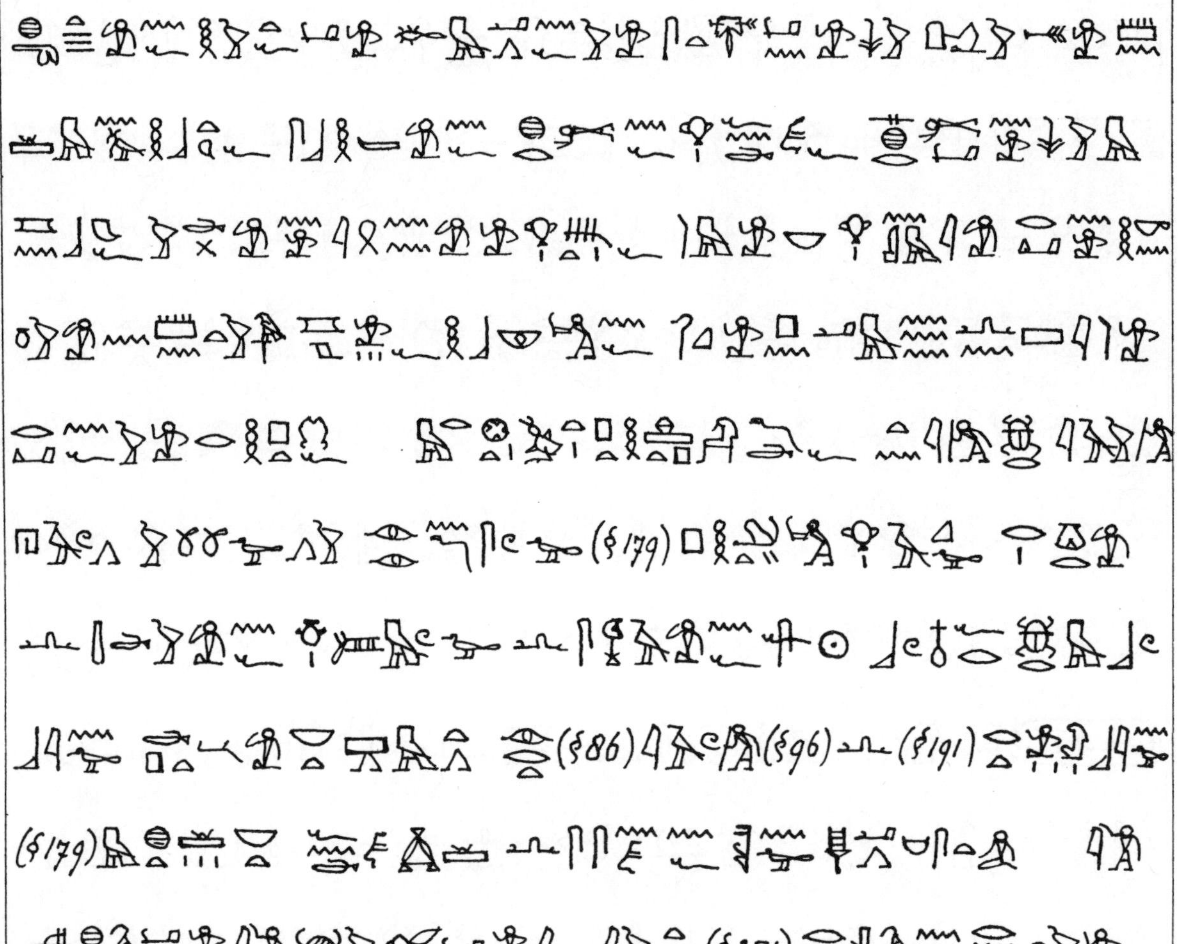
(§179)
(§86)
(§96)
(§191)
(§179)
(§251)
(§254)
(§235)
(§249,2)

128; 120) [illegible]

[illegible] (§164) [illegible]

[illegible] (§184) [illegible]

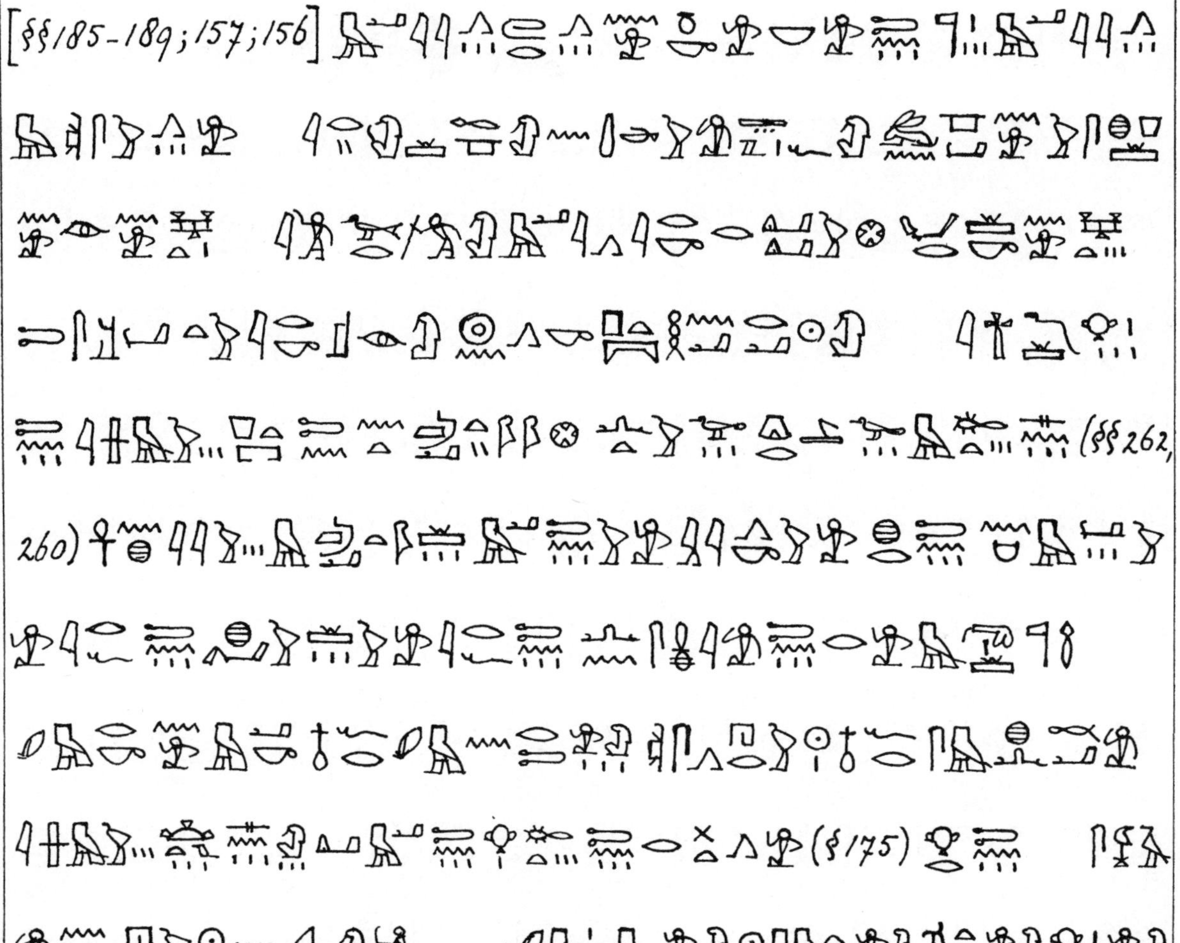
[§§185-189; 157; 156]
(§§262, 260)
(§175)
(§191)
(ḳt ḫt §53)

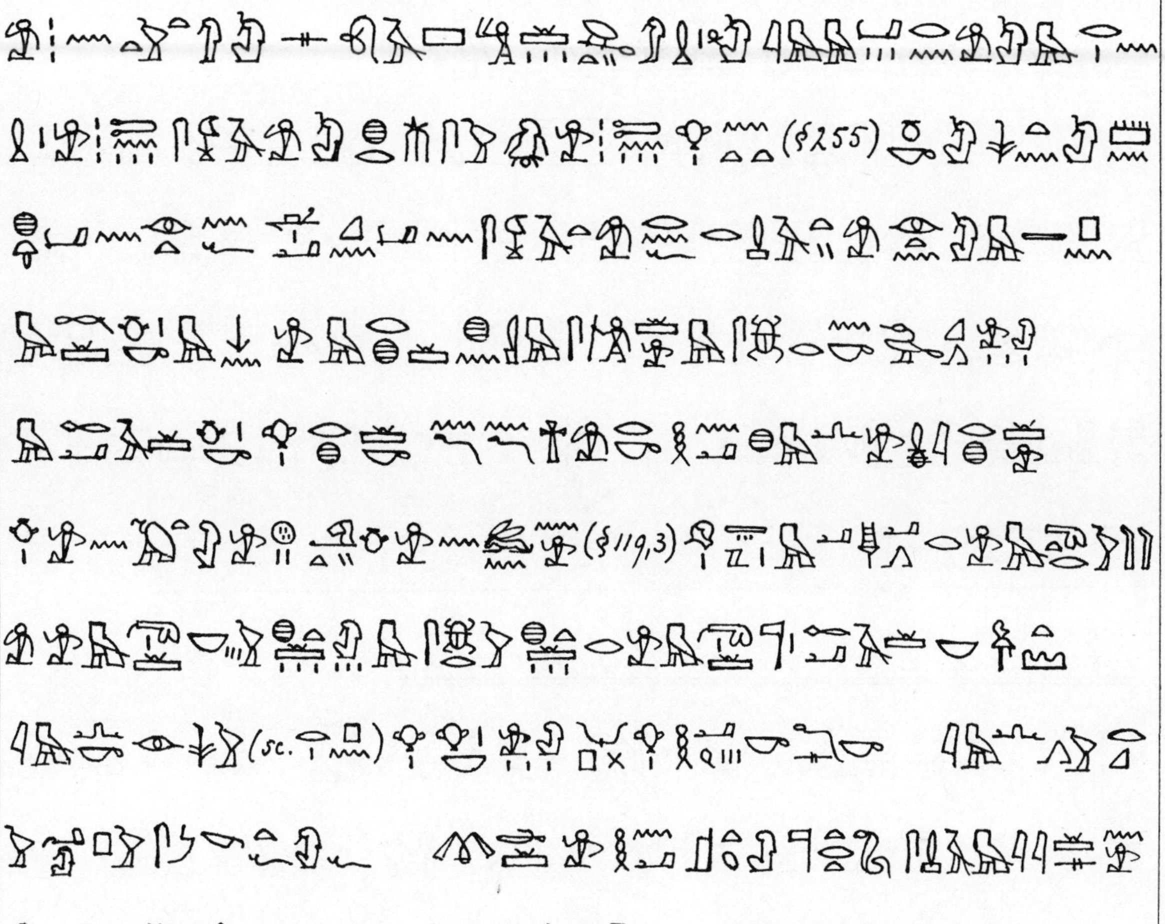
(§255)
(§119,3)
(sc.
[§§170-176]
(§153)

Canal inscription of Tuthmosis III.

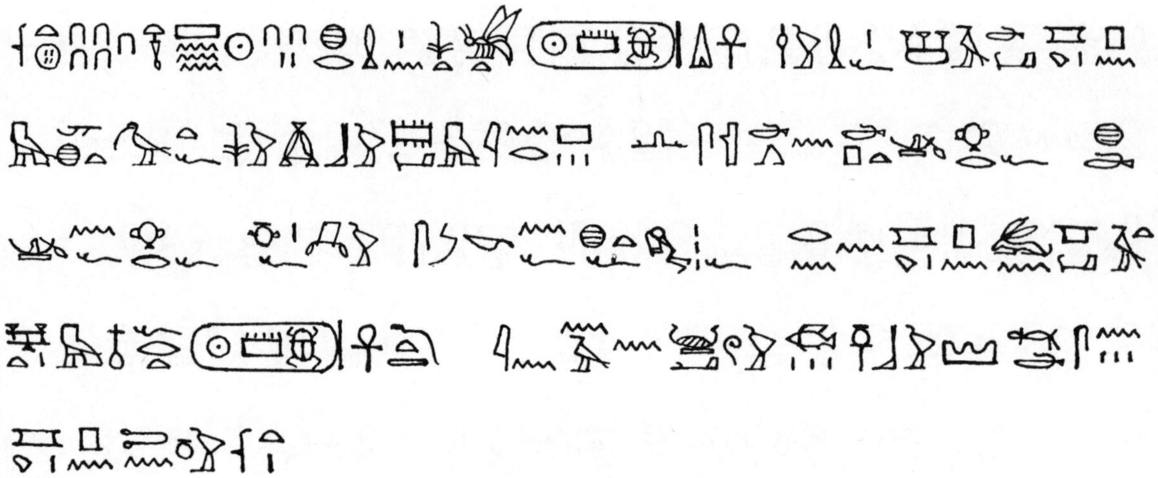

Coronation decree of Tuthmosis I.

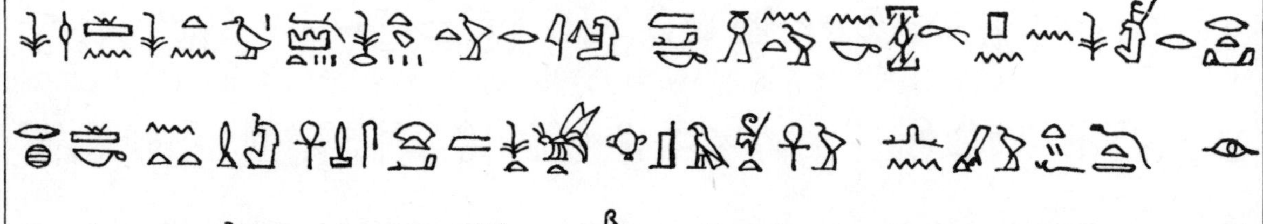

Inscription of Tuthmosis II, recording a rebellion in Nubia.

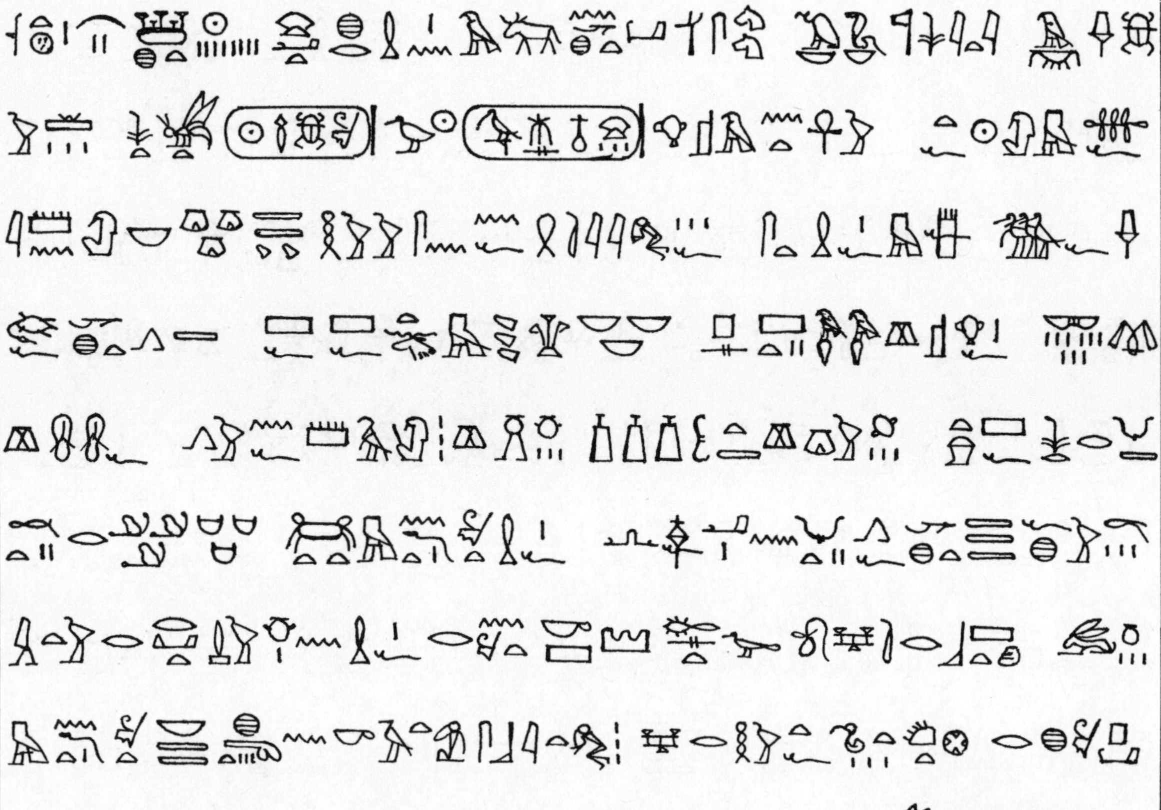

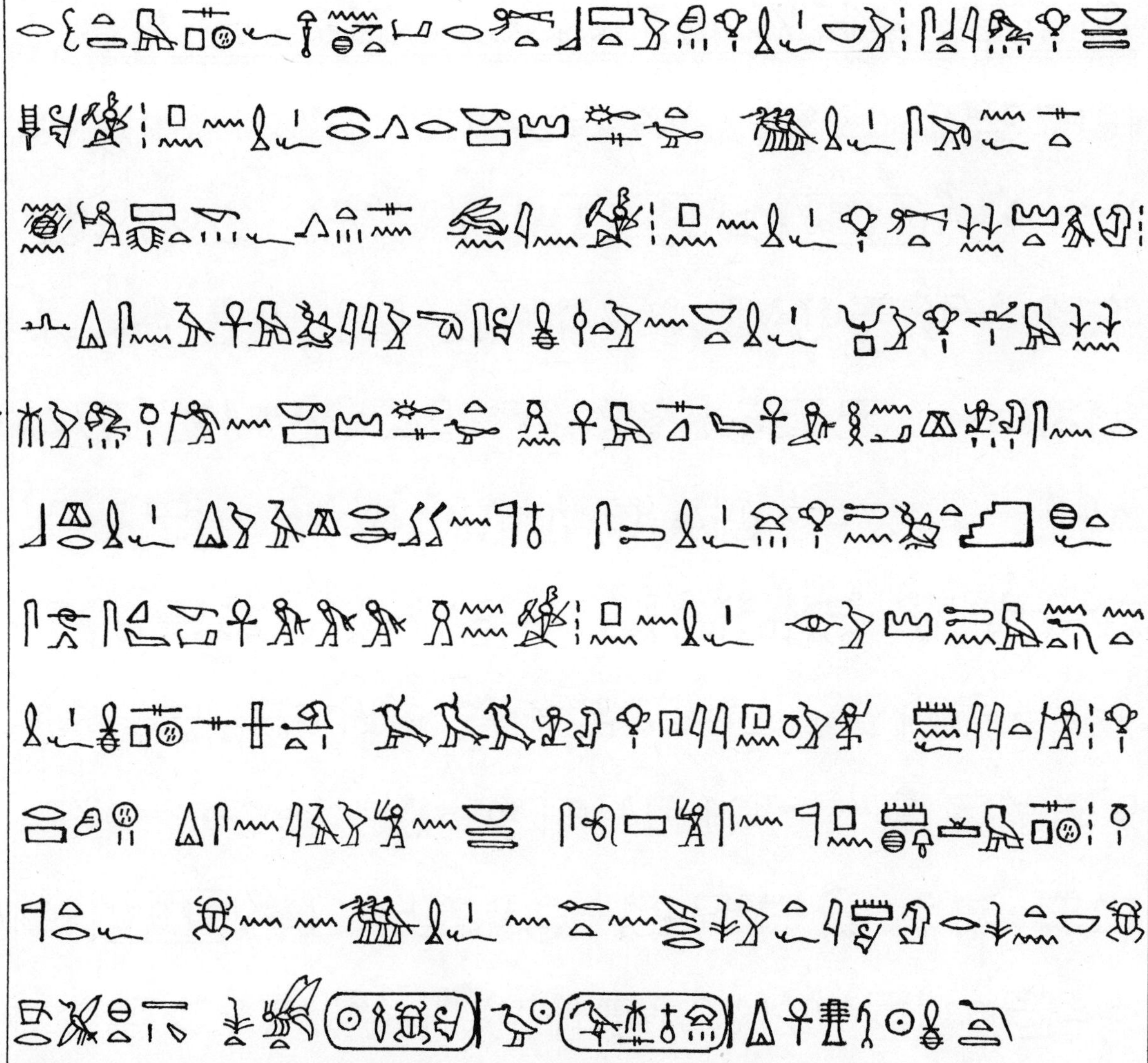

The Punt expedition of Queen Hatshepsut.

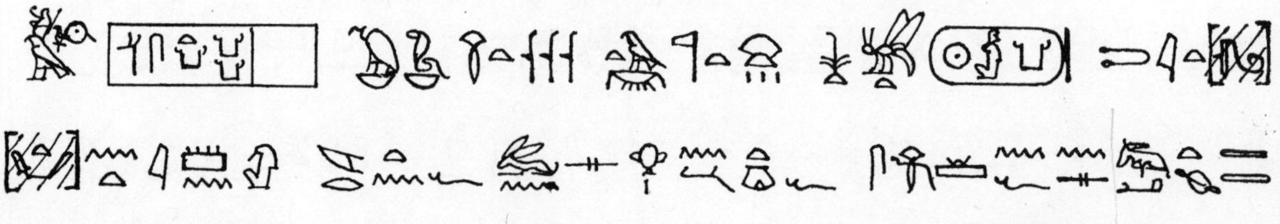

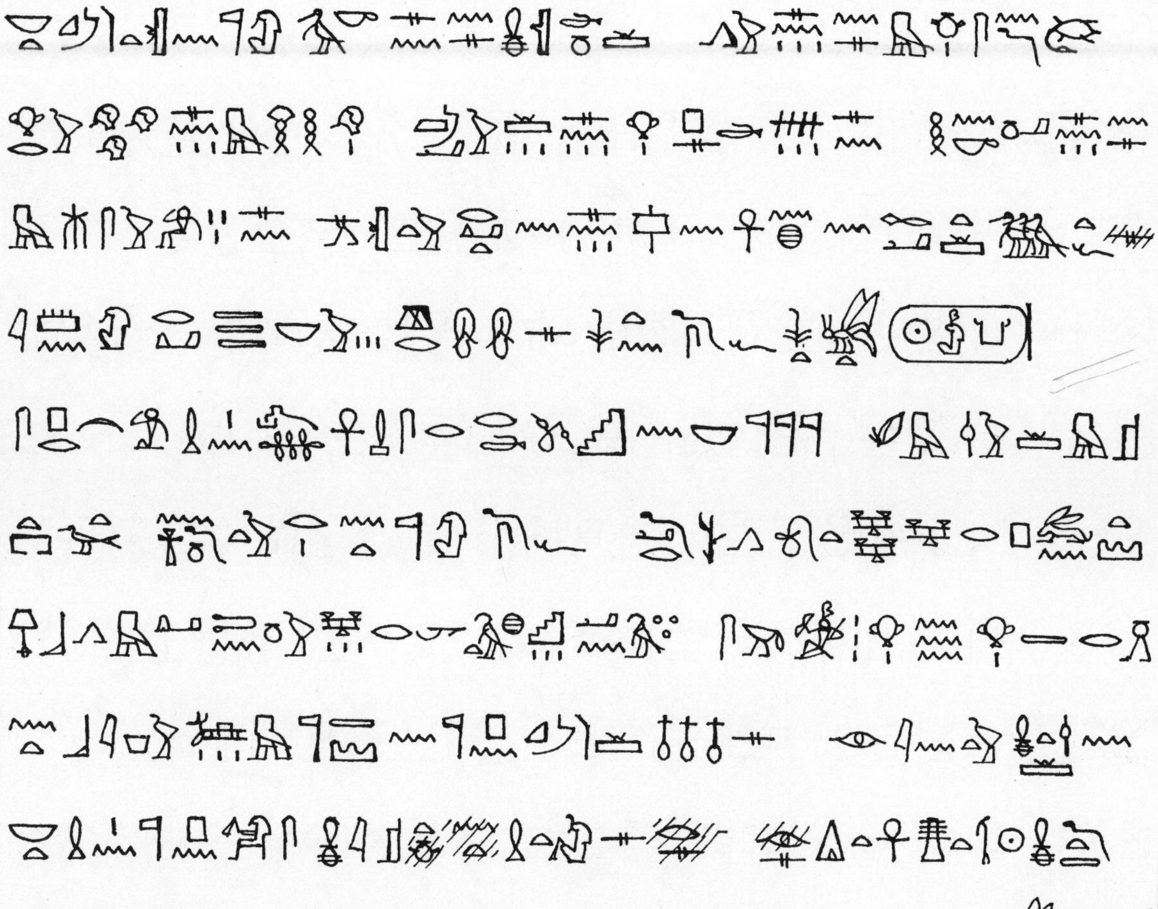

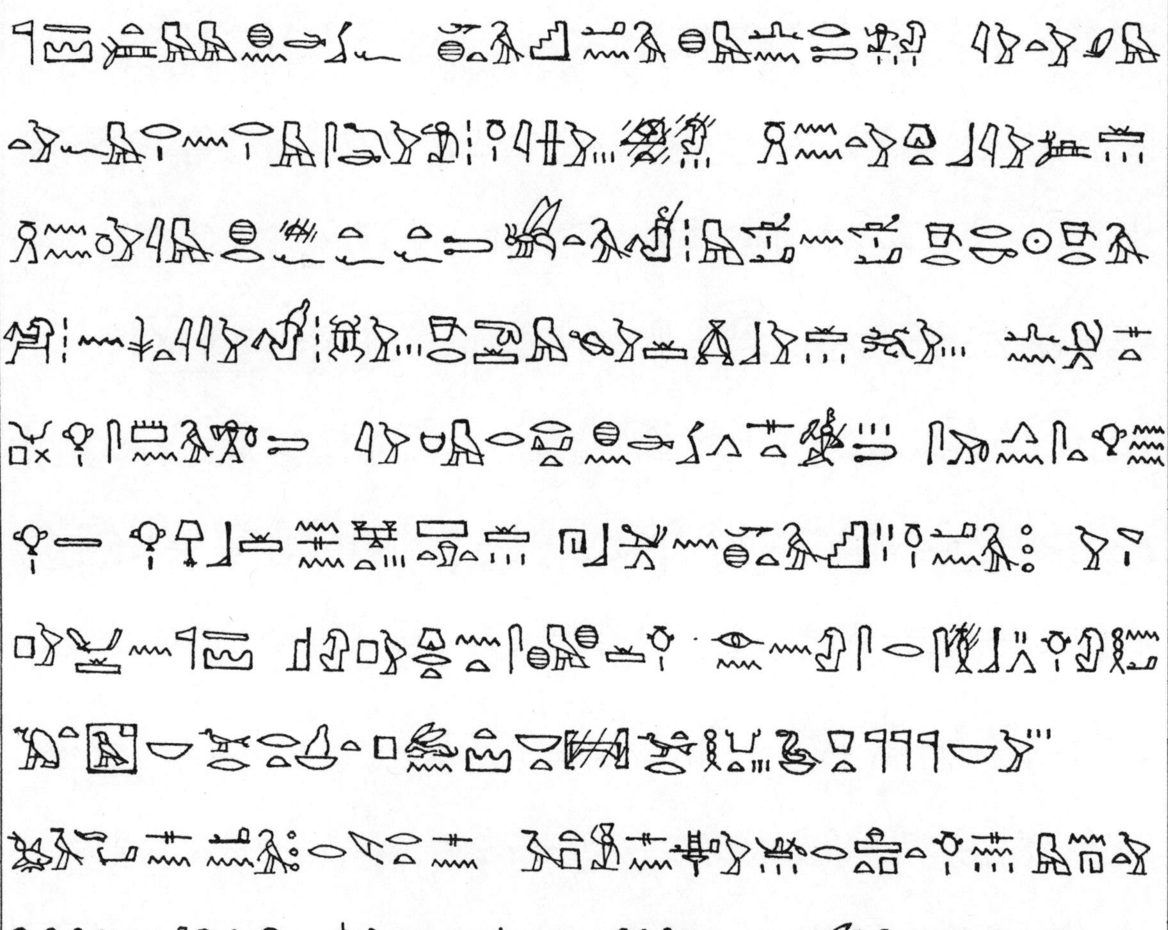

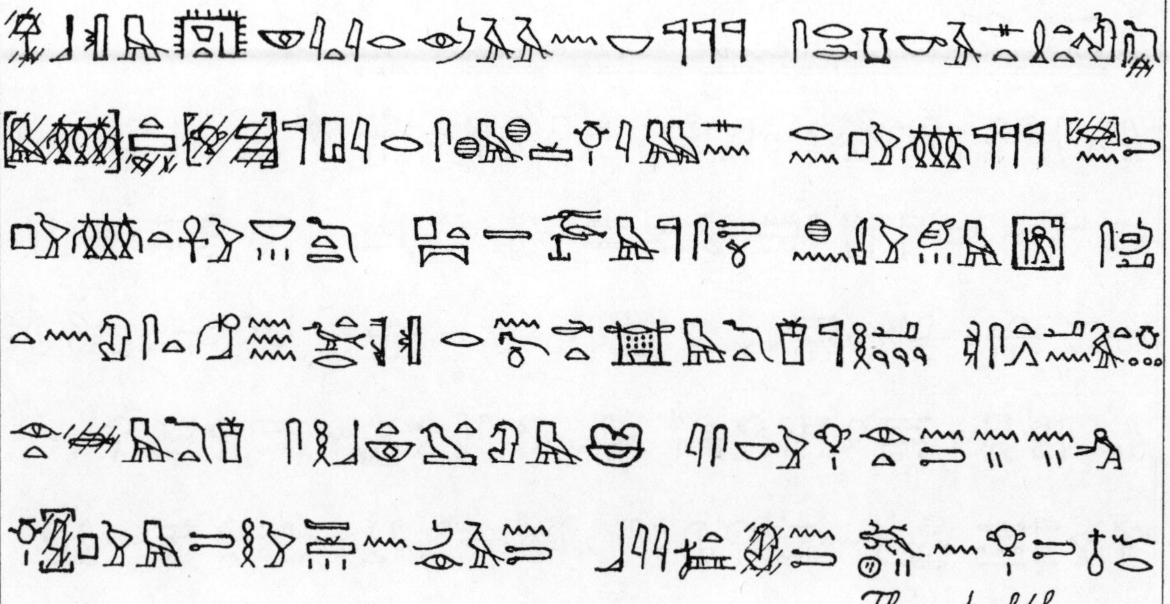

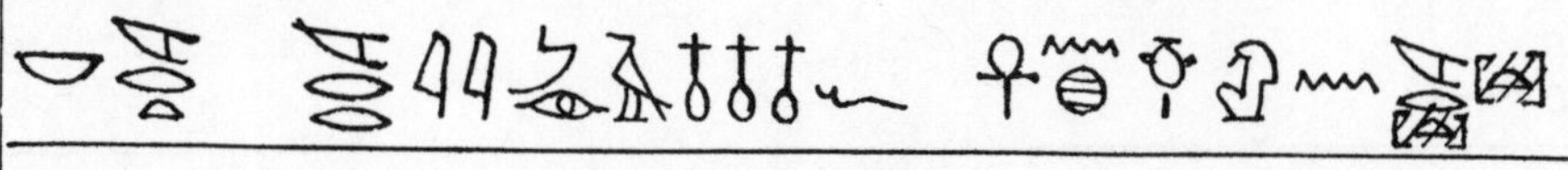

The rest of the inscr. is very fragmentary.

Departure of the Punt expedition.

Arrival of the expedition in Punt.

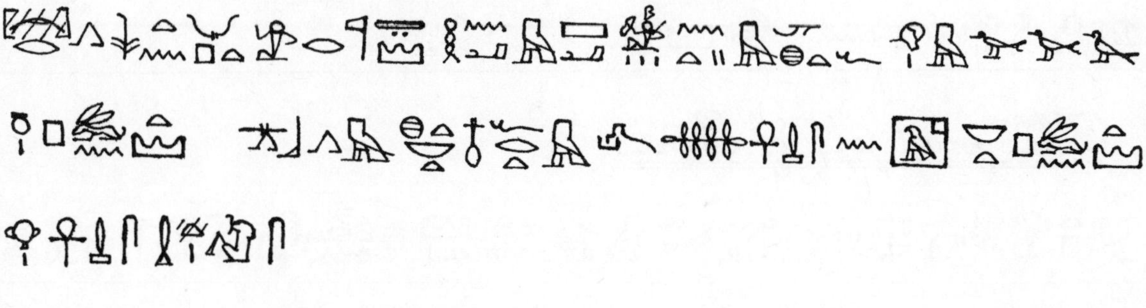

The Puntites receive the expedition.

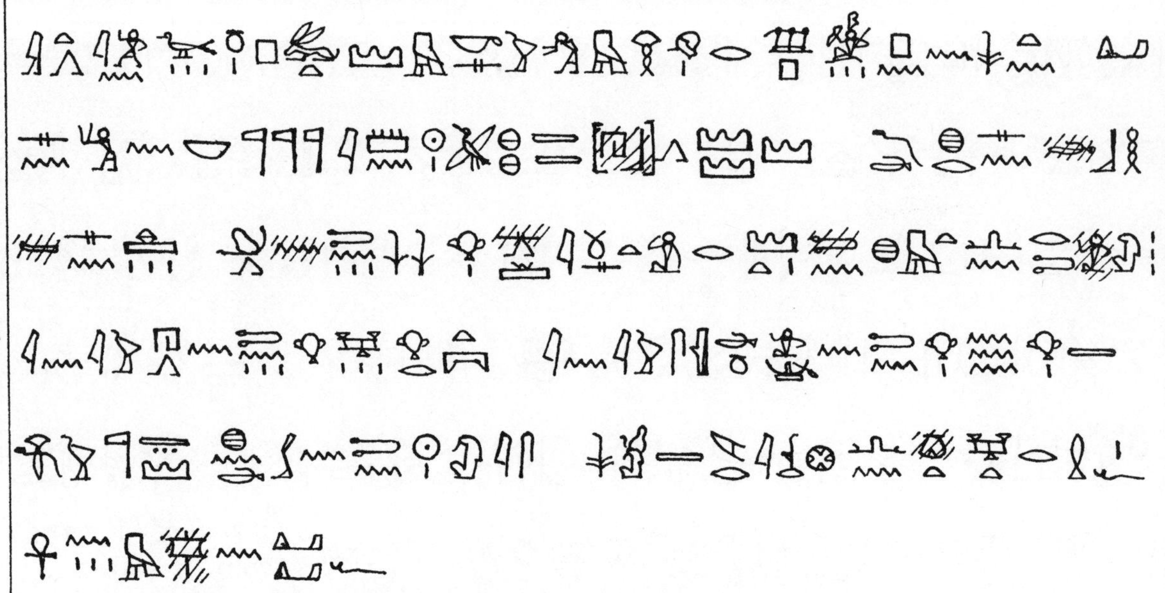

Pitching a camp for the expedition.

Reception of the tribute of the Puntites.

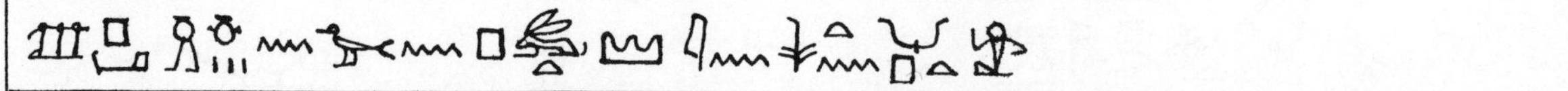

The products of Punt.

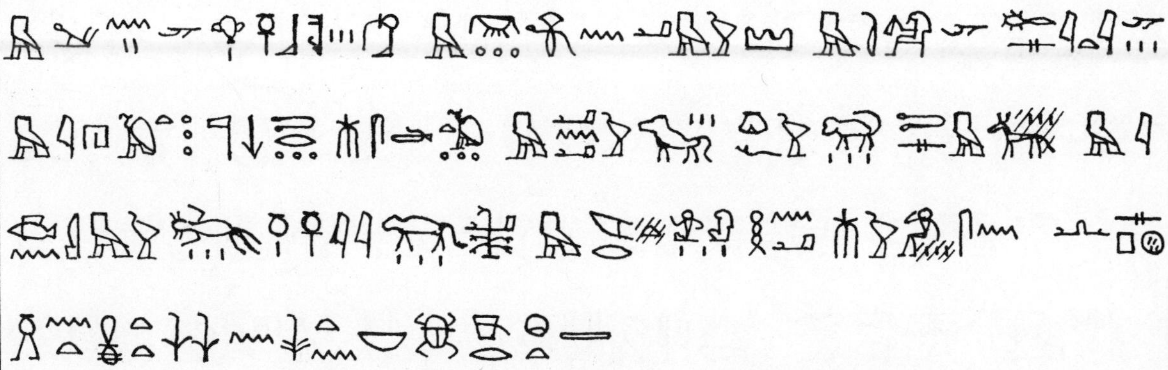

The return voyage of the expedition.

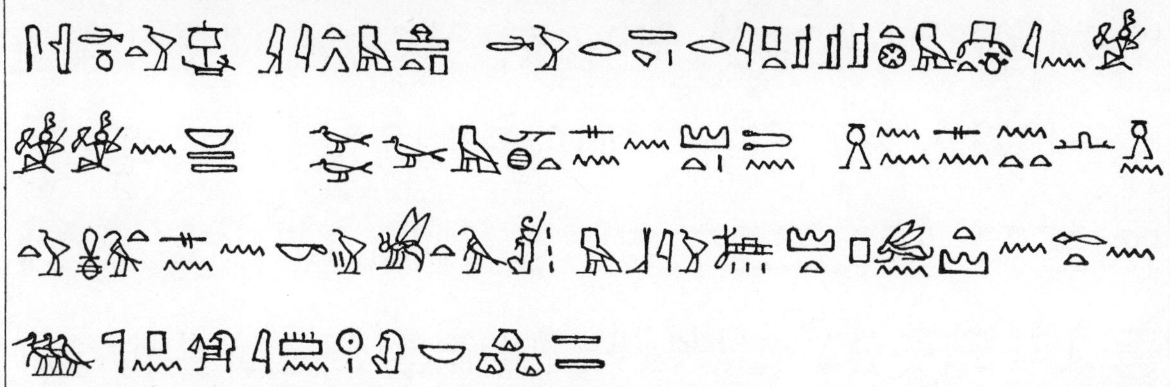

The 'poetical' stela of Tuthmosis III.

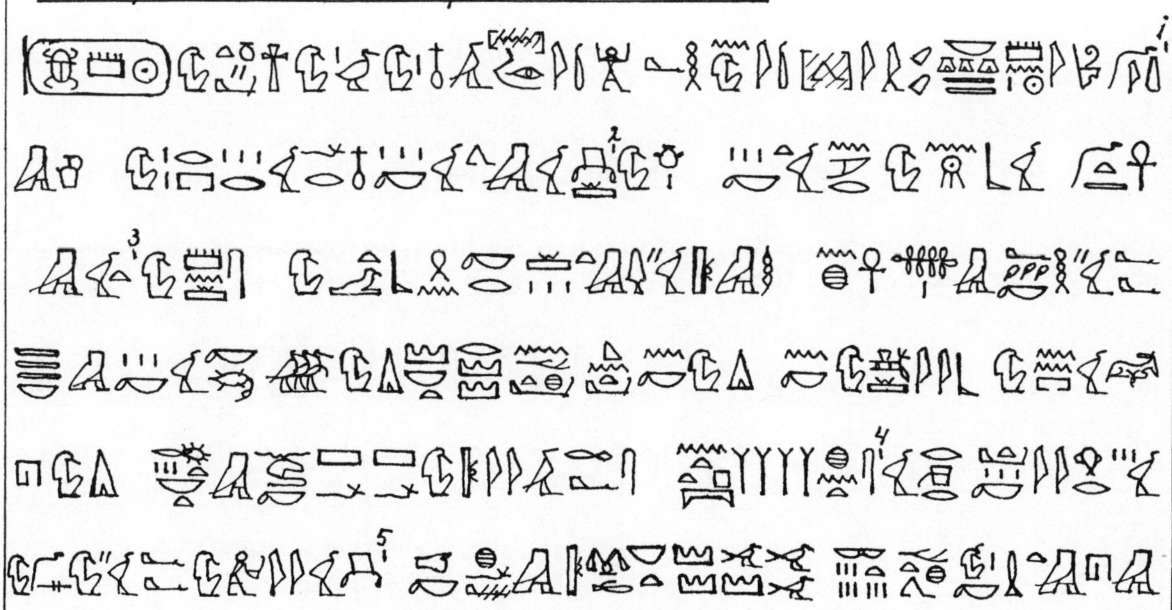

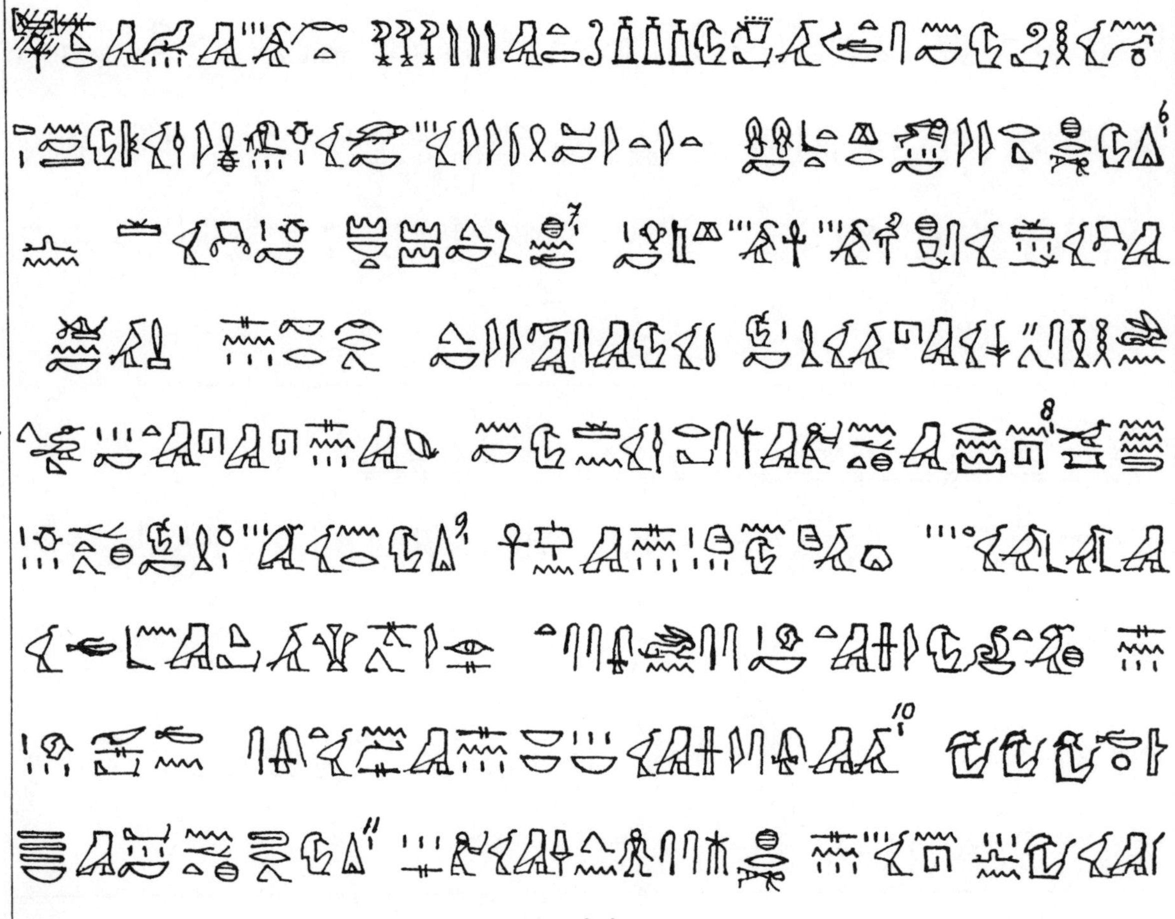

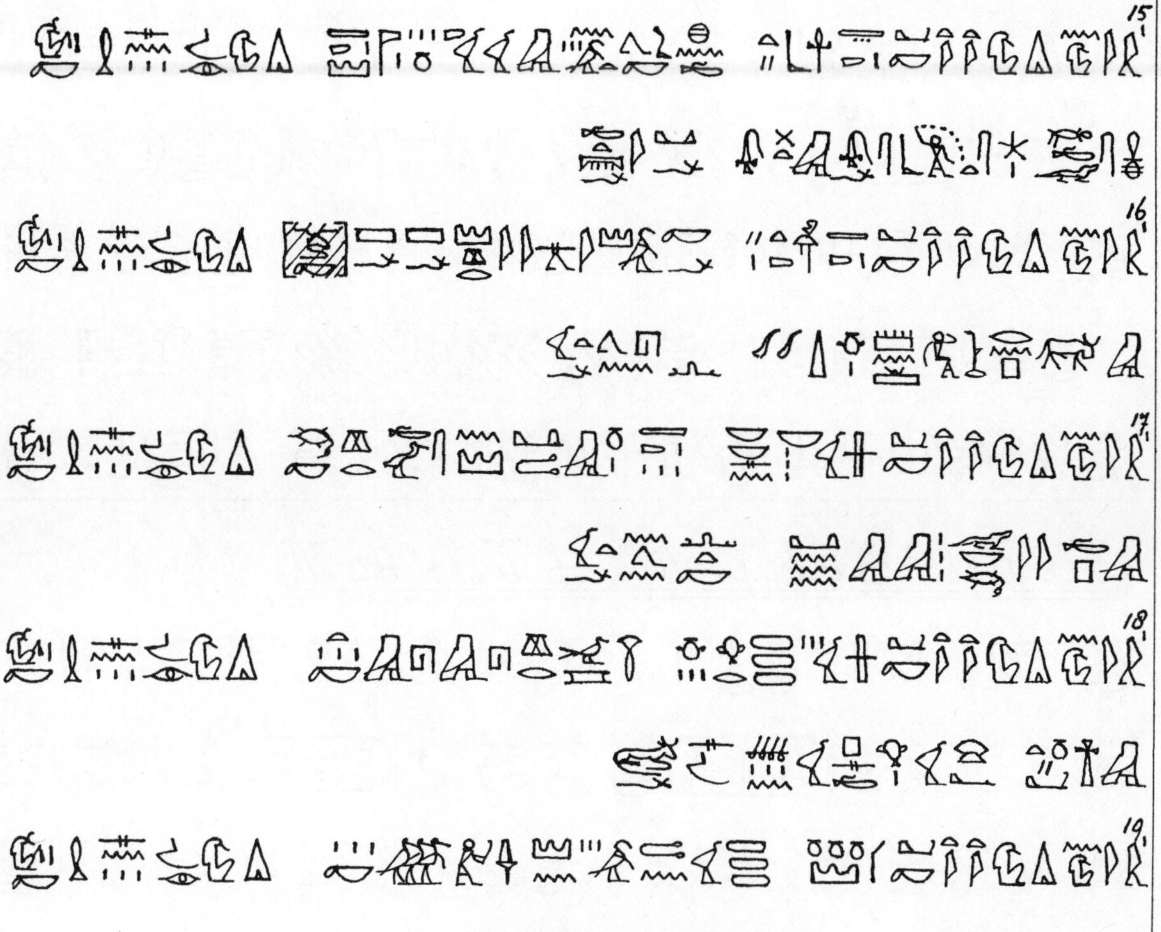

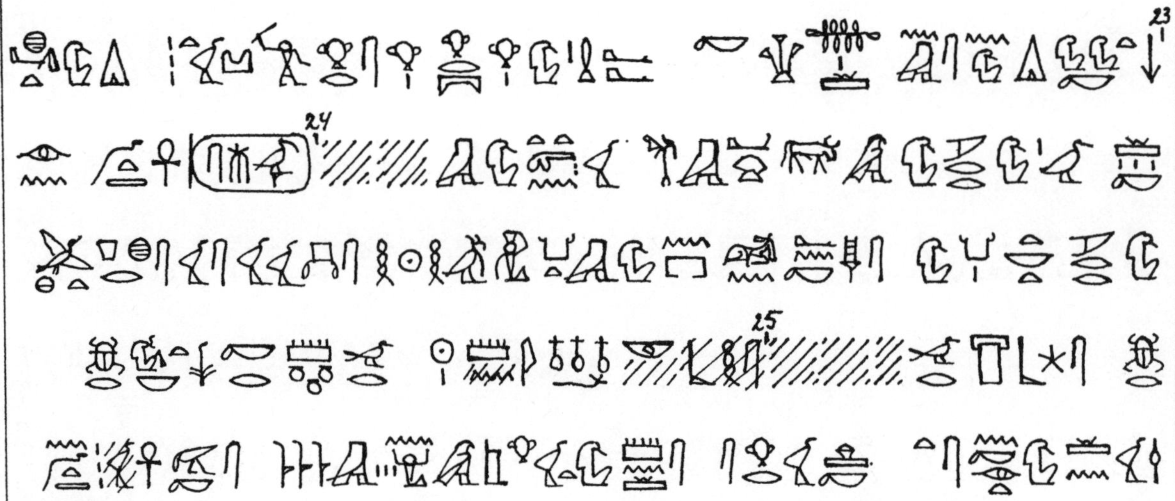

The Gebel Barkal stela of Tuthmosis III.

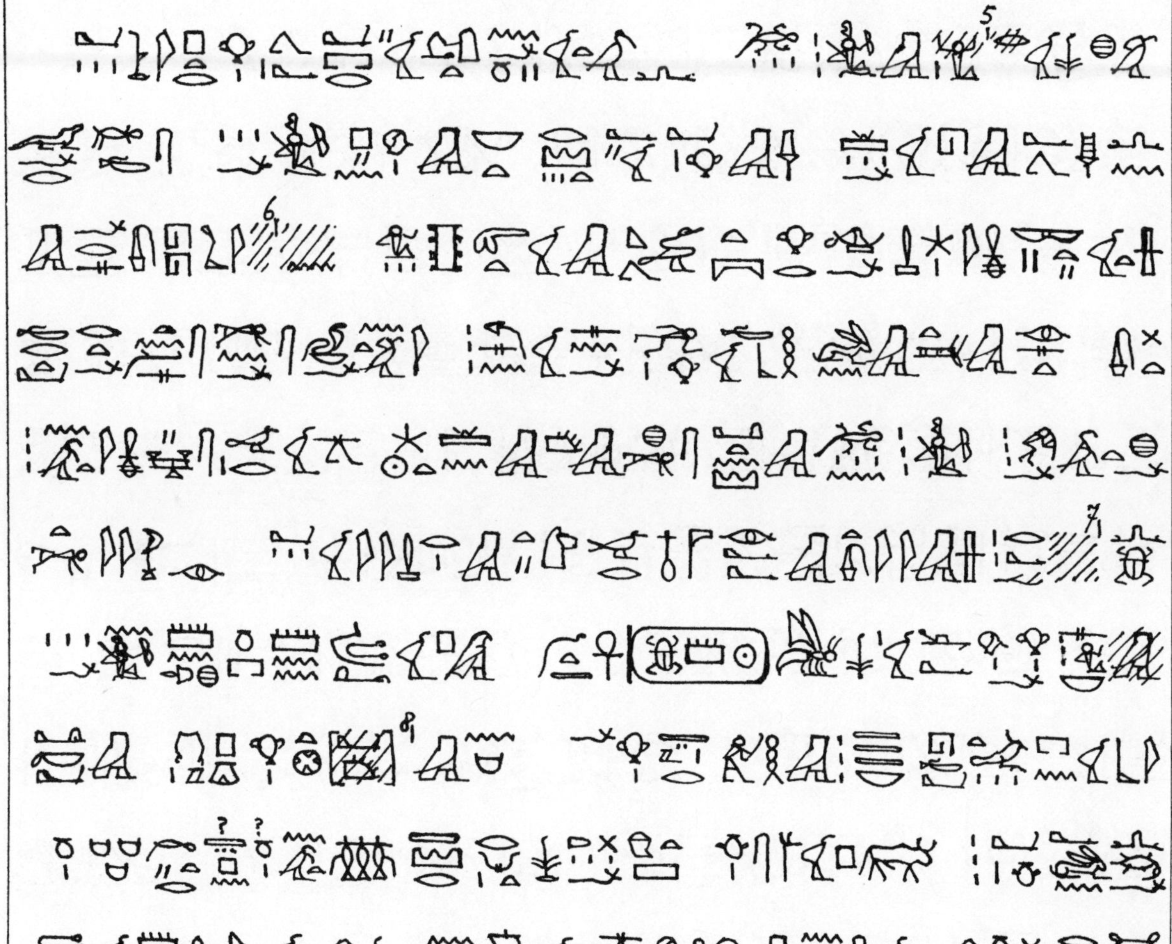

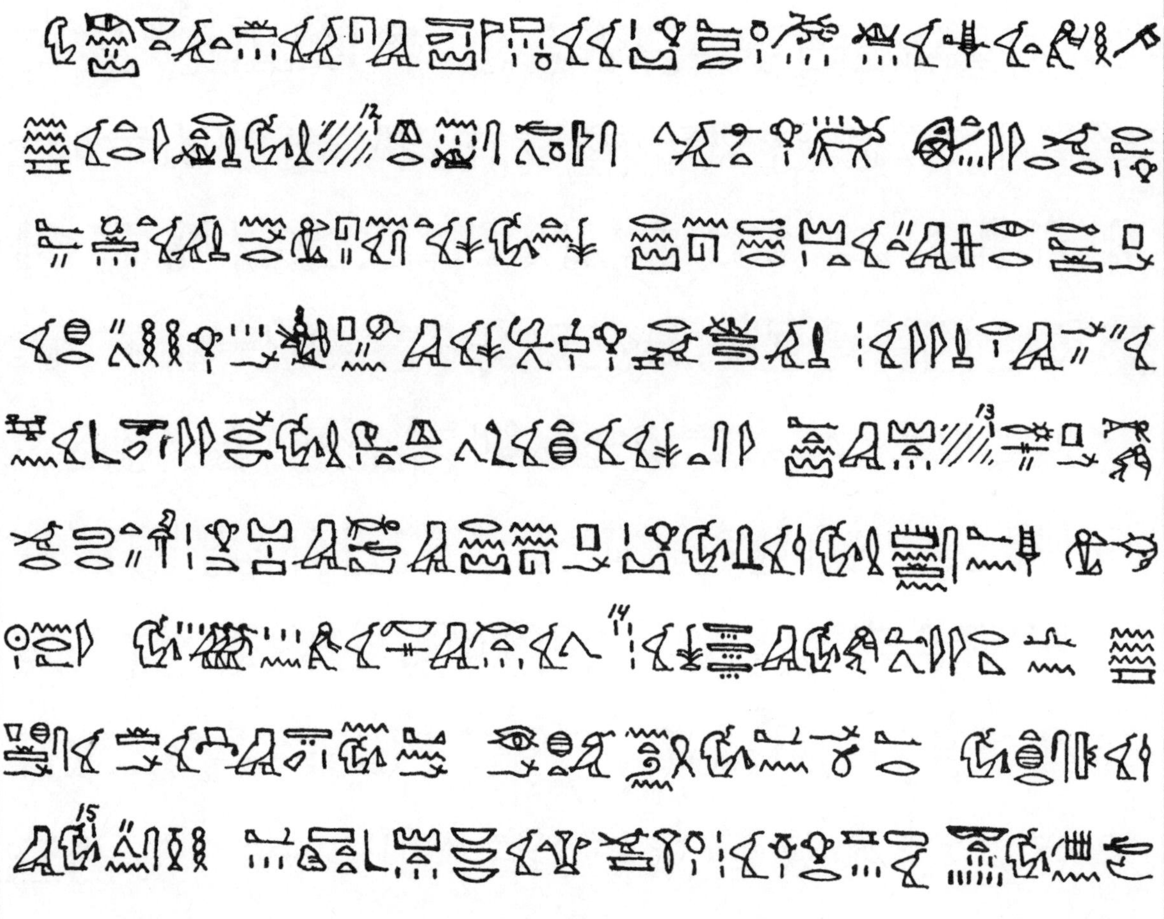

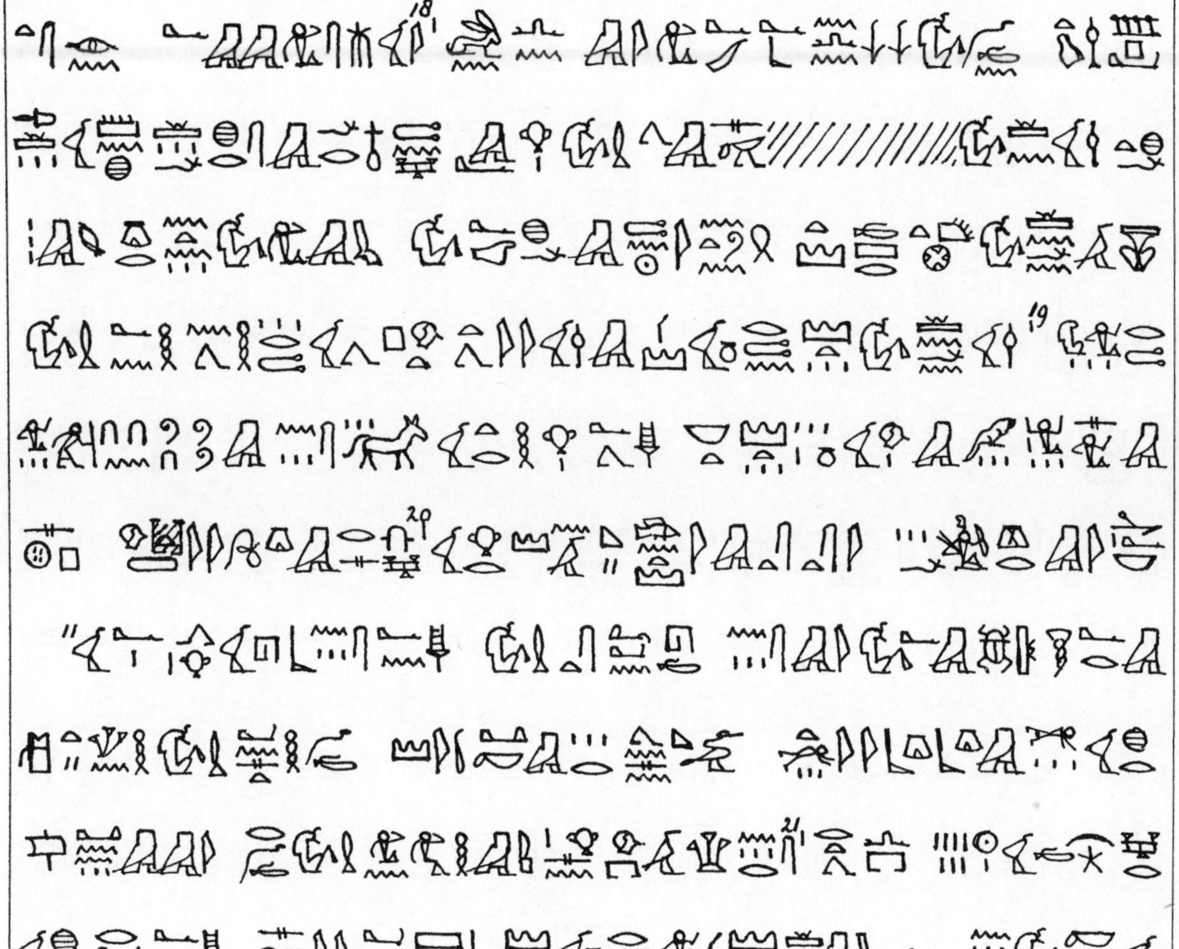

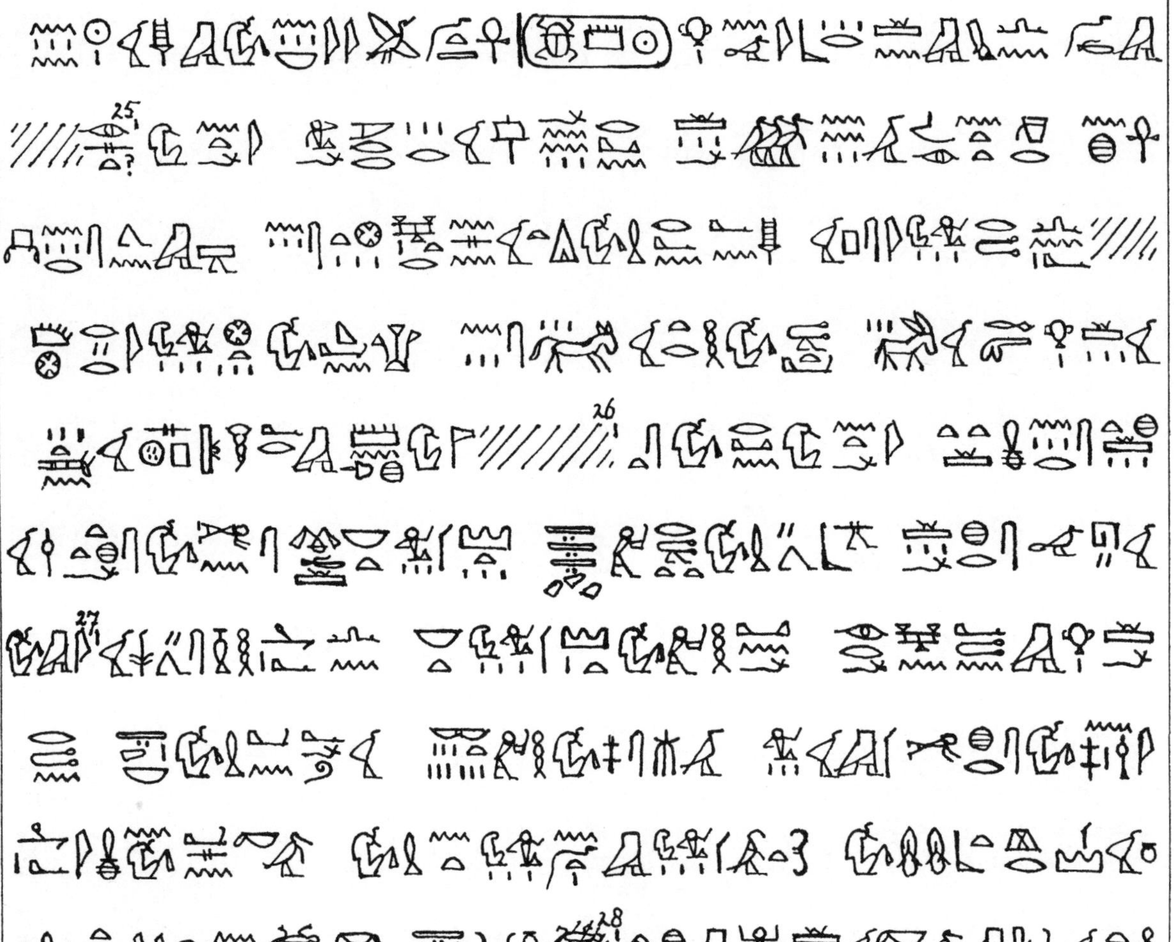

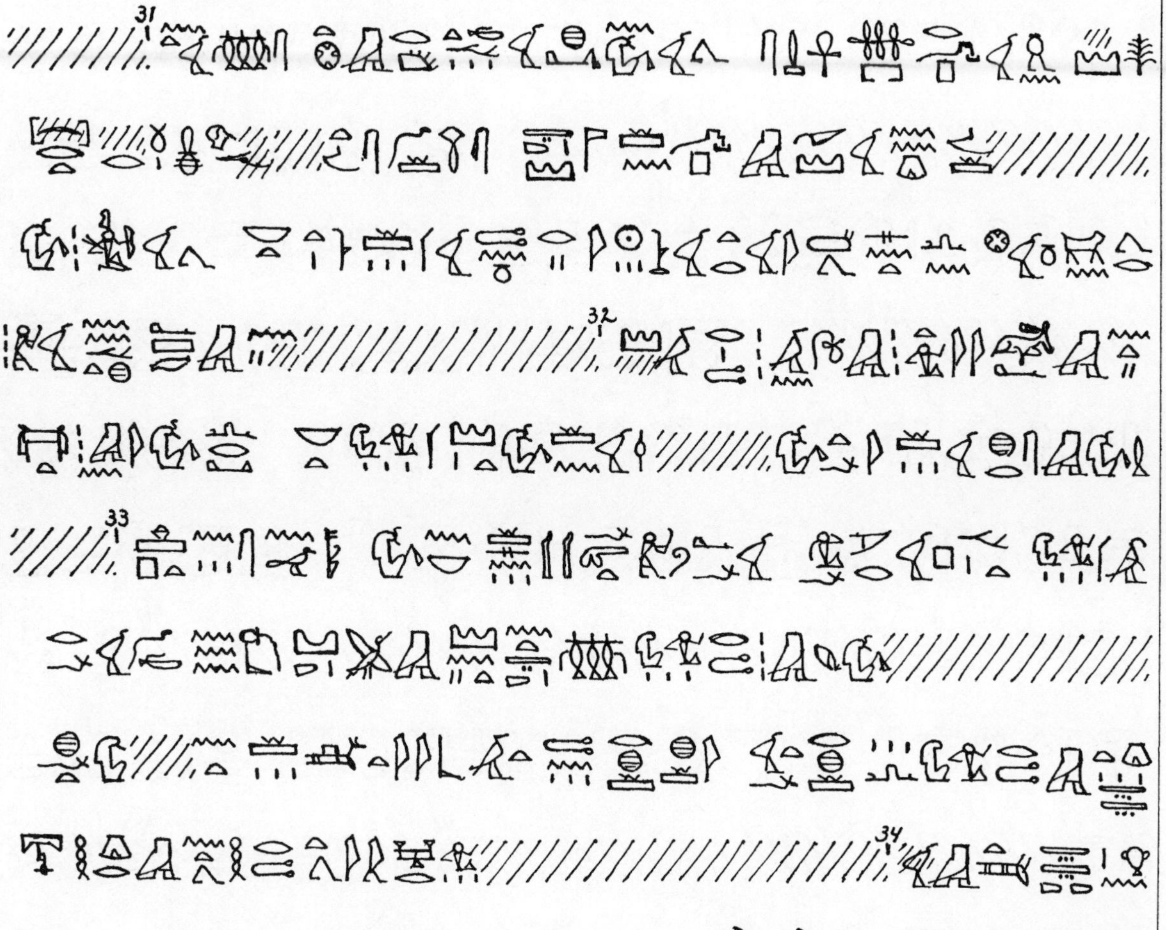

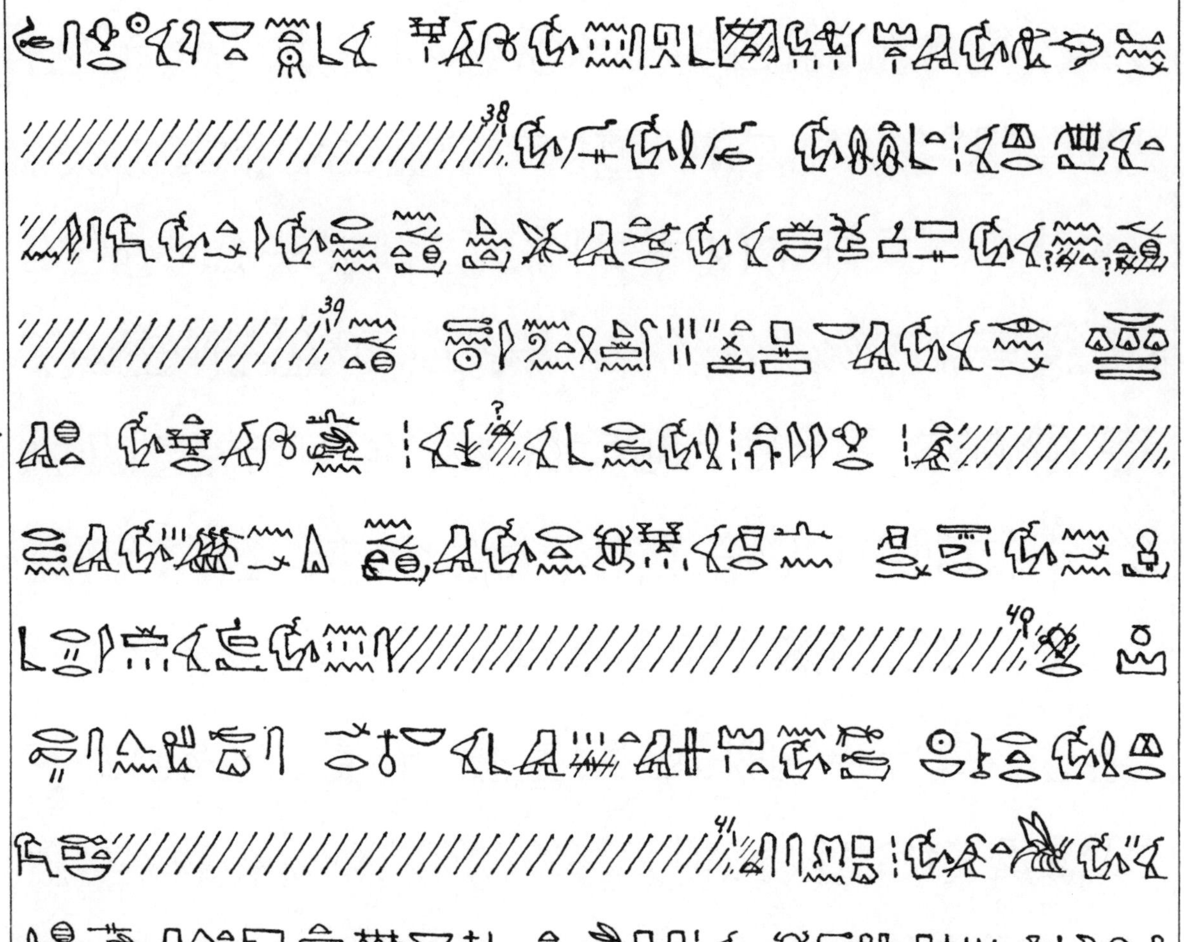

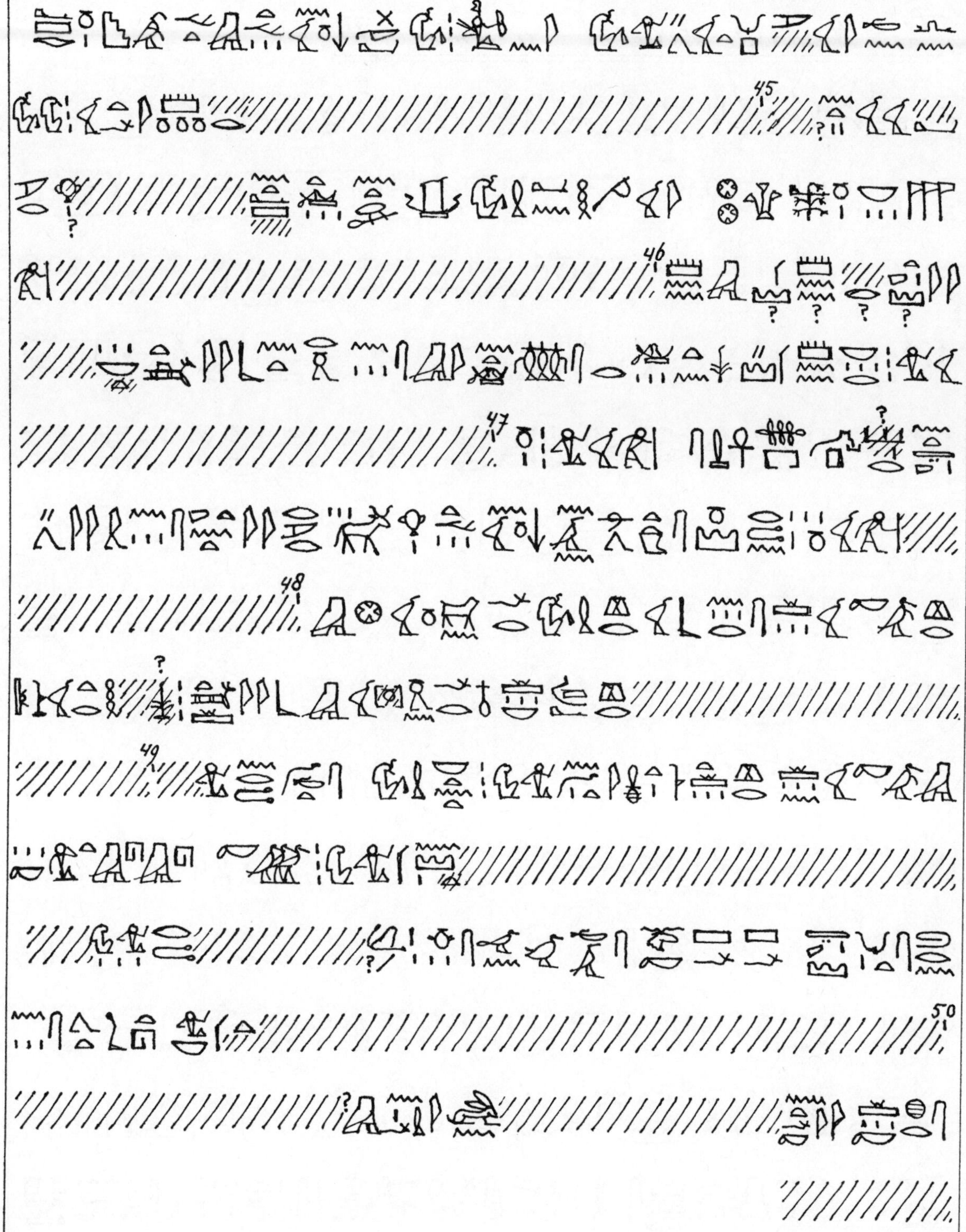

The Armant stela of Tuthmosis III.

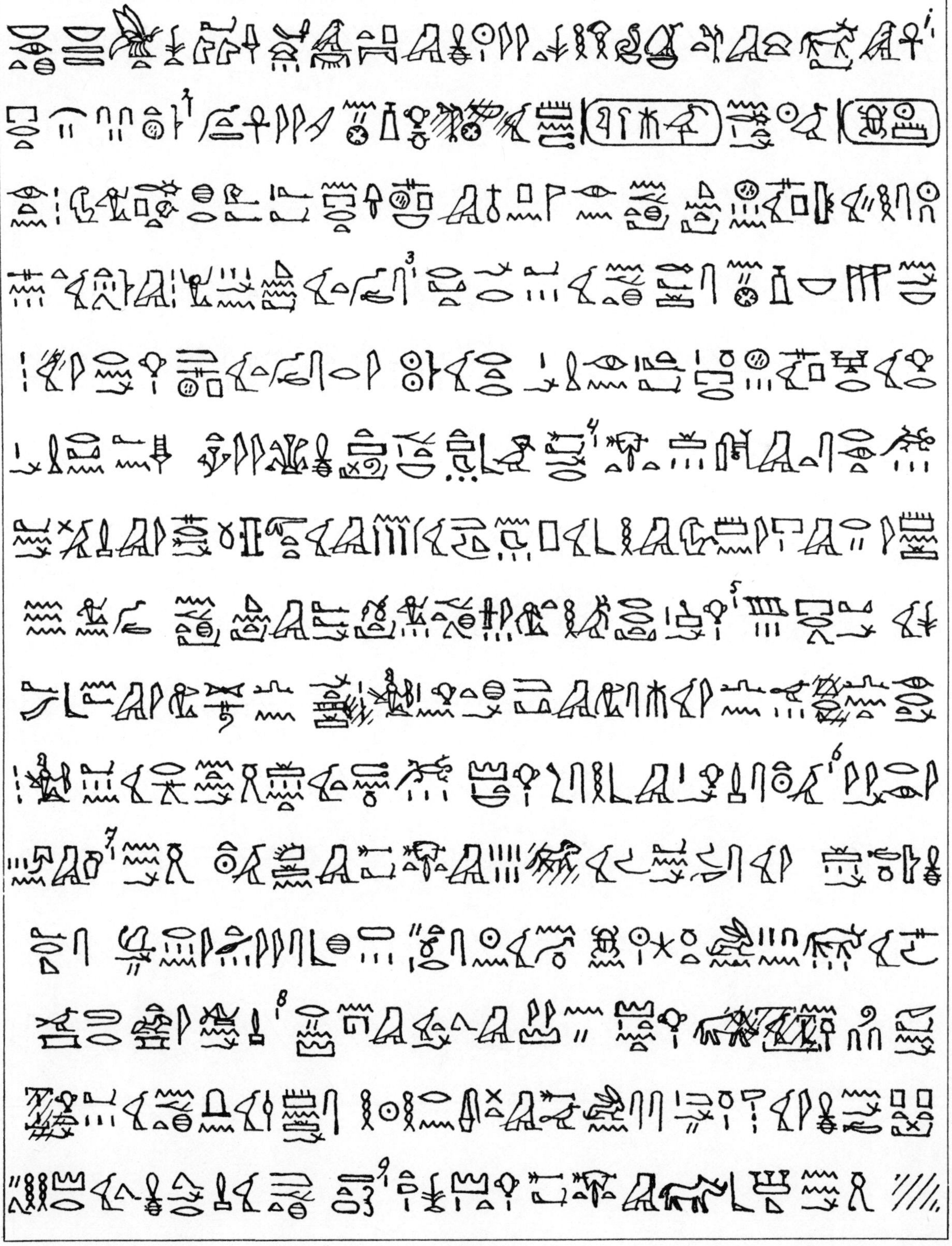

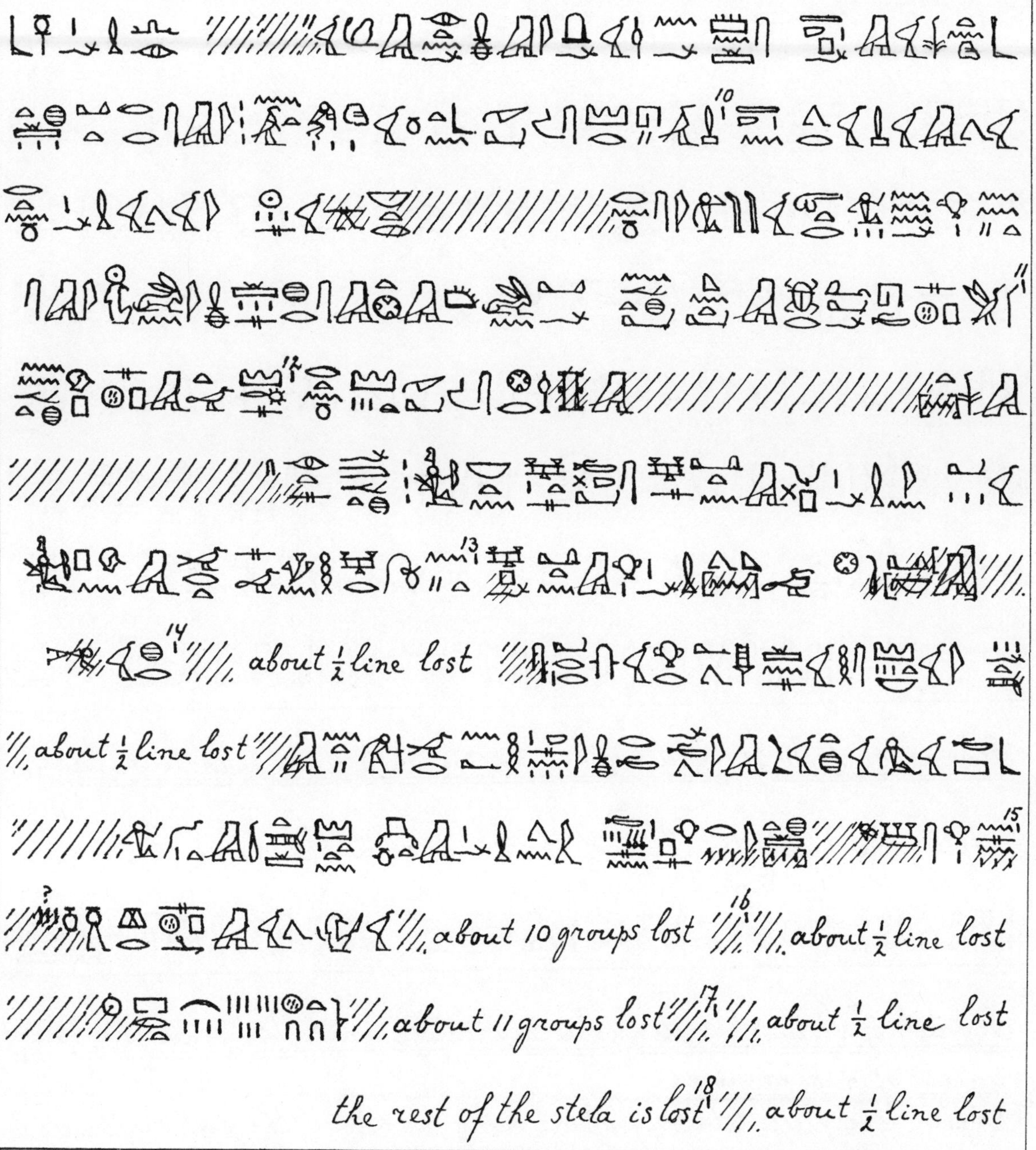
about ½ line lost
about ½ line lost
about 10 groups lost
about ½ line lost
about 11 groups lost
about ½ line lost
the rest of the stela is lost
about ½ line lost

Scarab of Amenophis III, recording a wild cattle hunt.

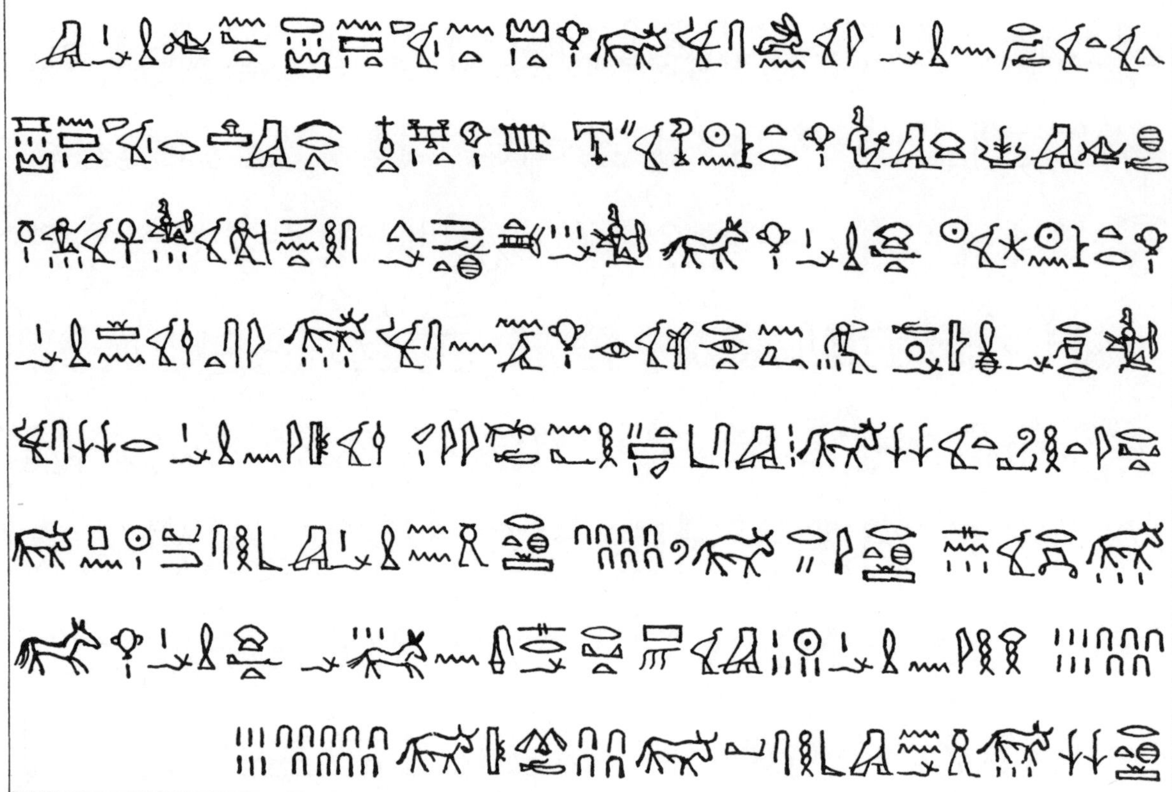

Scarab of A. III, recording his success in 10 years' lion-hunting.

After the full titulary of the king and the name of the queen, as above, the text continues:

Scarab of A. III, recording his marriage with Tiy and the boundaries of his empire.

After the full titulary of the king, as above, the text continues:

Scarab of A. III, recording the arrival of the princess Gilukhipa.

The full titulary of the king follows 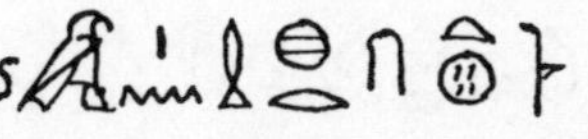

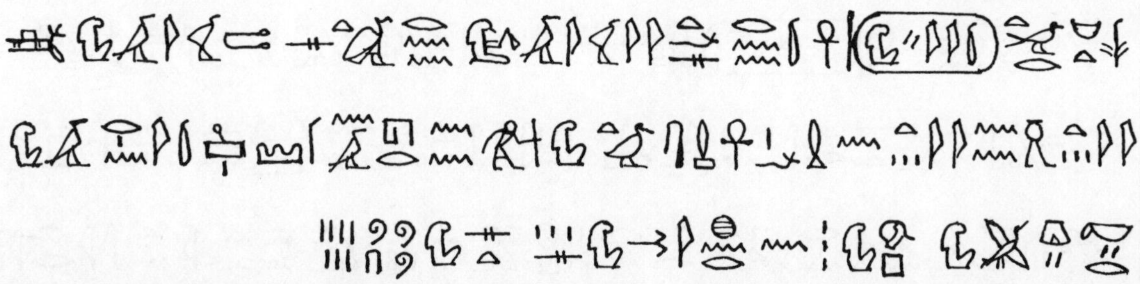

Scarab of A. III, recording the construction of a pleasure-lake.

The full titulary of the king follows 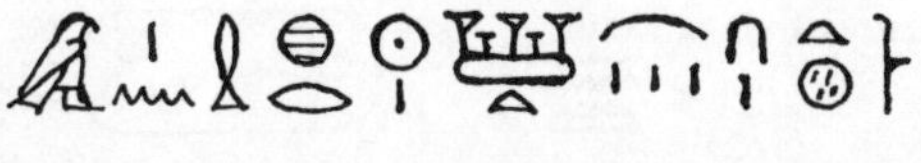

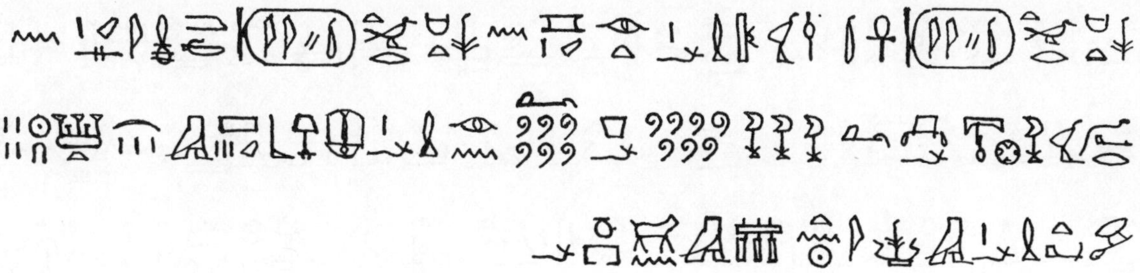

The biography of Khnumhotpe, prince of Beni Hasan.

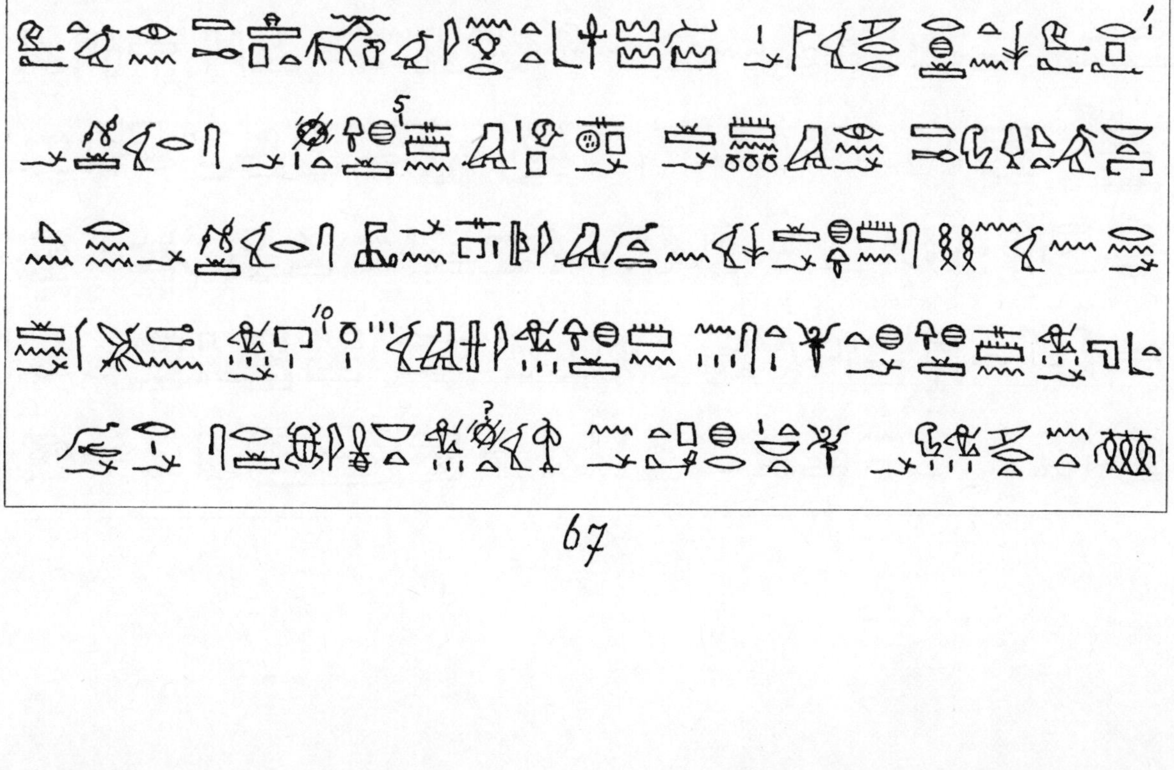

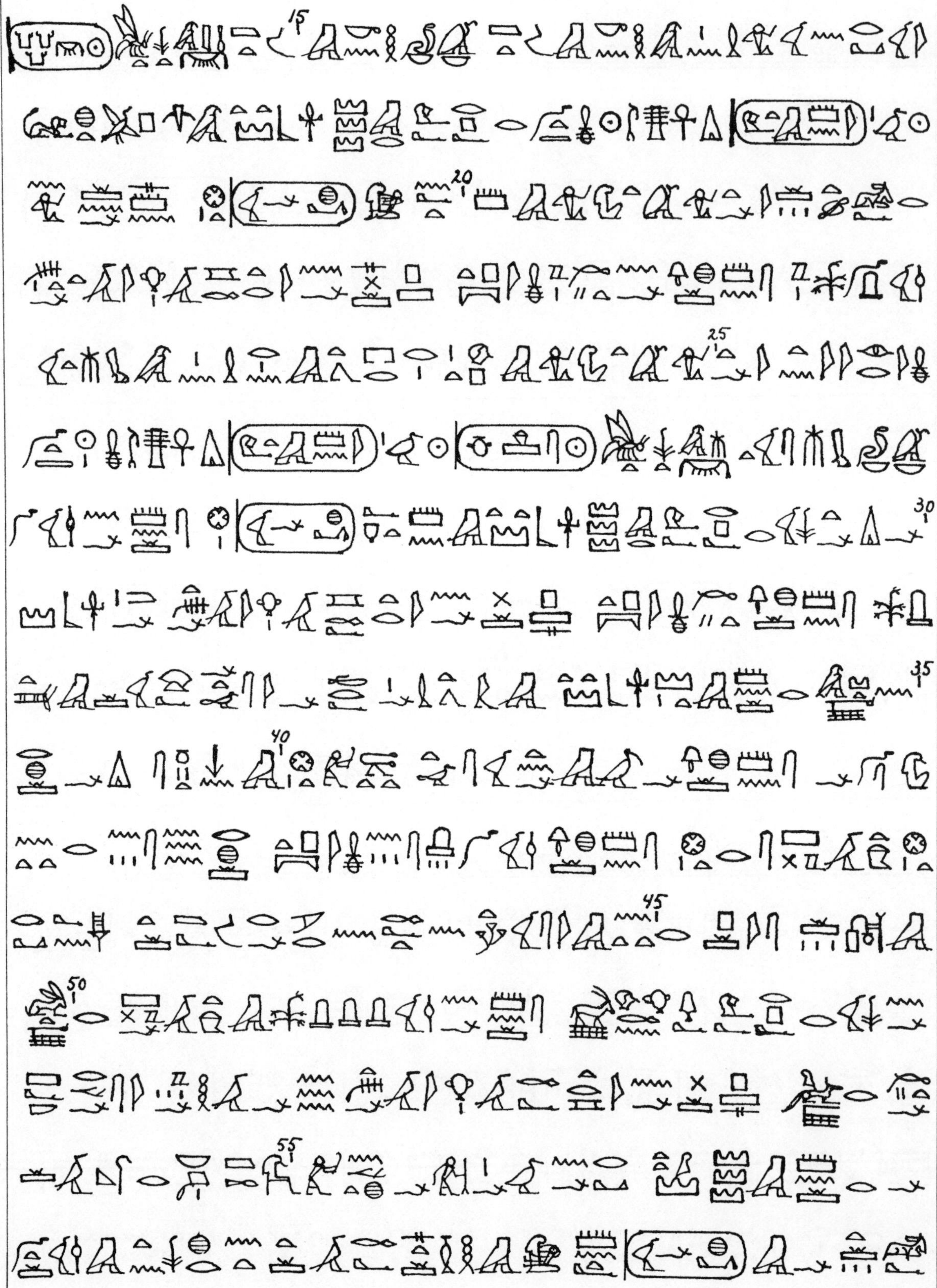

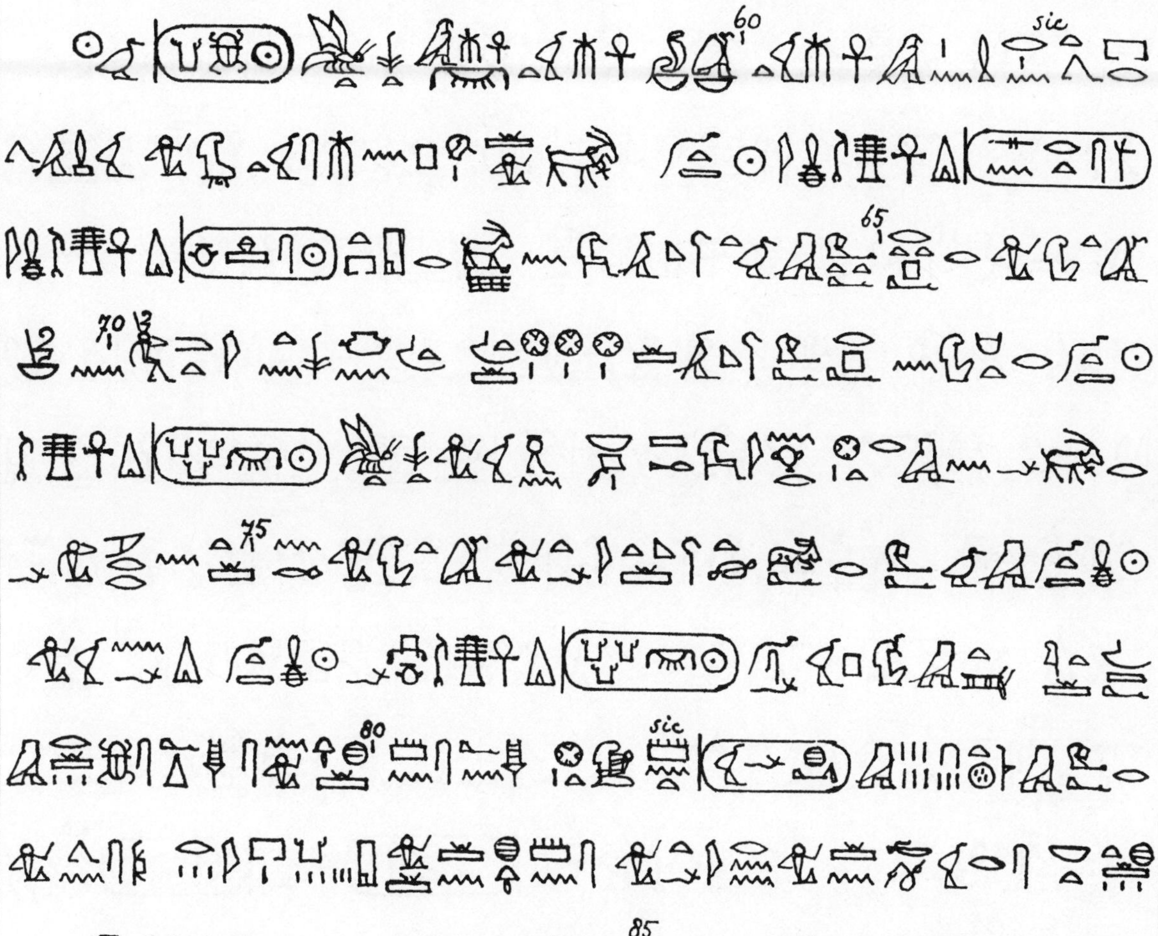

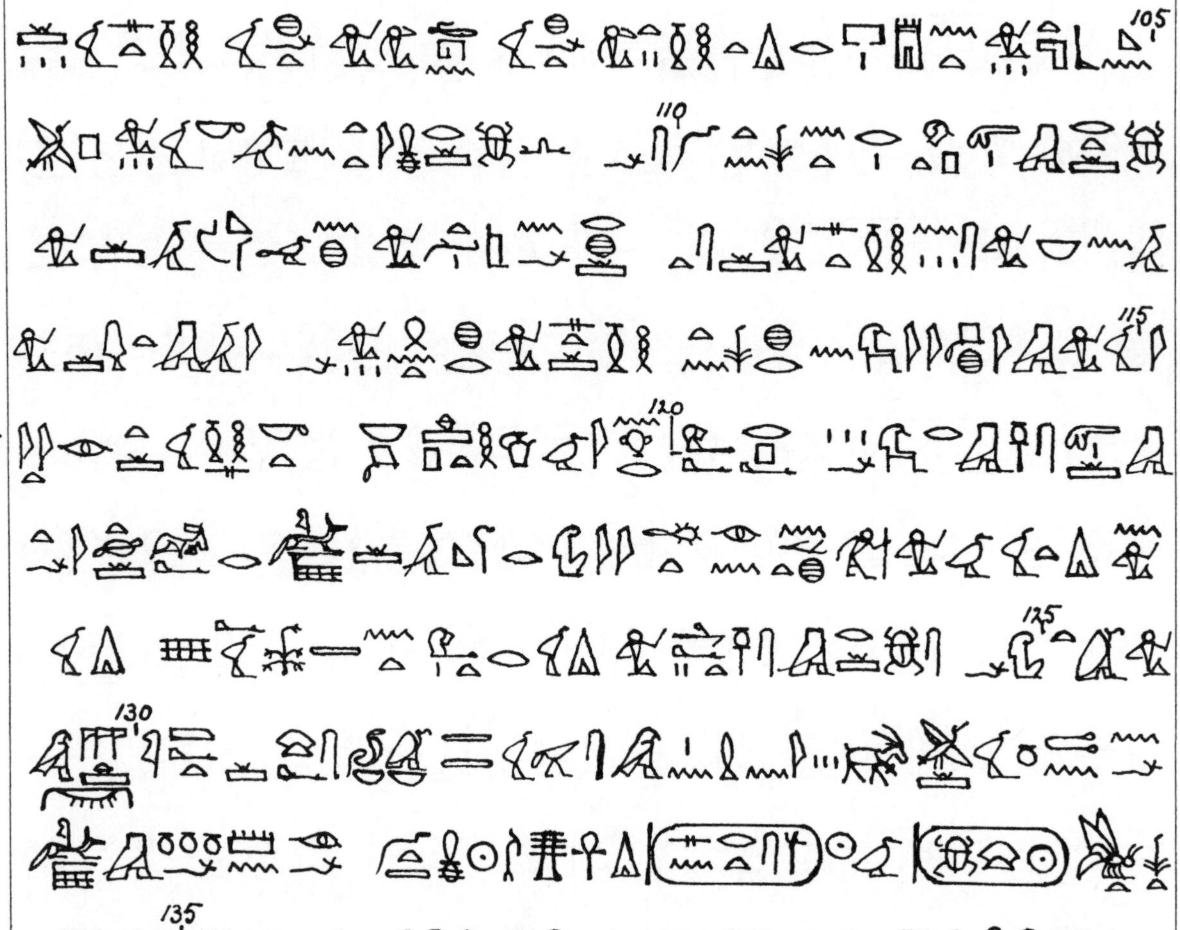

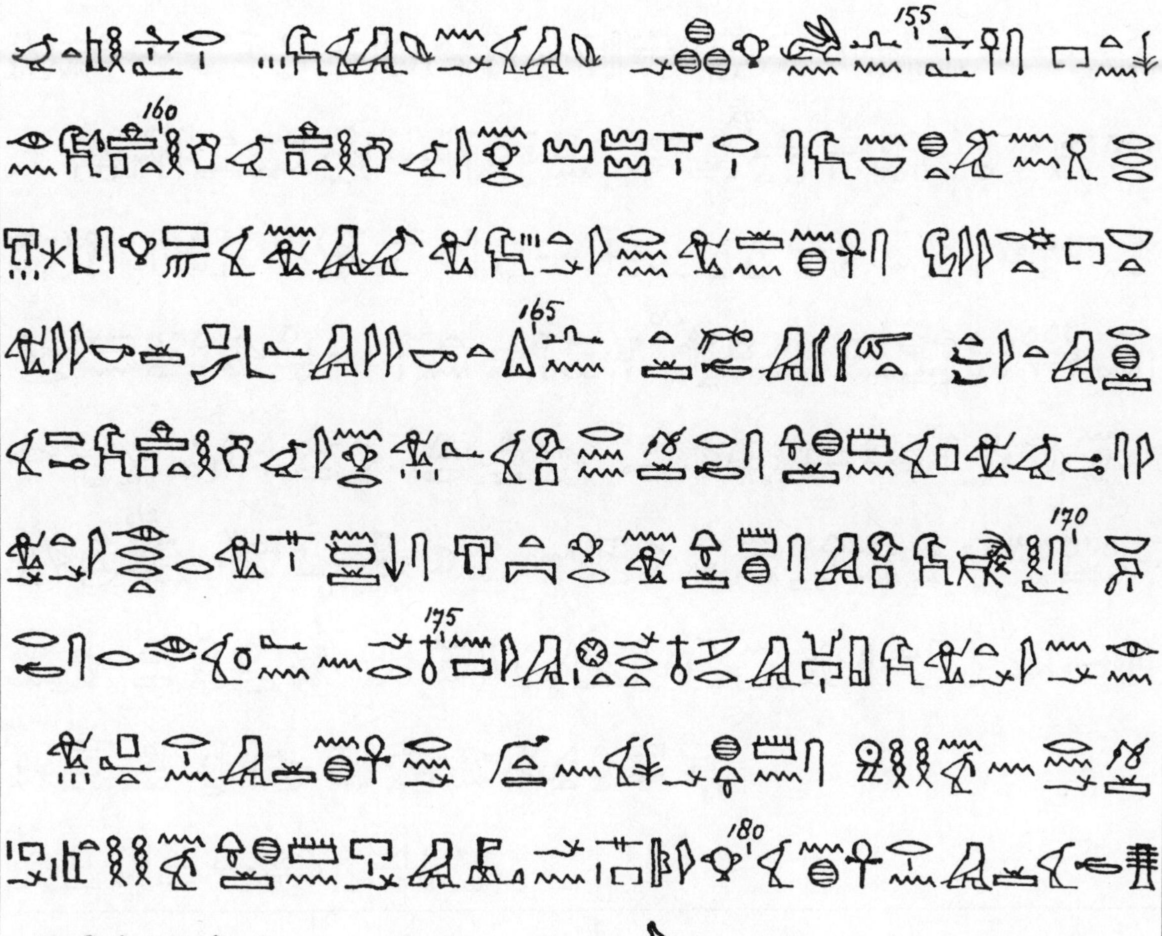

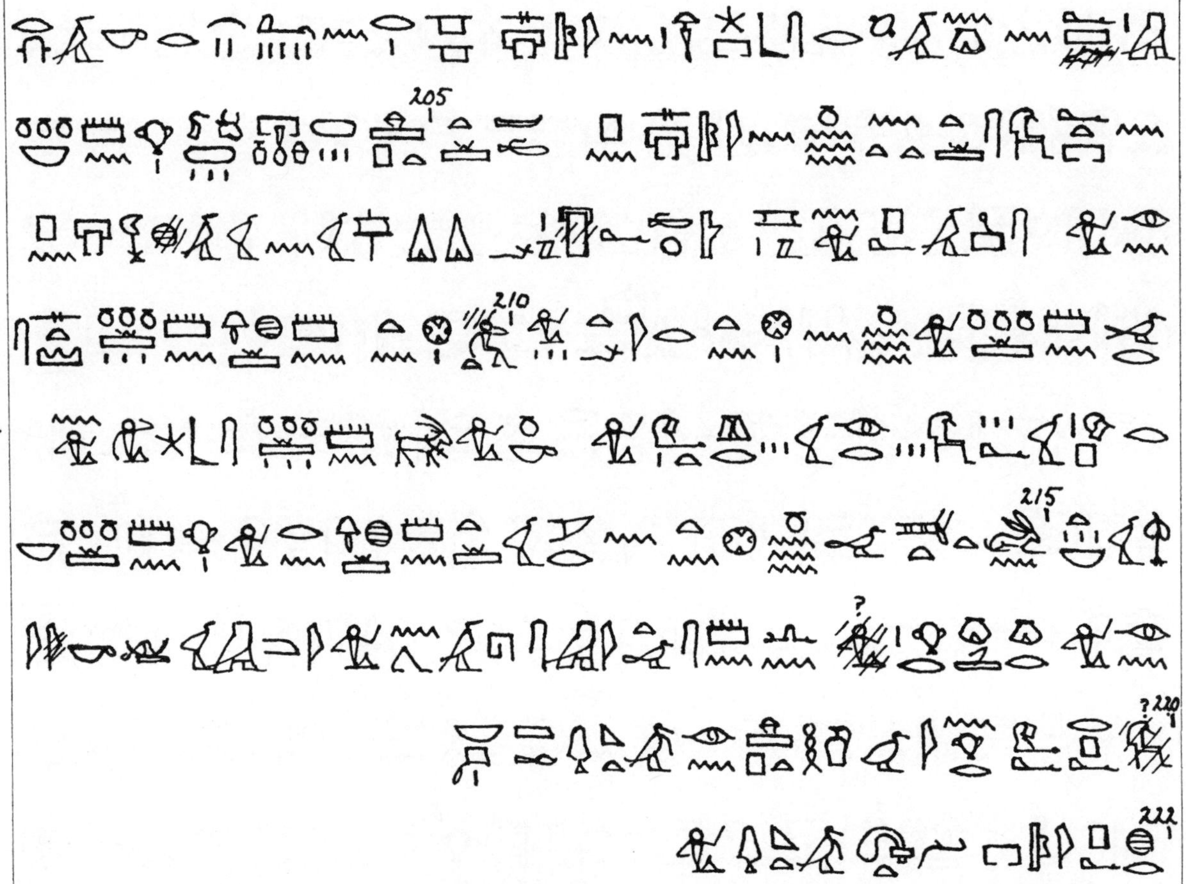

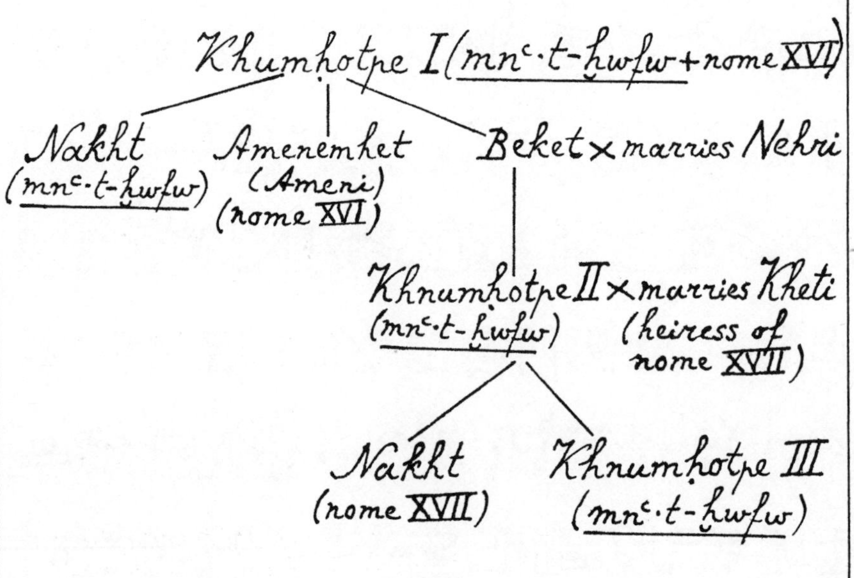
Khumhotpe I (mnᶜ·t-ḫwfw + nome XVI)
Nakht (mnᶜ·t-ḫwfw)
Amenemhet (Ameni) (nome XVI)
Beket × marries Nehri
Khnumhotpe II × marries Kheti (heiress of nome XVII)
(mnᶜ·t-ḫwfw)
Nakht (nome XVII)
Khnumhotpe III (mnᶜ·t-ḫwfw)

XIX
XVIII
XVII
XVI
Beni-Hasan
Hermopolis
XV
XV
Amarna

The laudatory autobiography of Kay (Hatnub, Gr. 24)

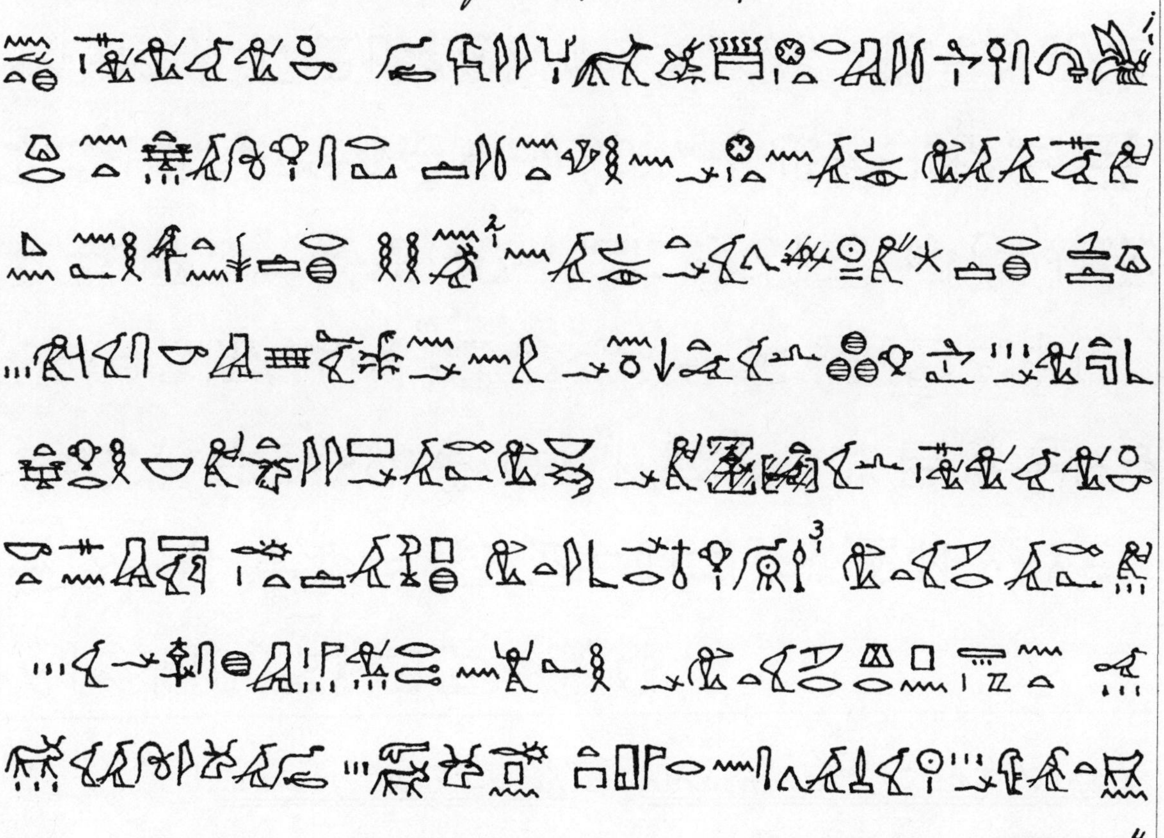

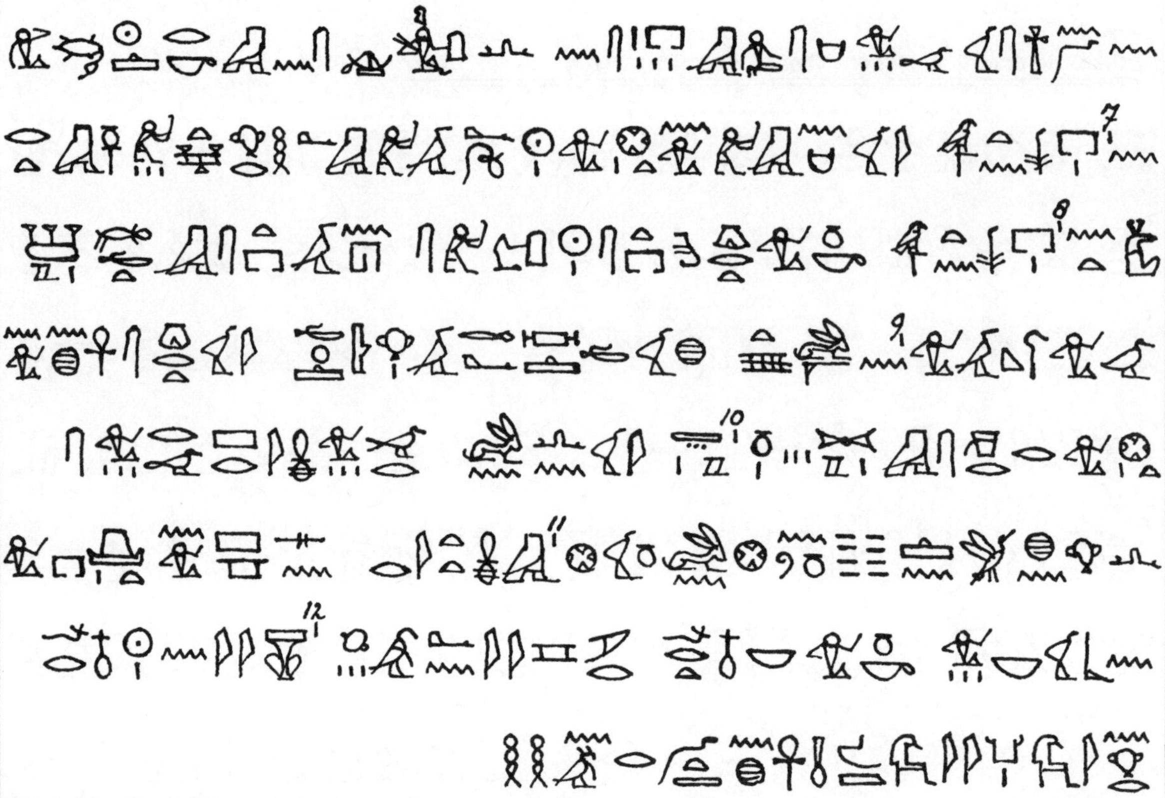

Expedition to Hammamat; the official record.

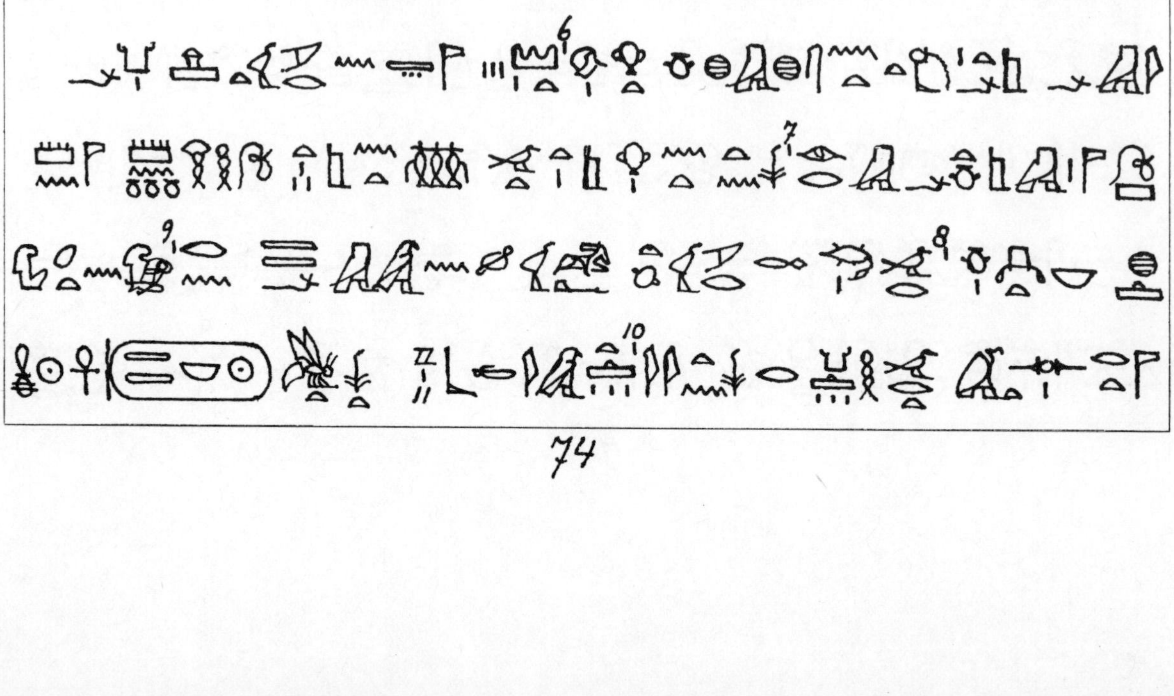

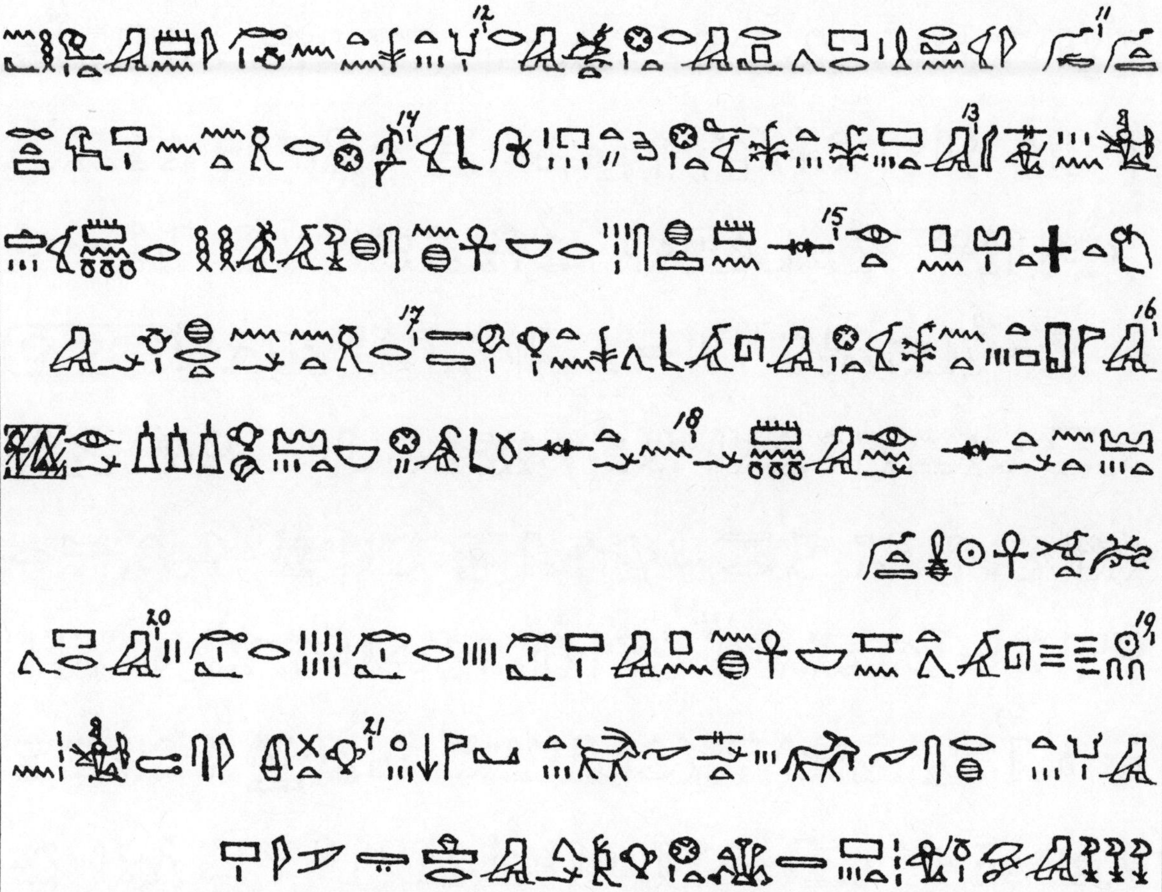

The same expedition; the commander's record.

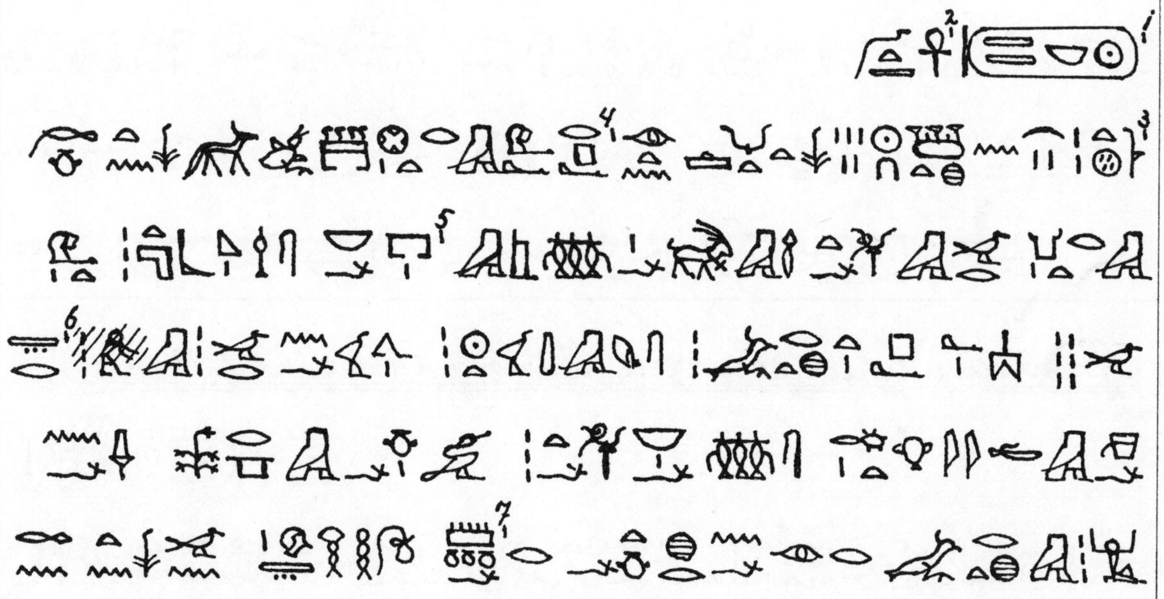

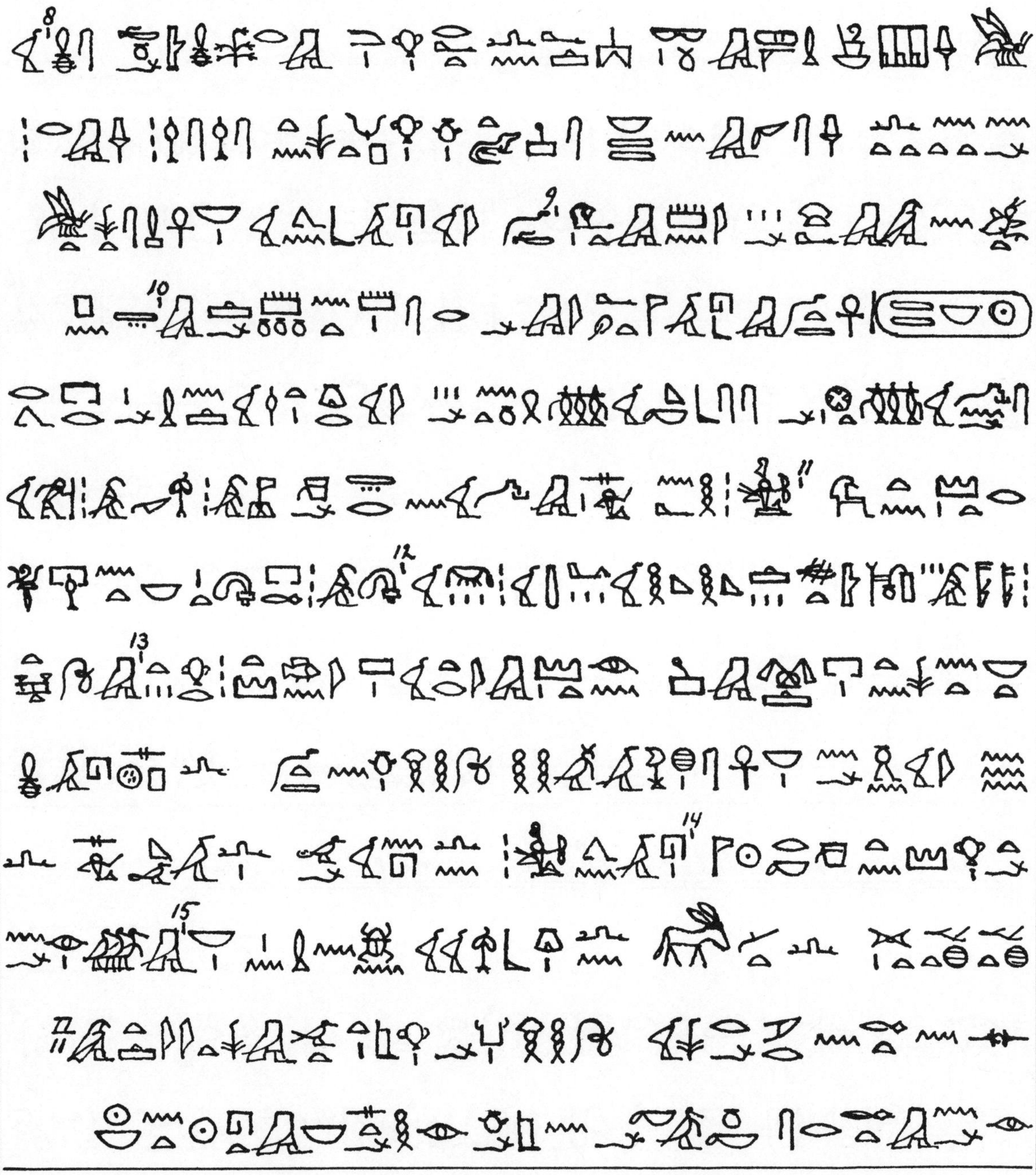

A wonder, which occurred during this expedition.

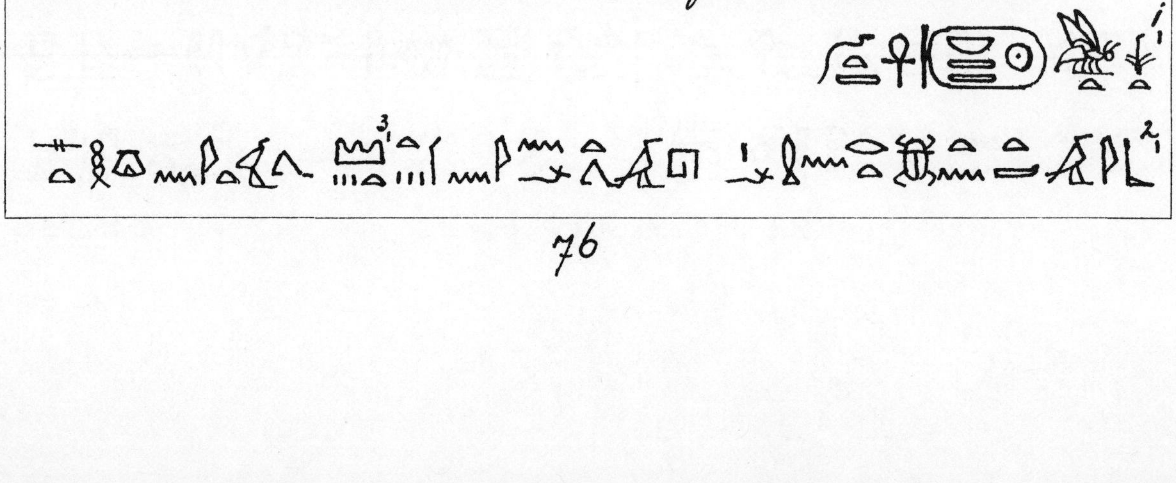

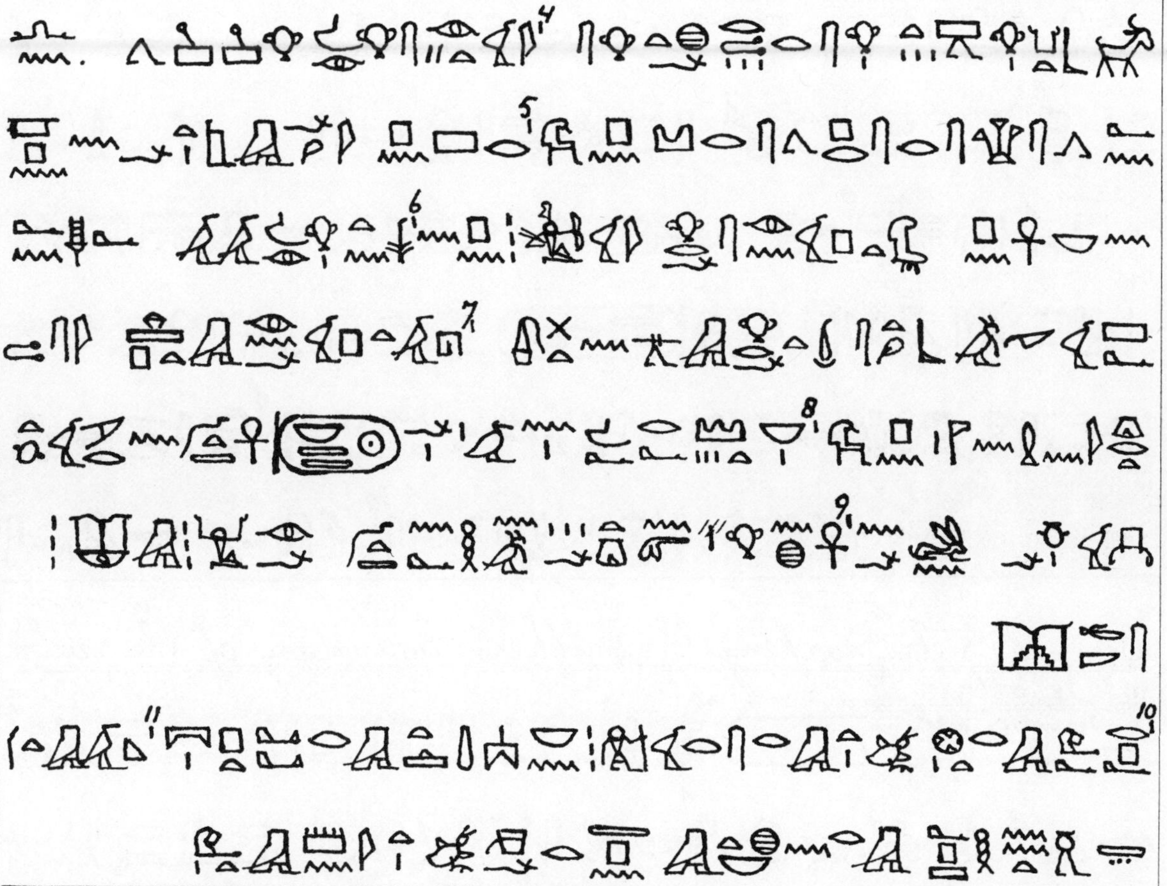

The second wonder which happened during this expedition.

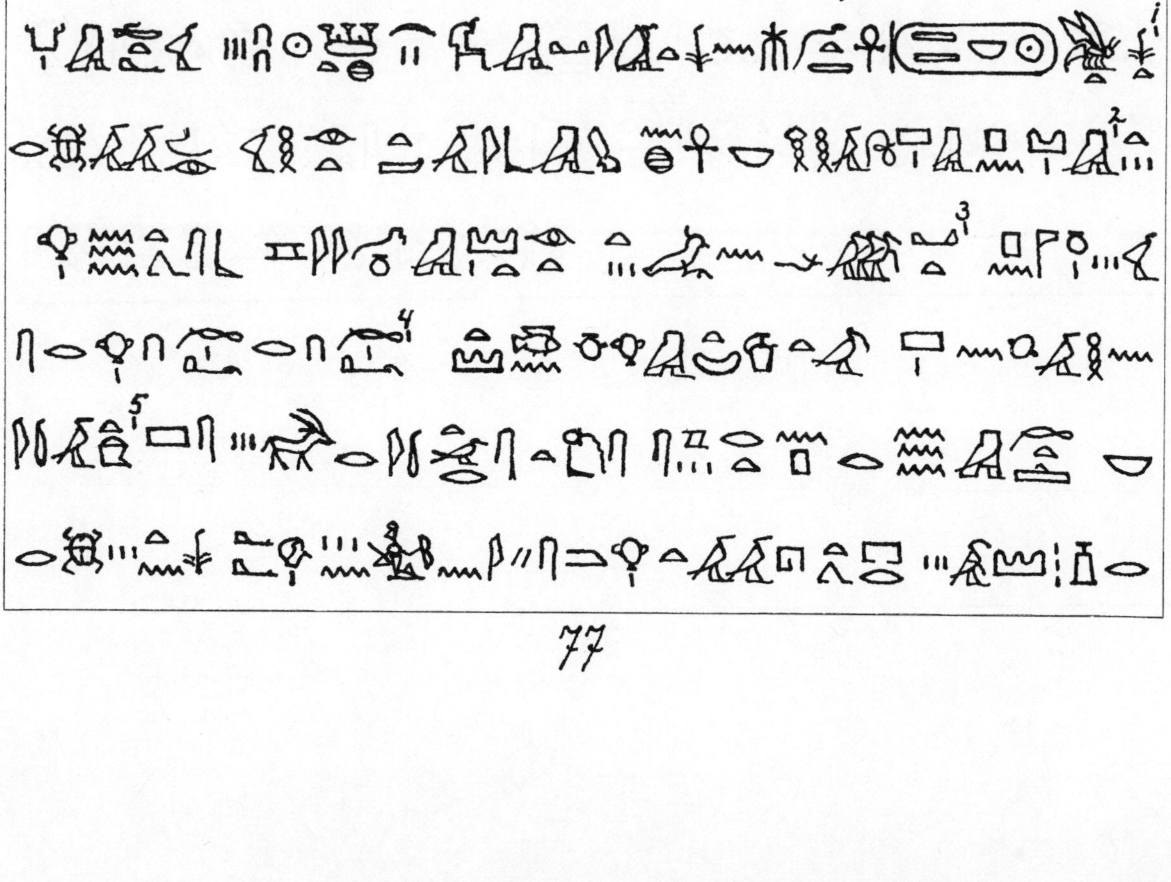

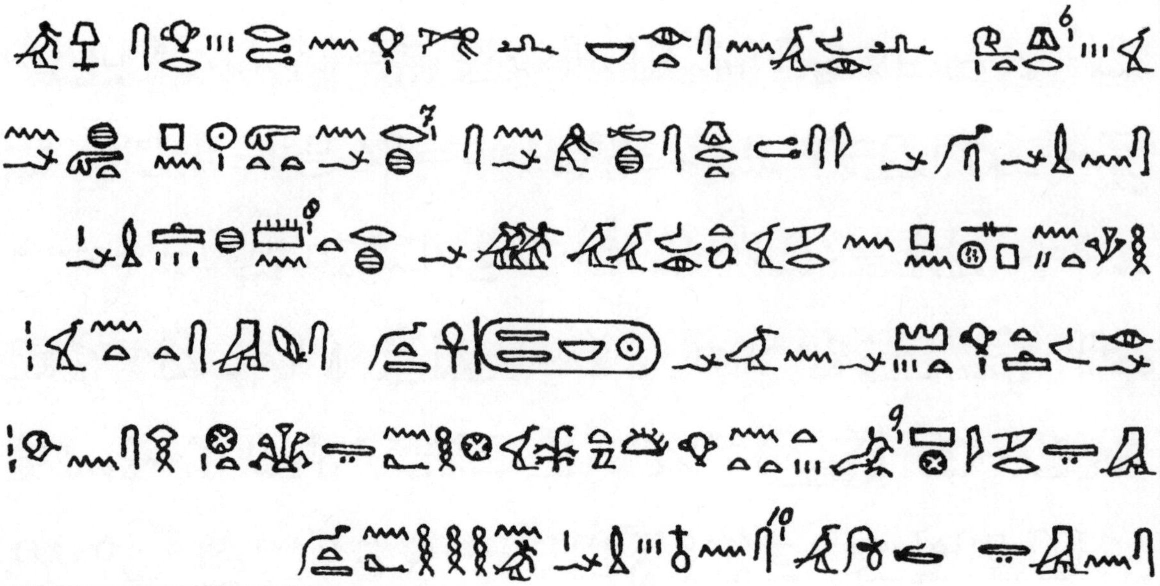

Semneh stela marking the southern boundary of the realm of Sesostris III.

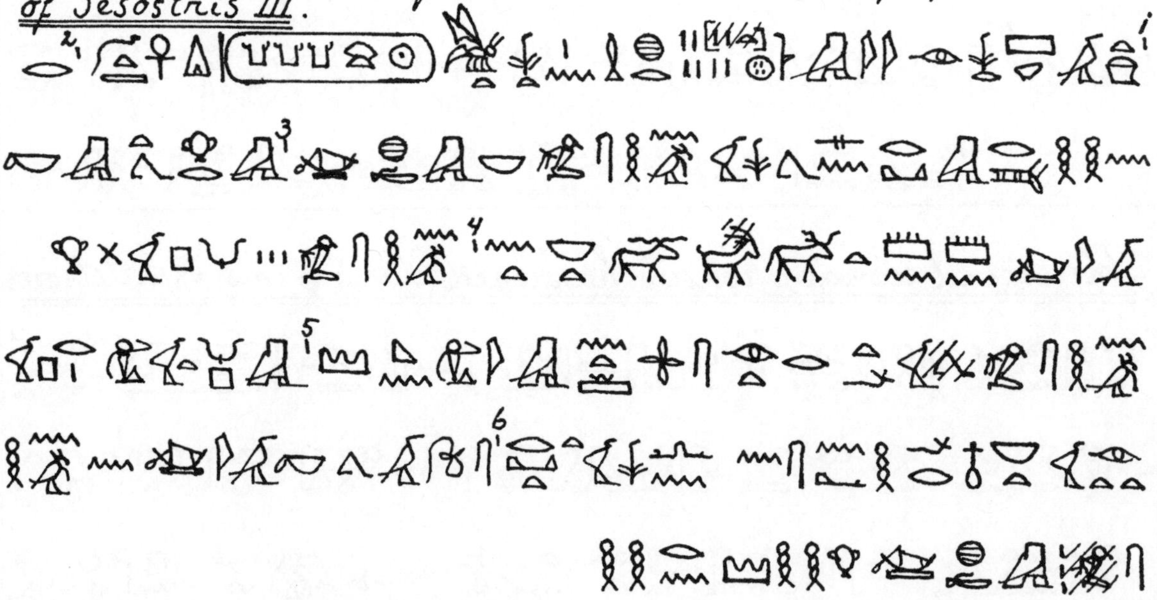

Story of the miracles which happened in the reign of Cheops.

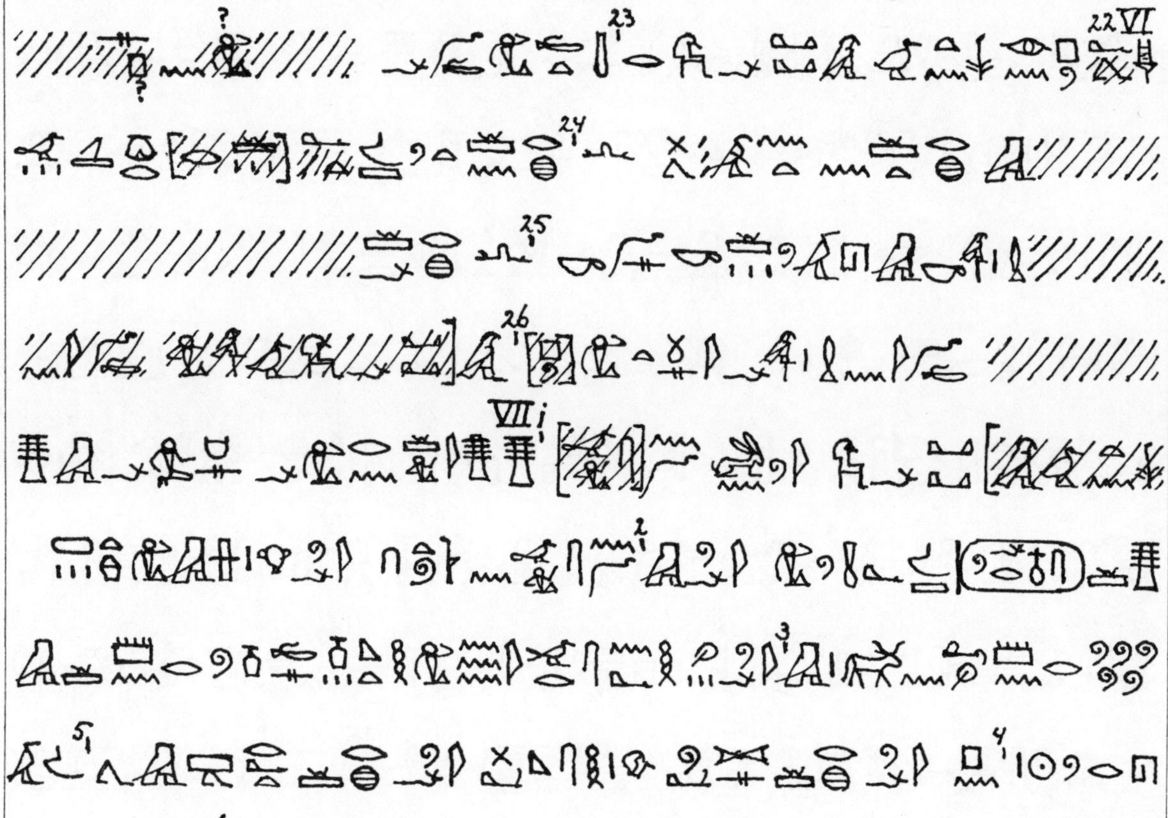

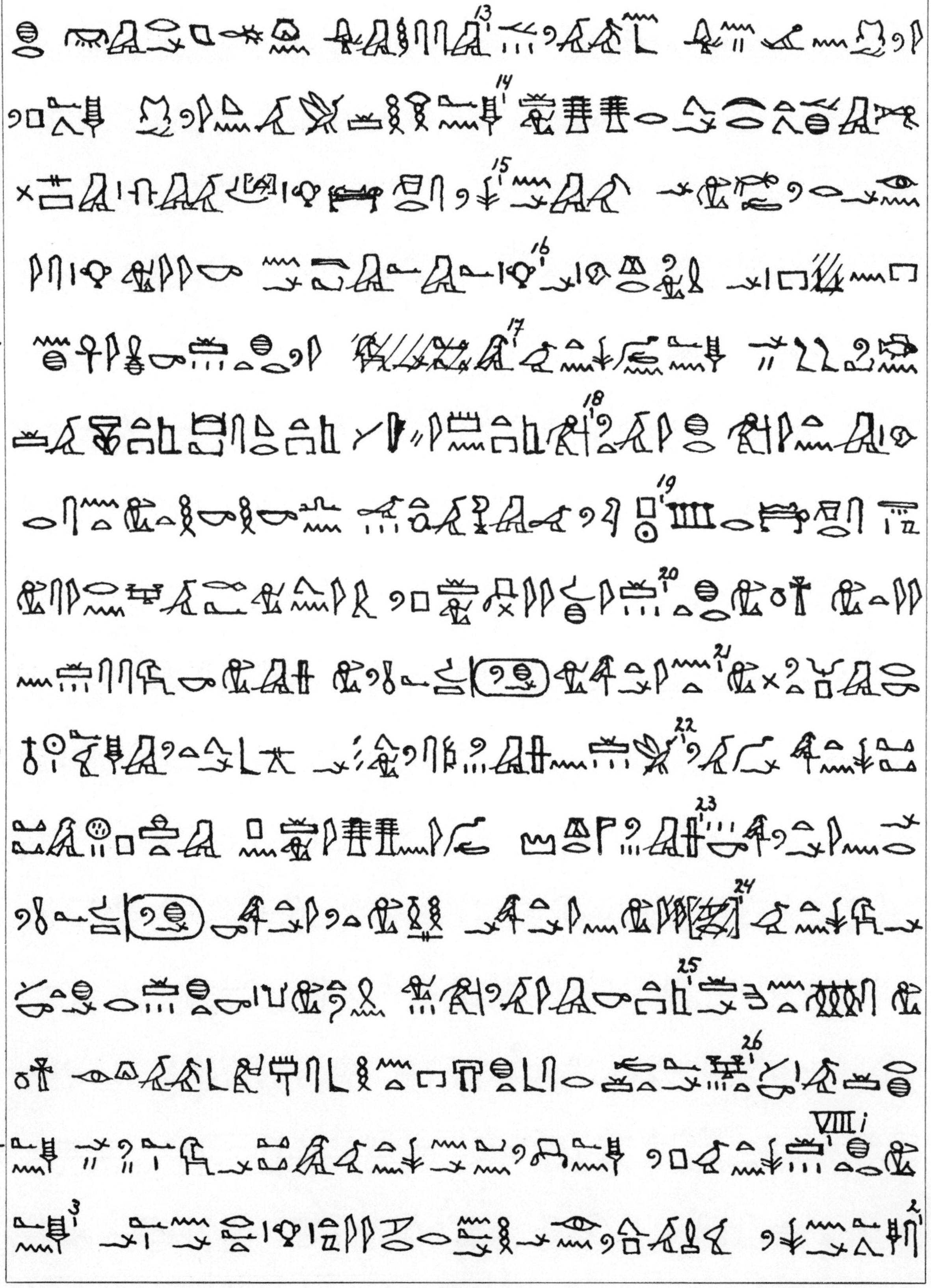

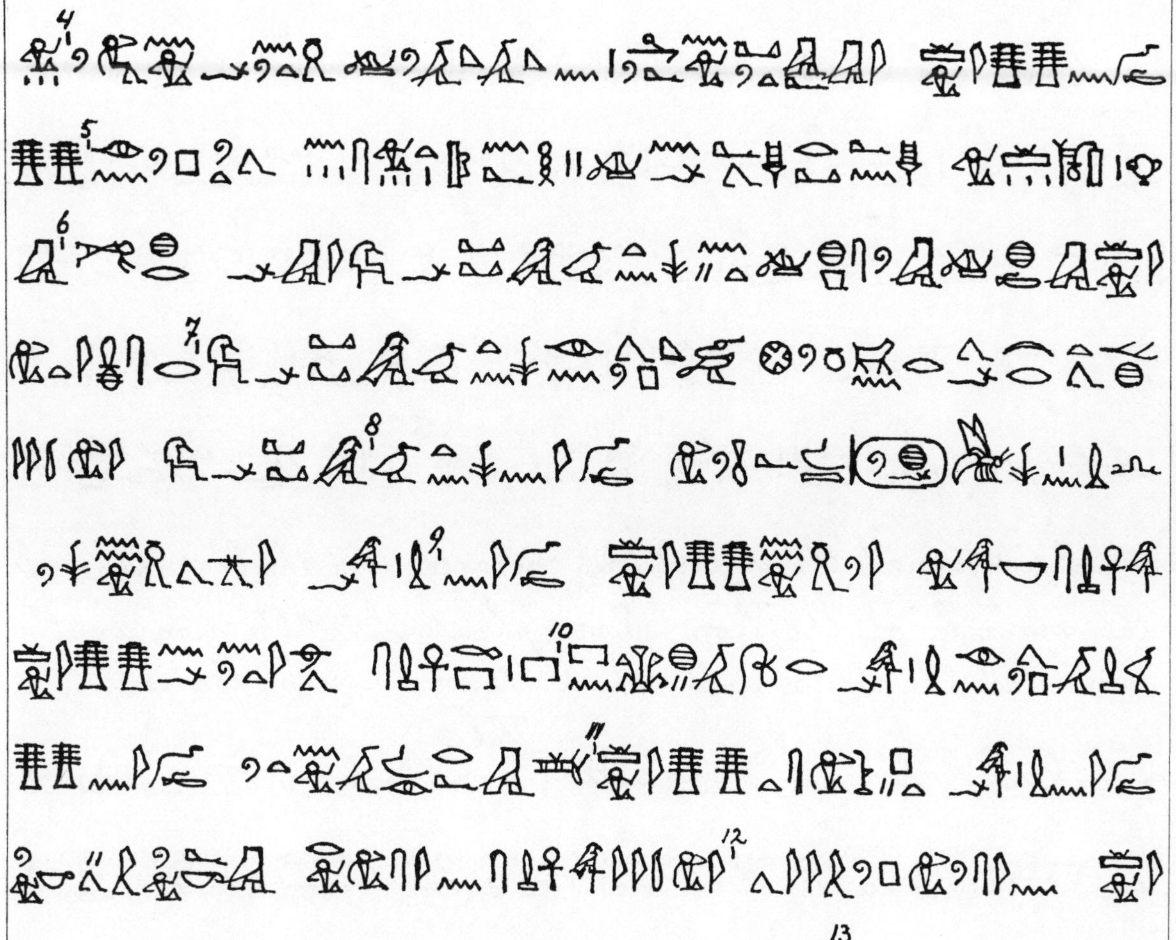

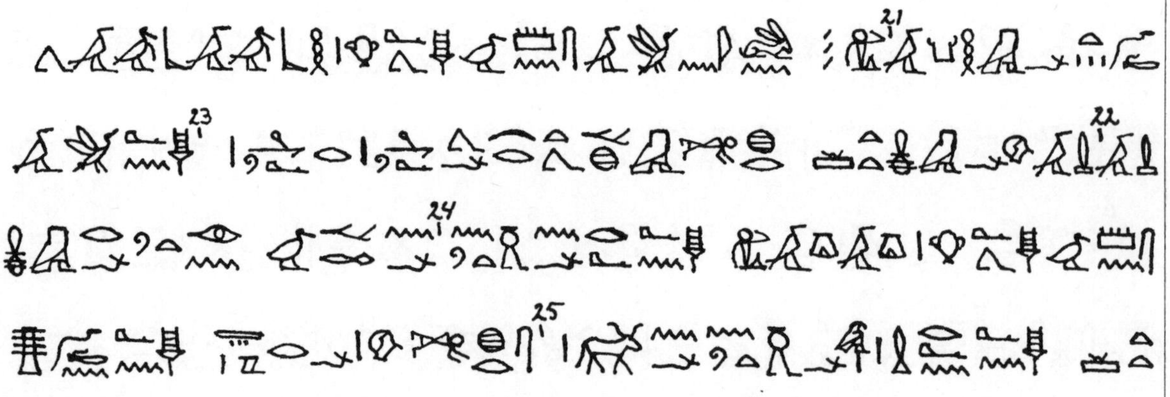

A long omission 

which contained the end of this miracle and the beginning of the miracle of the lion. Some phrase like "the lion went" preceded the words with which the manuscript continues.

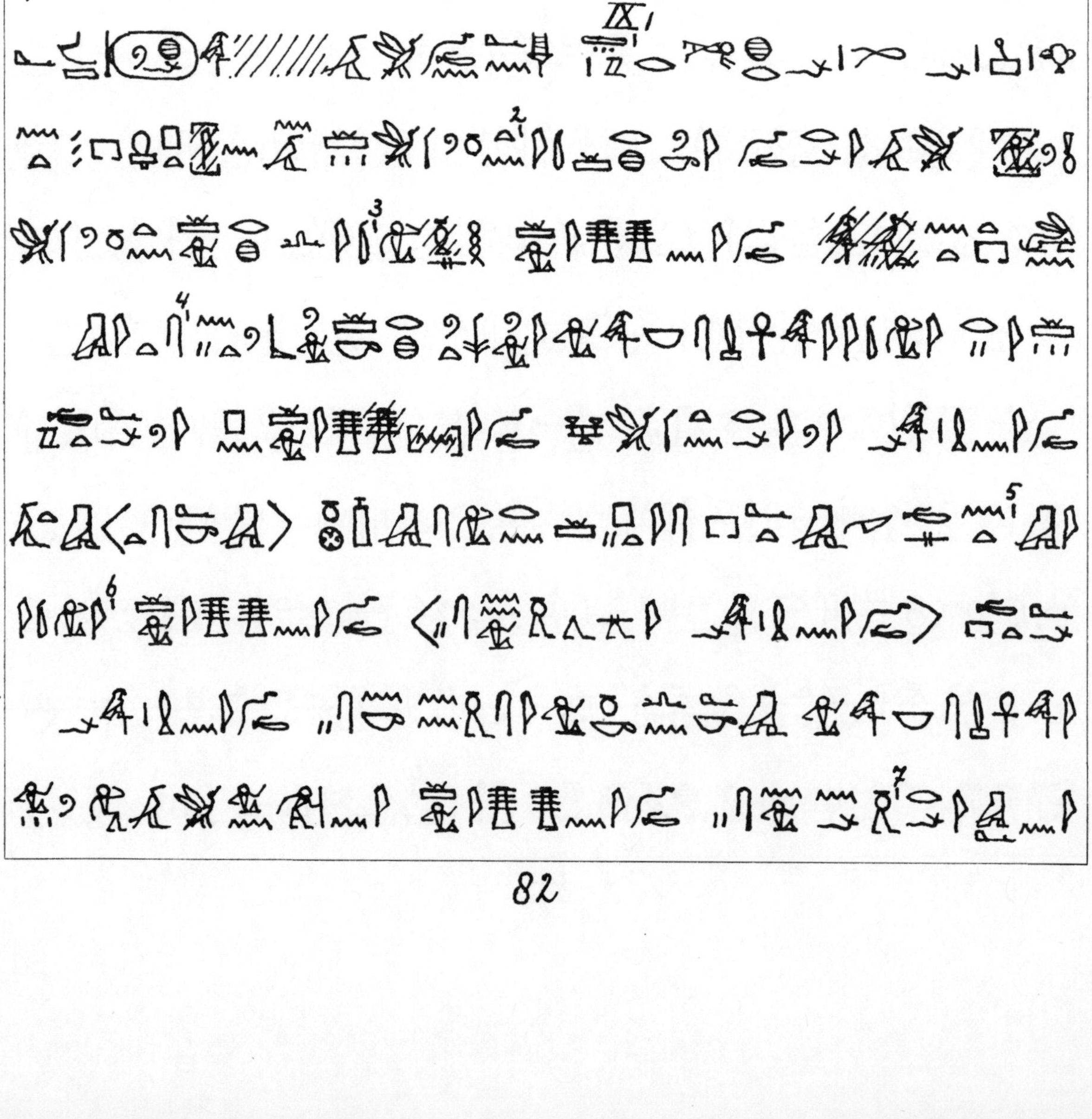

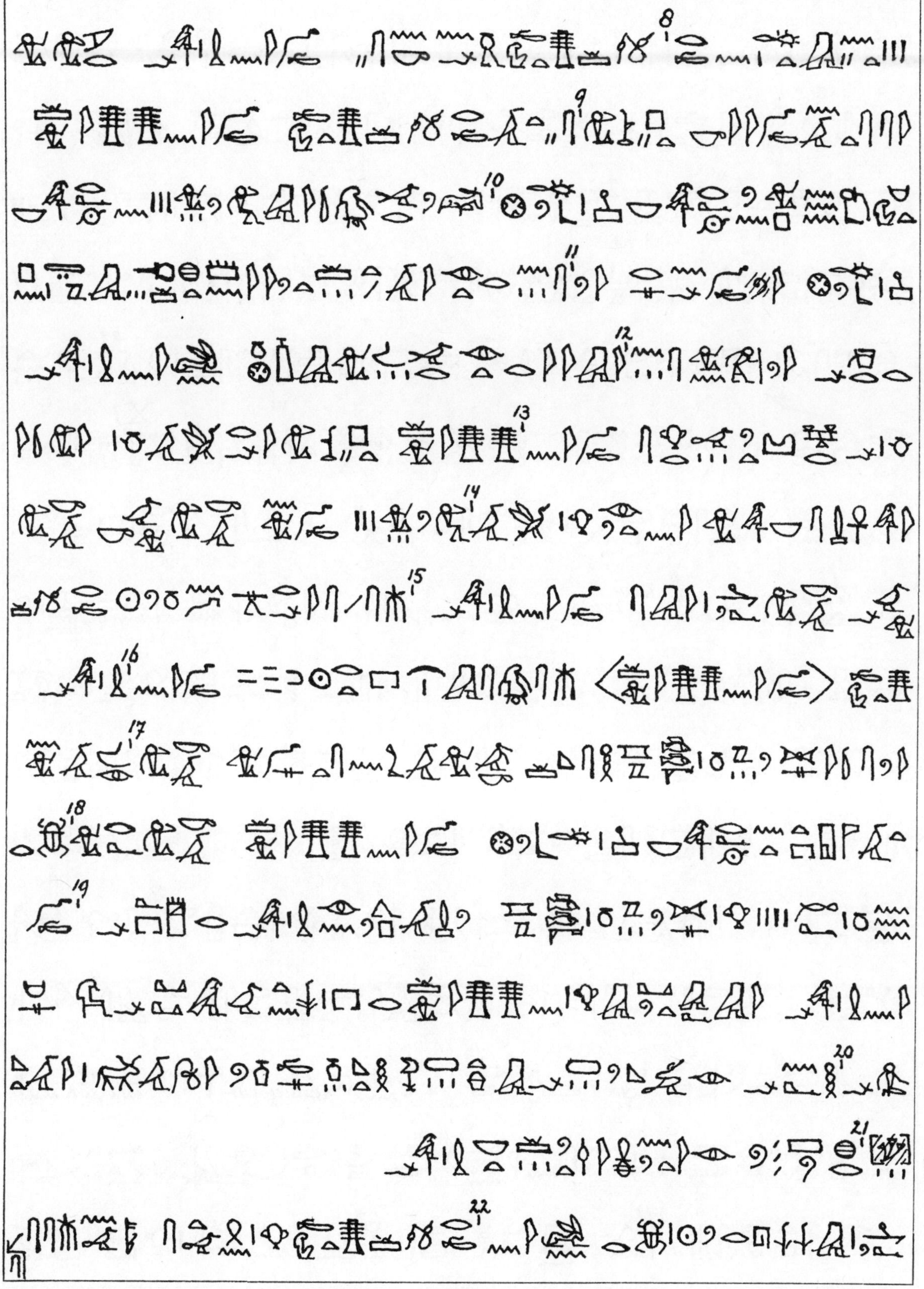

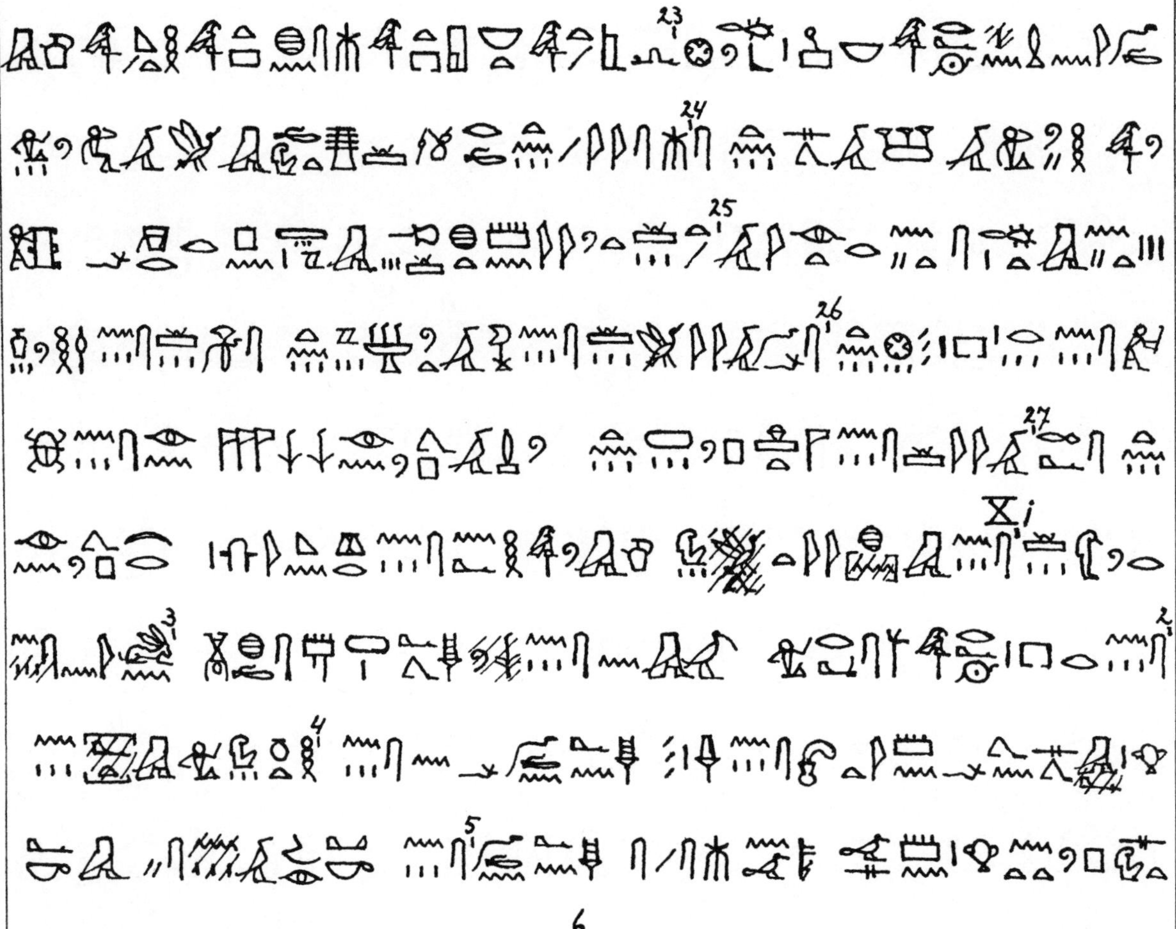

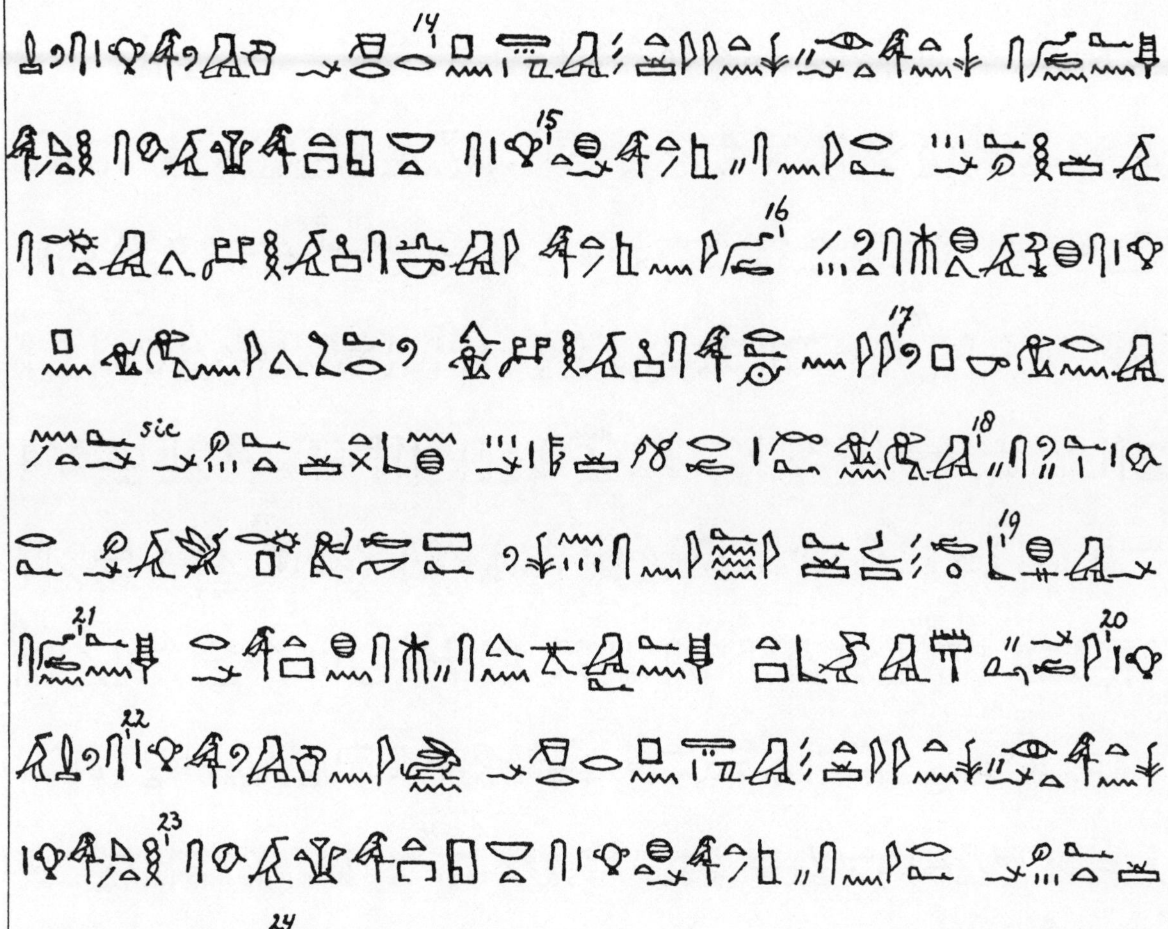

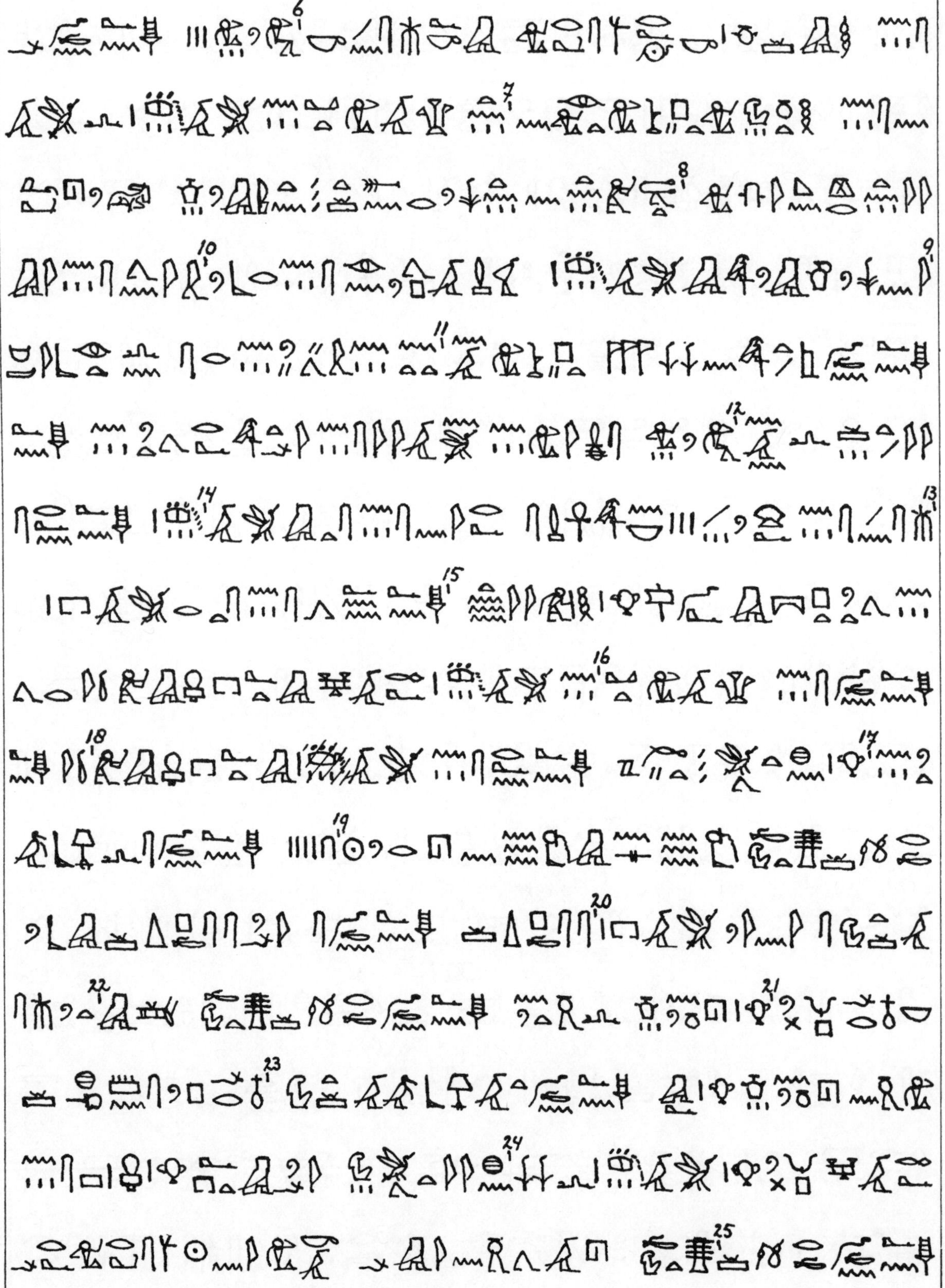

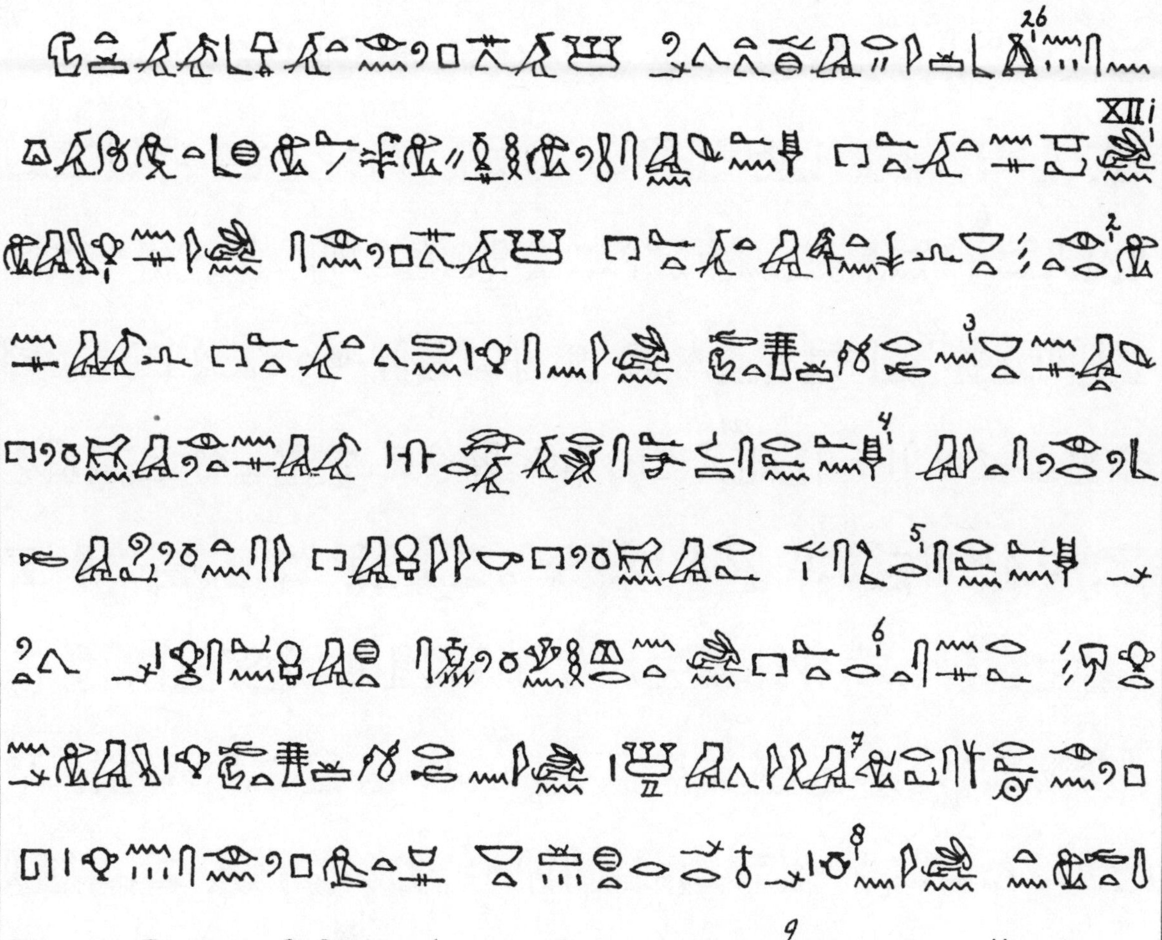

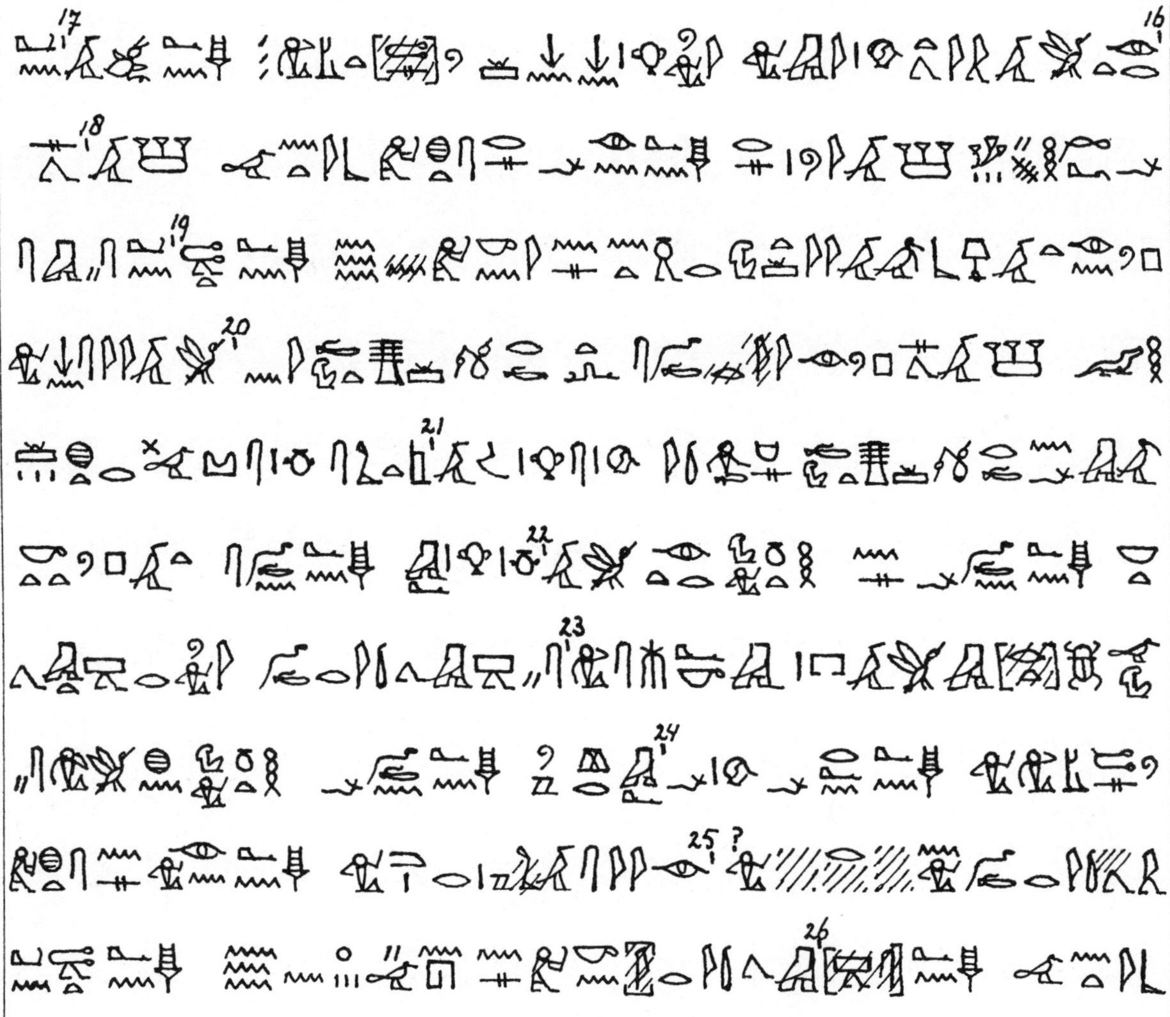

End of page and papyrus. 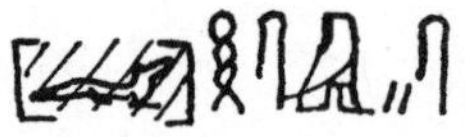

The story of the Eloquent Peasant.

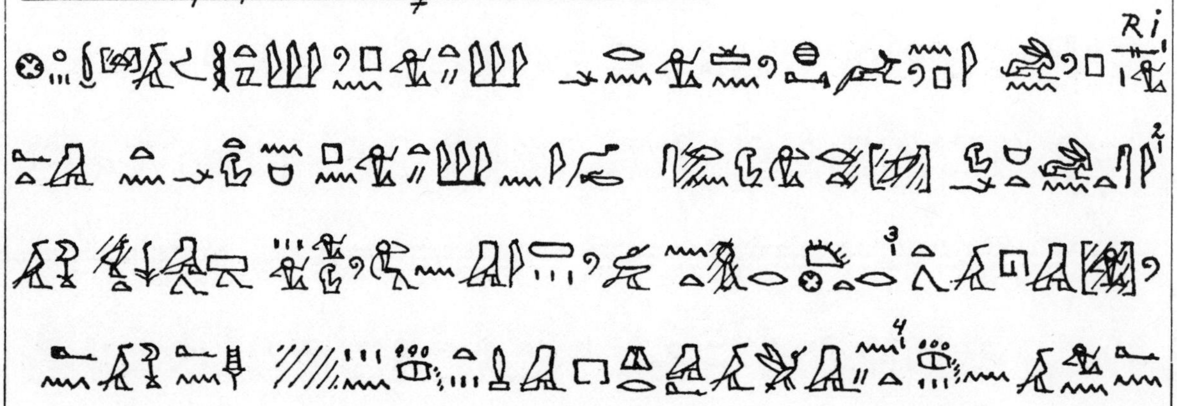

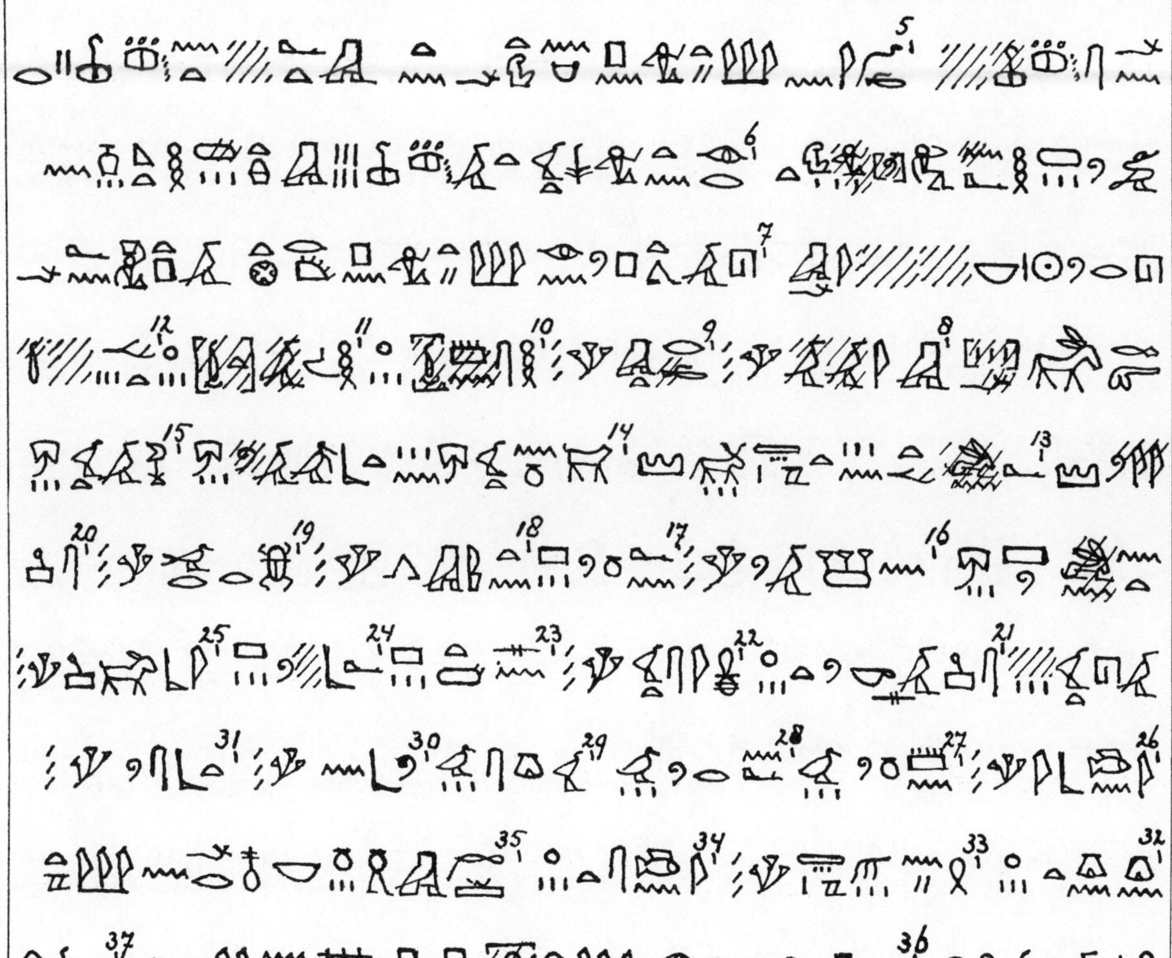

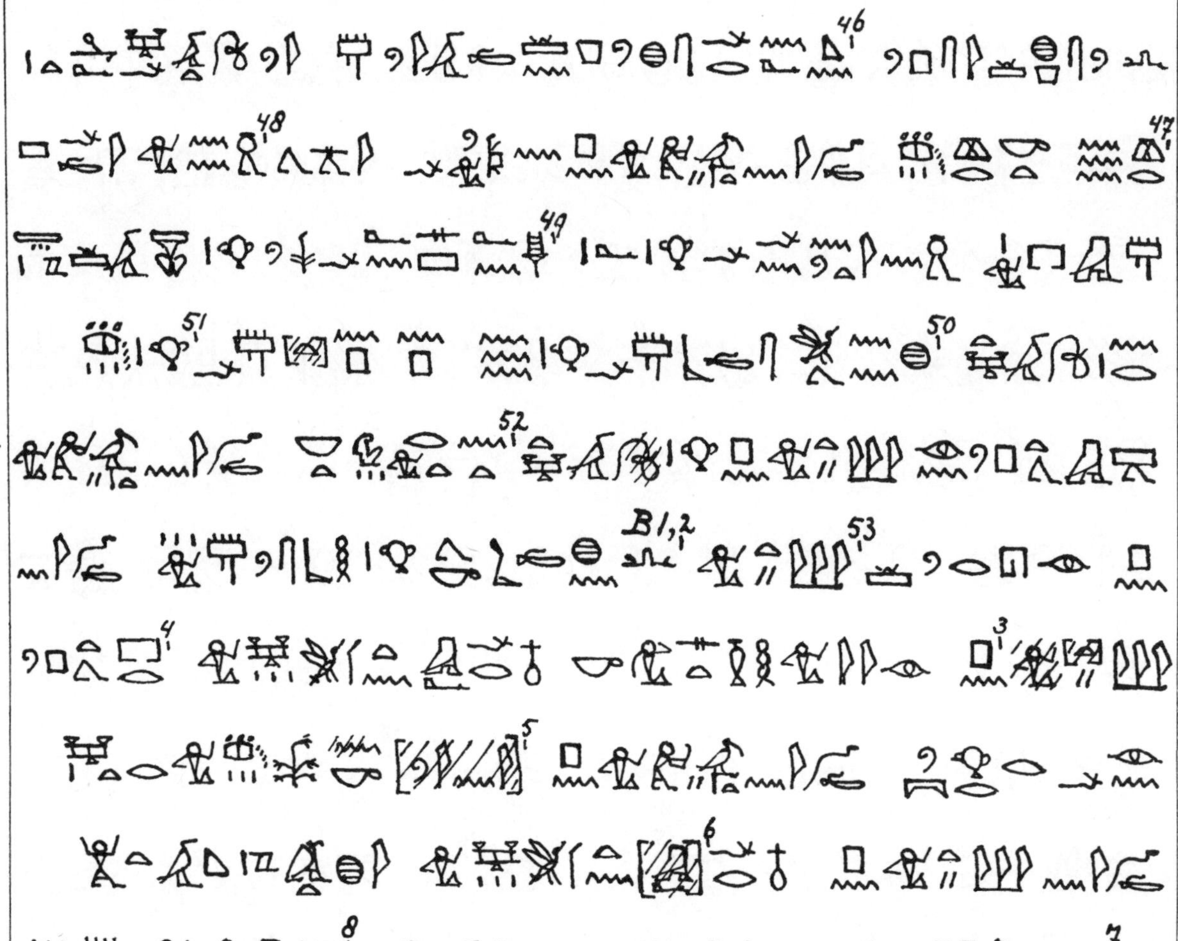

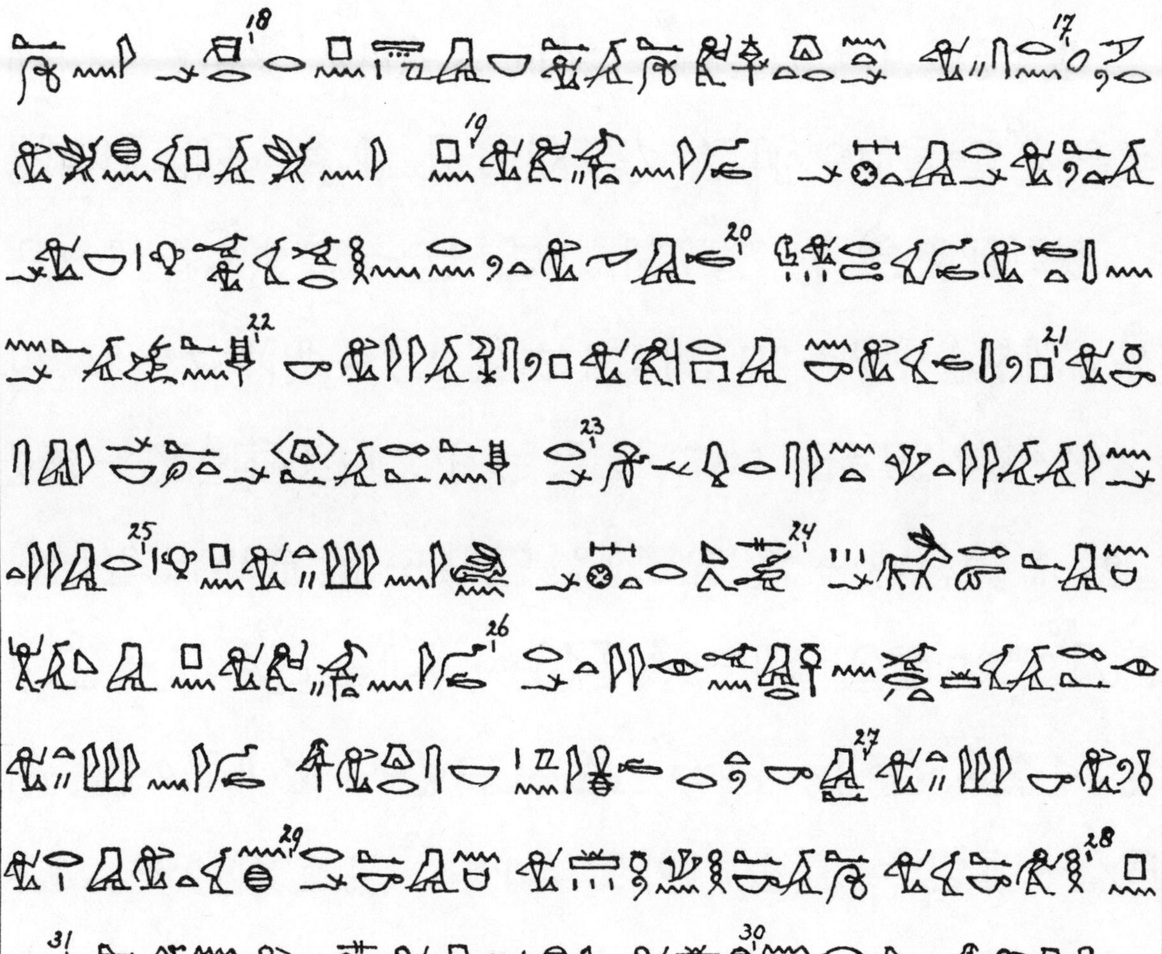

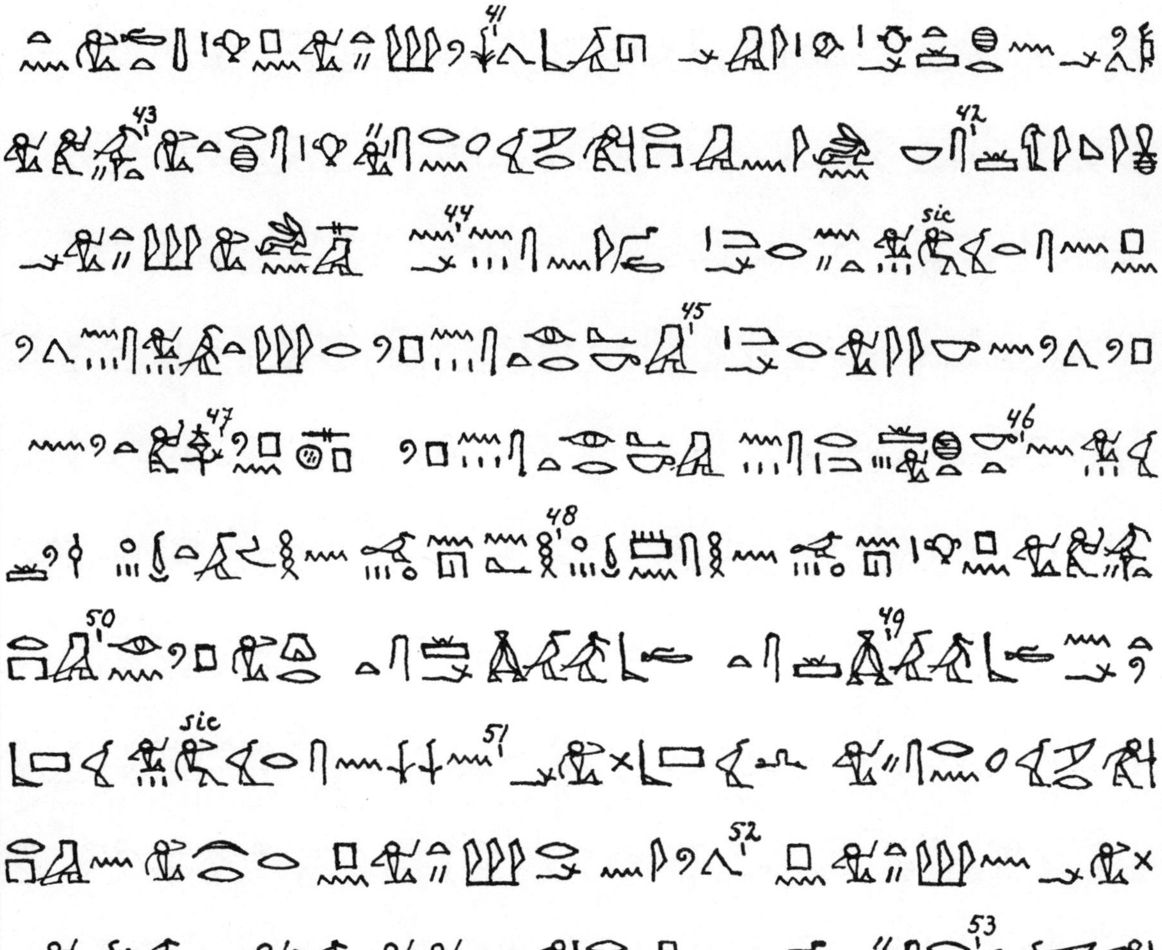

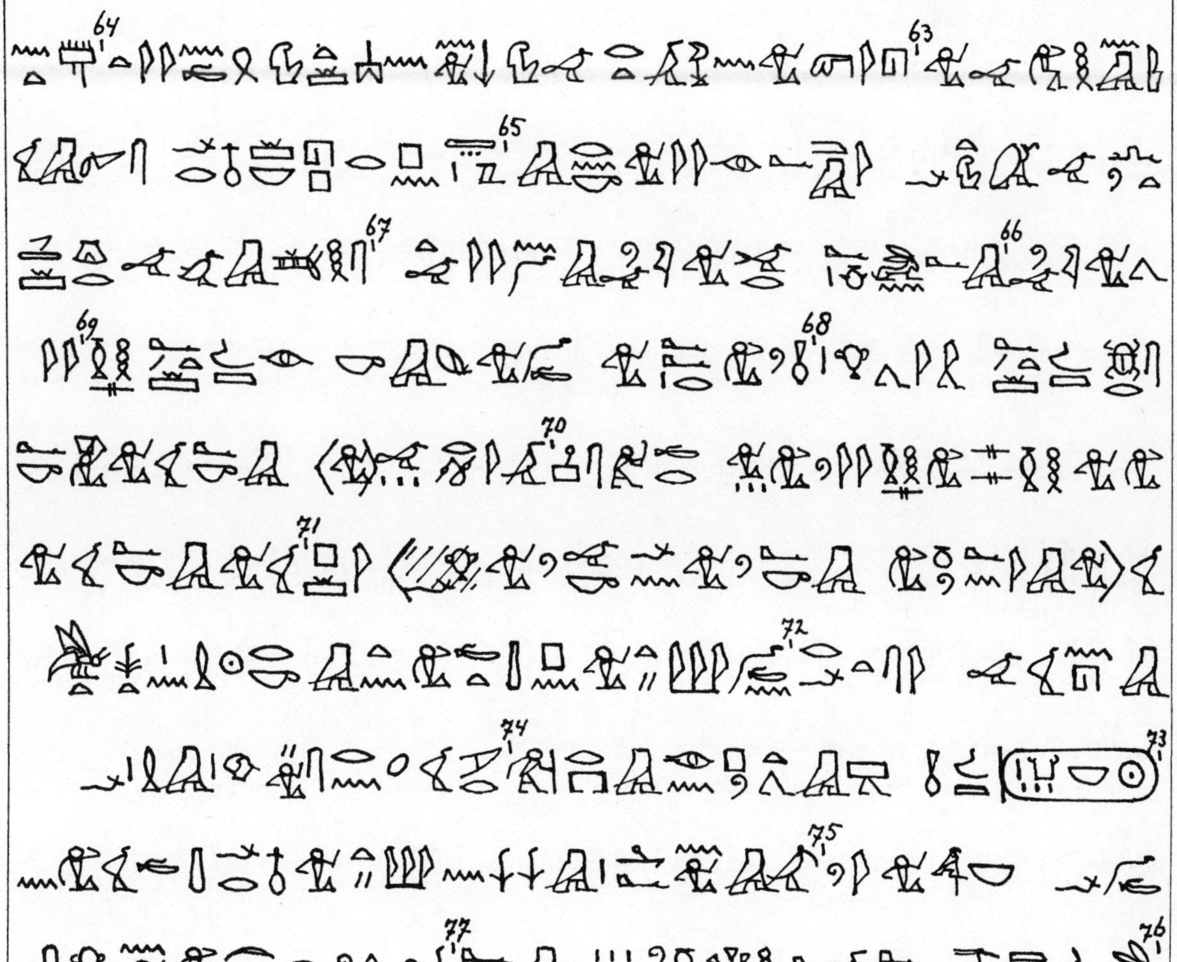

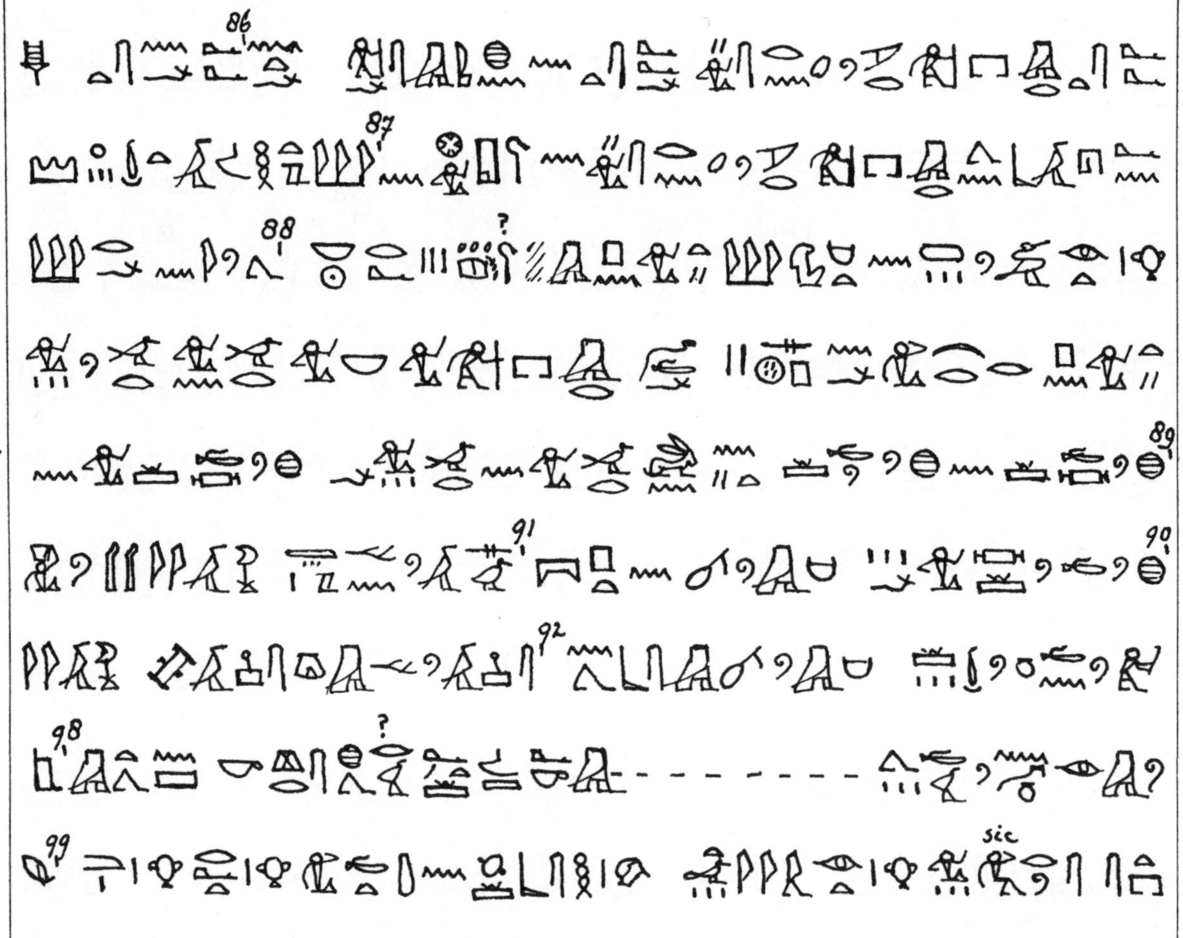

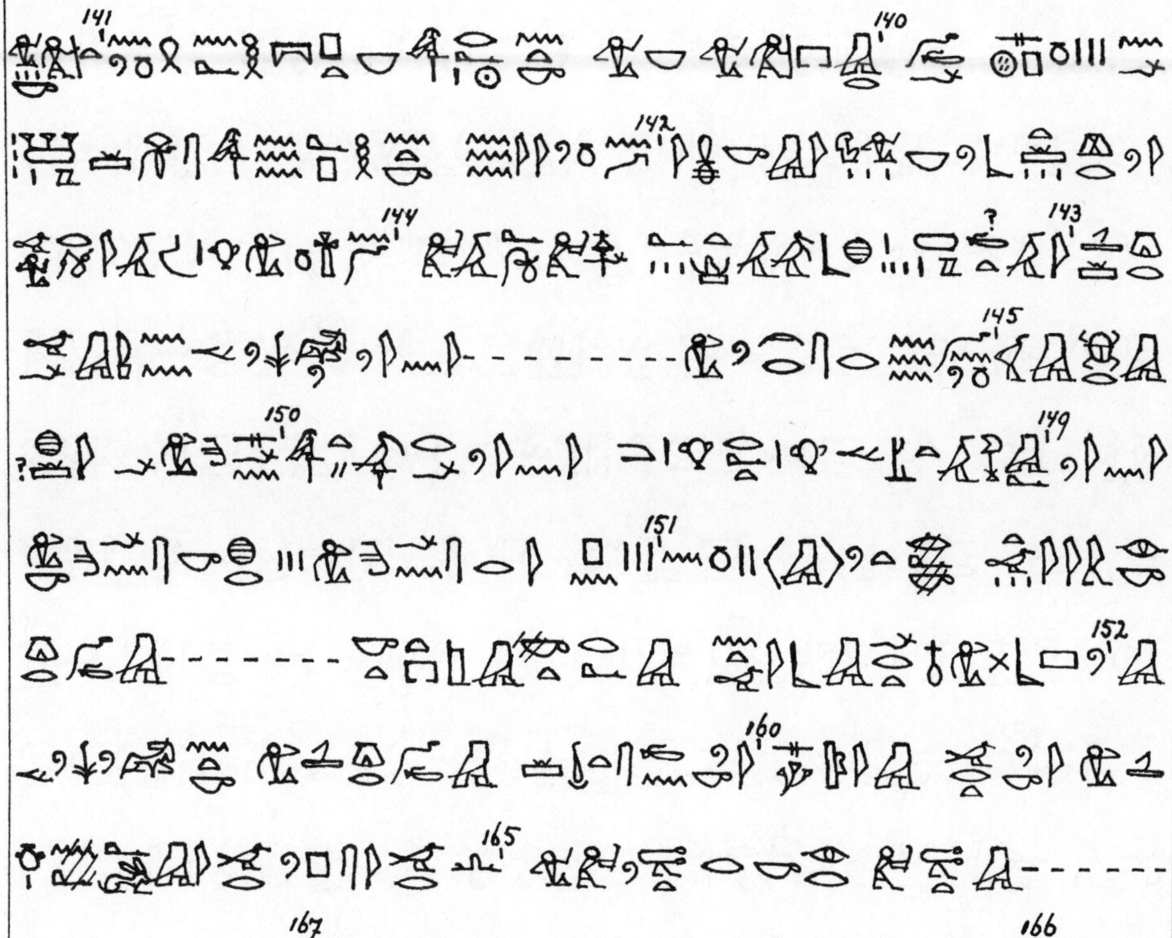

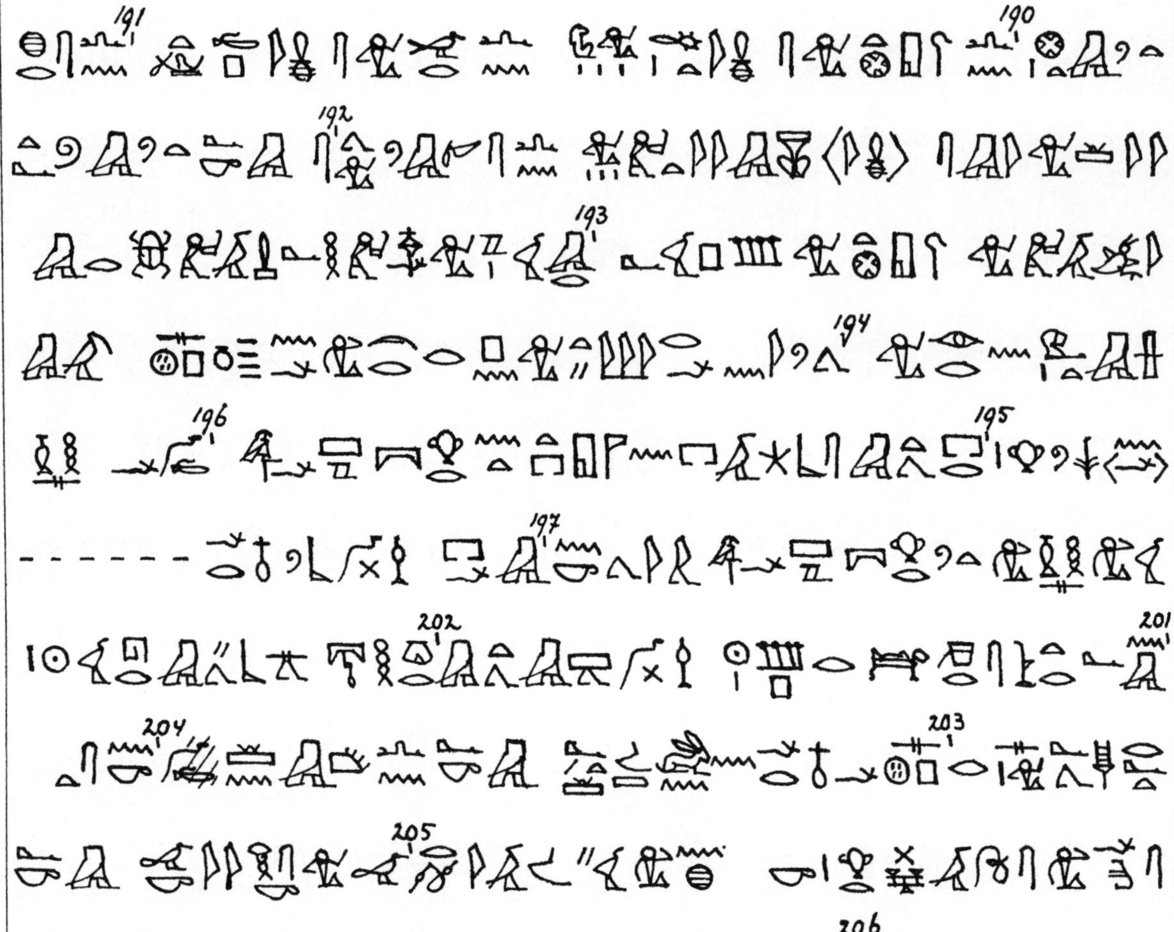

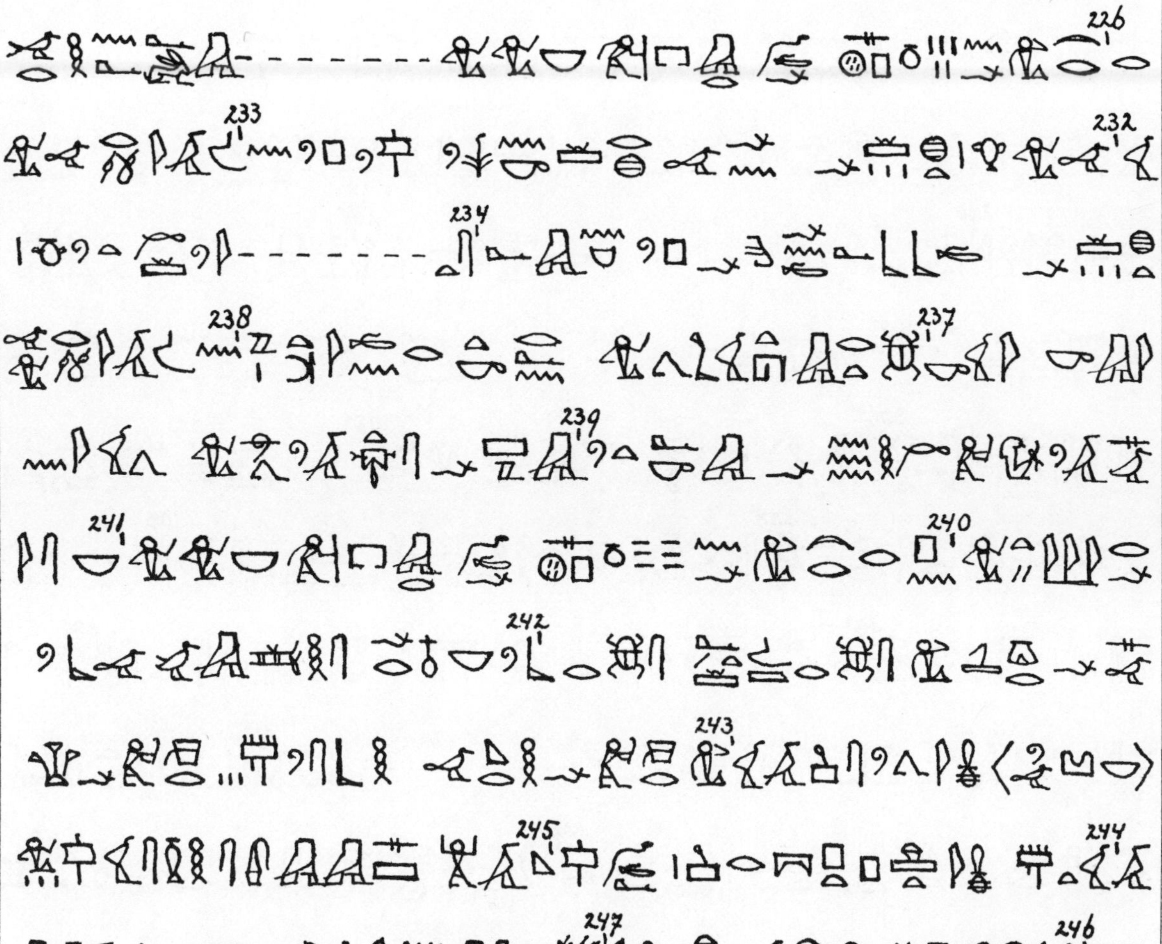

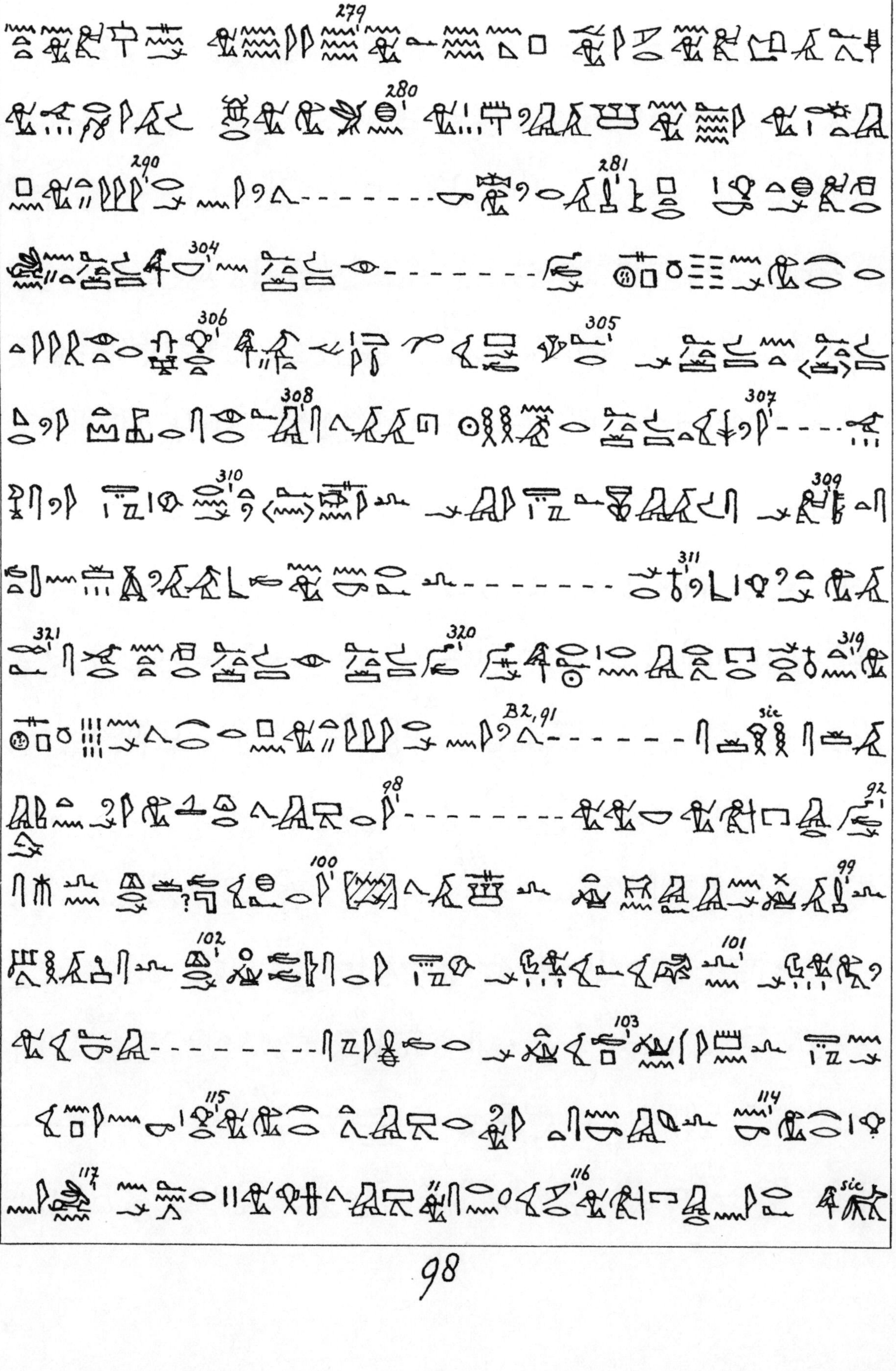

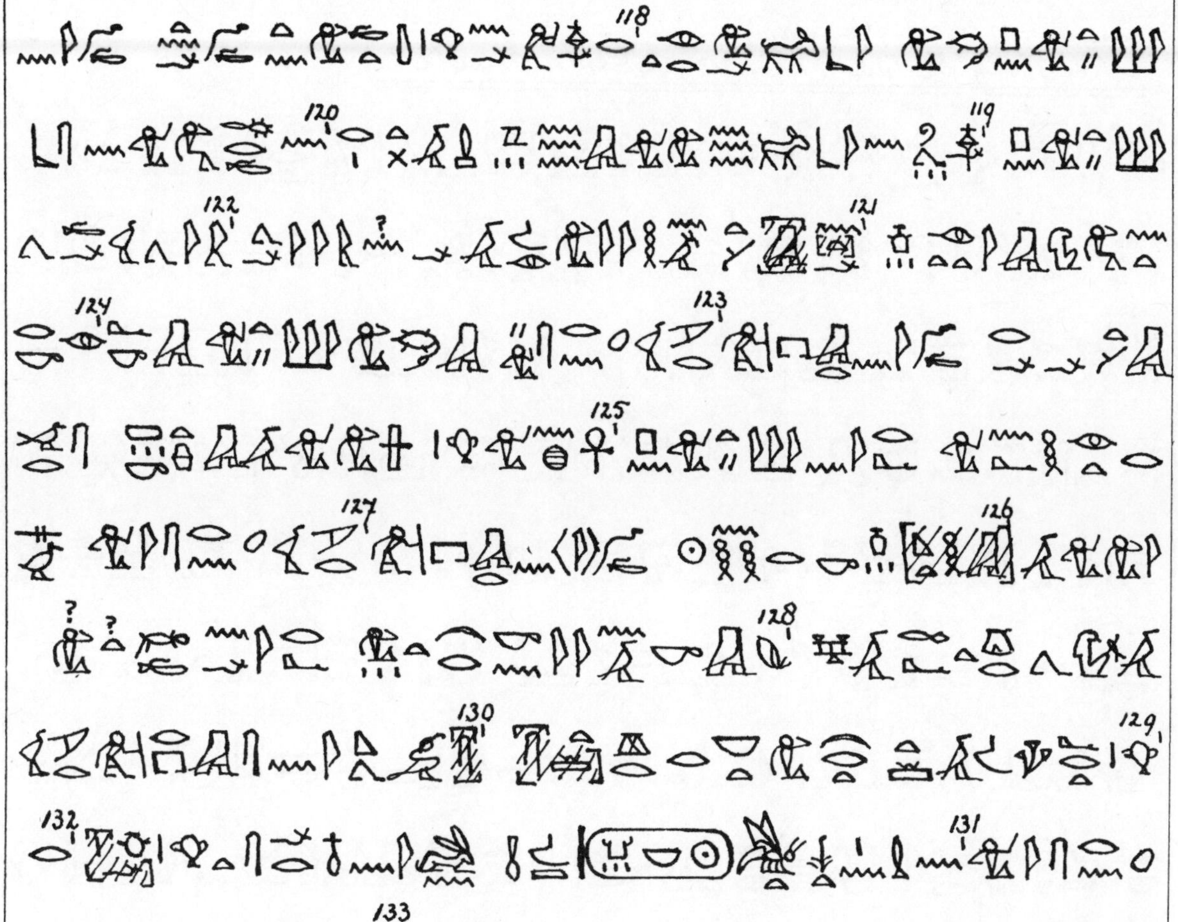

The story of the Shipwrecked Sailor.

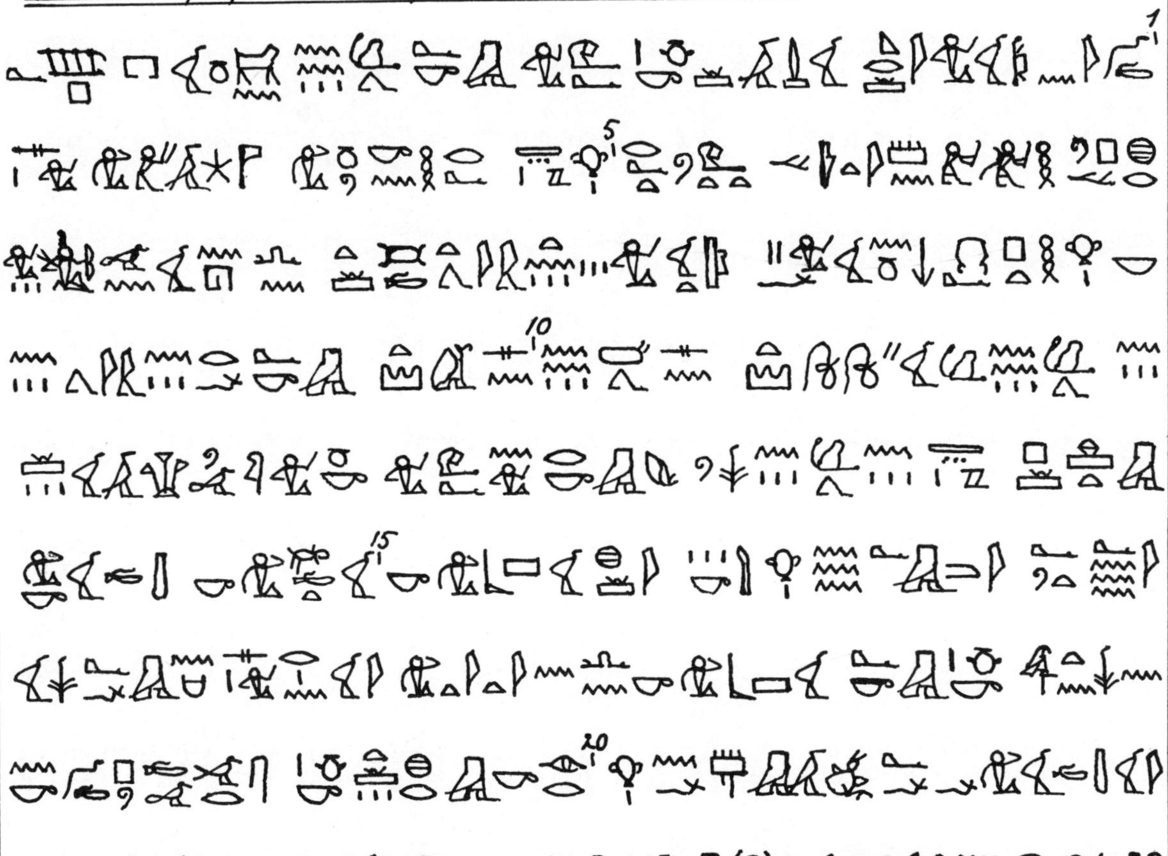

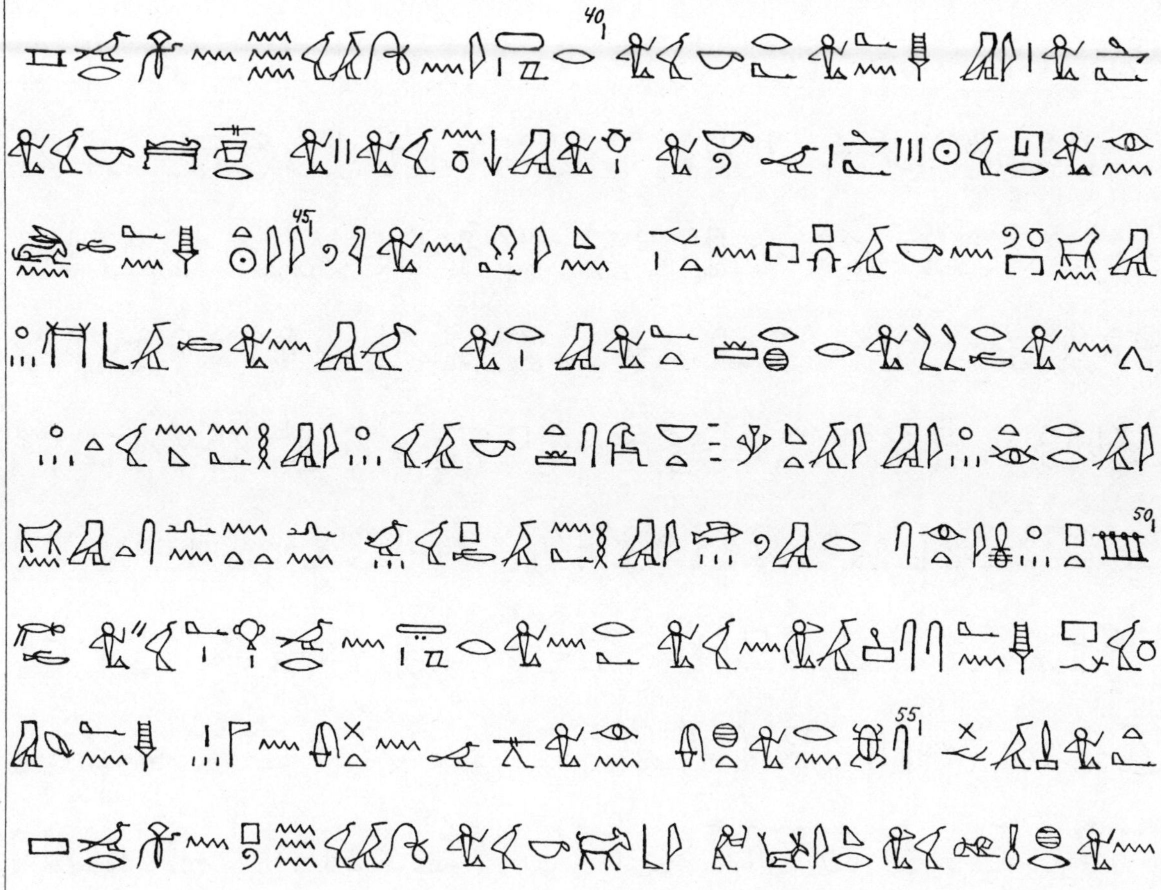

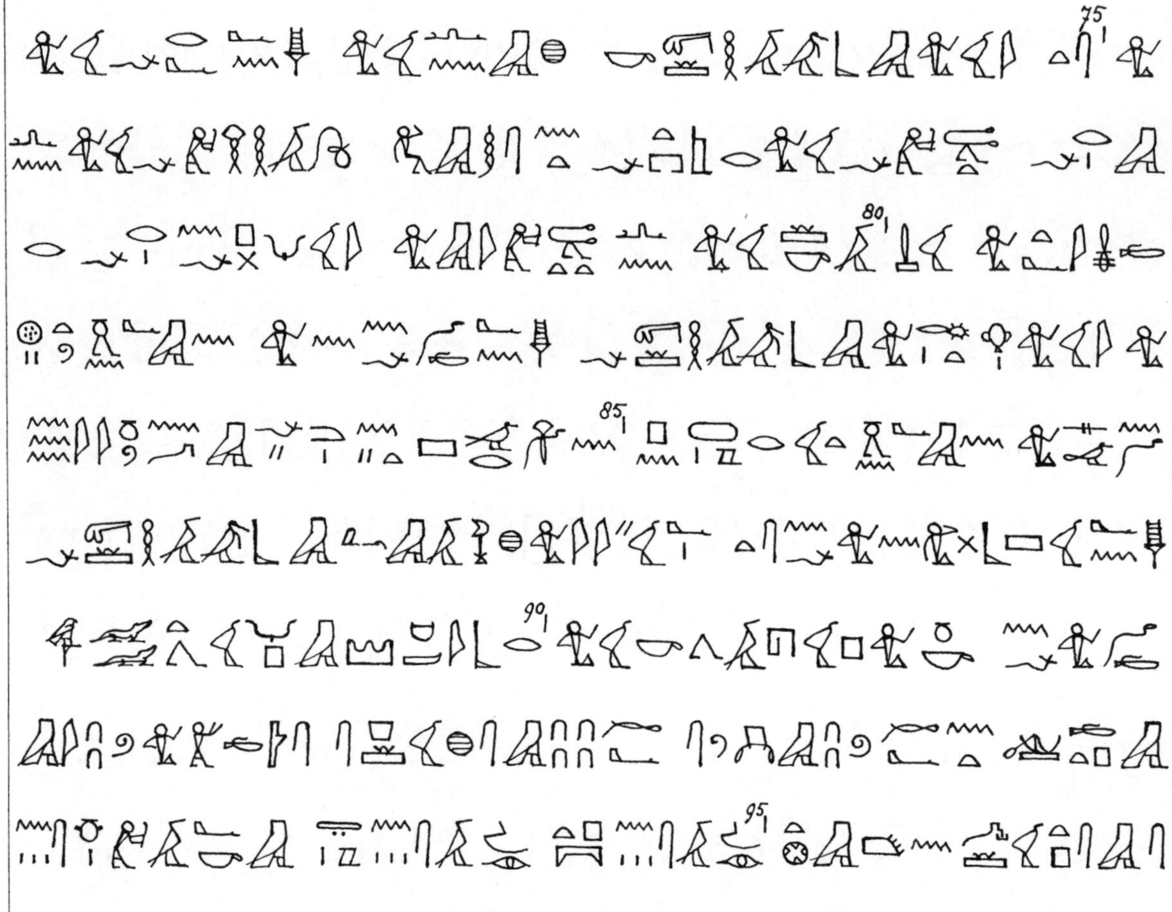

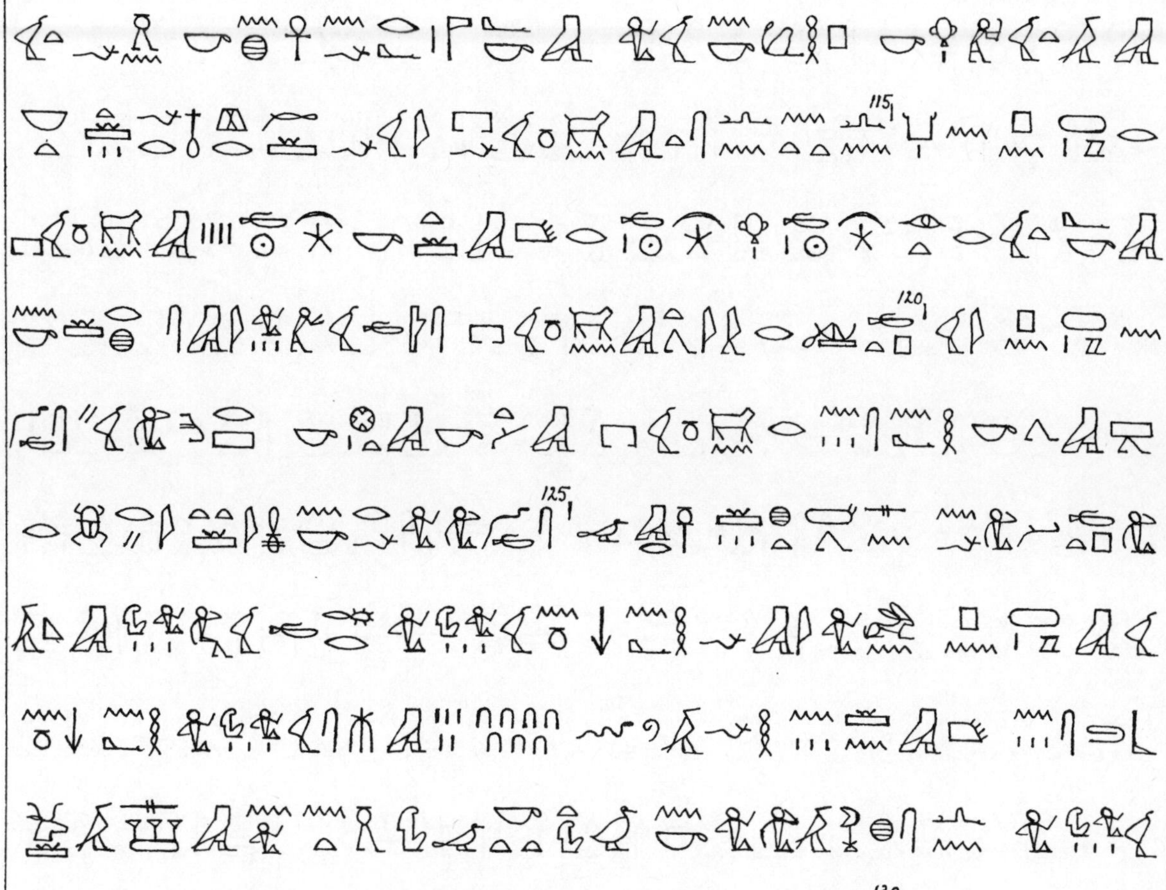

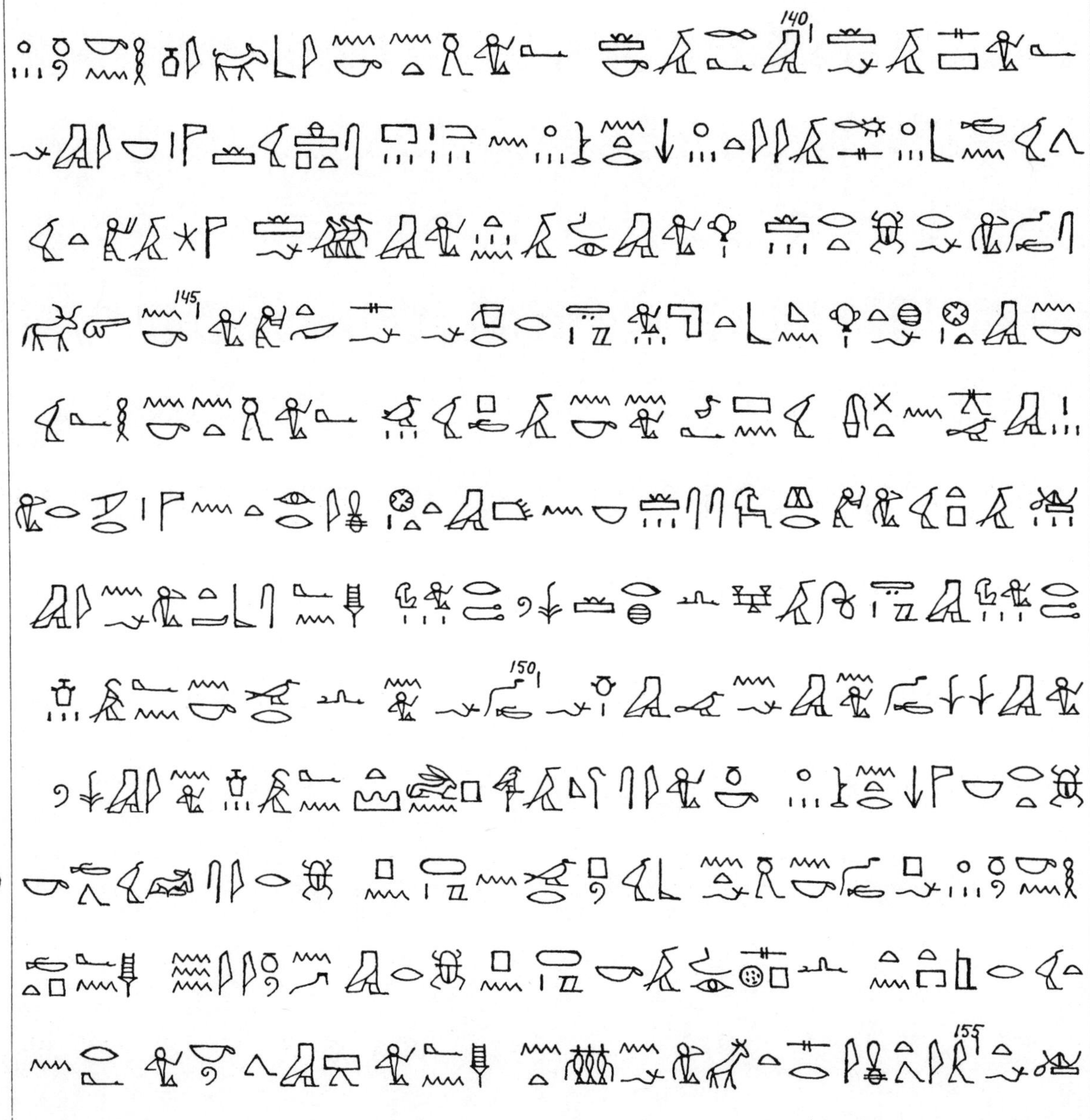

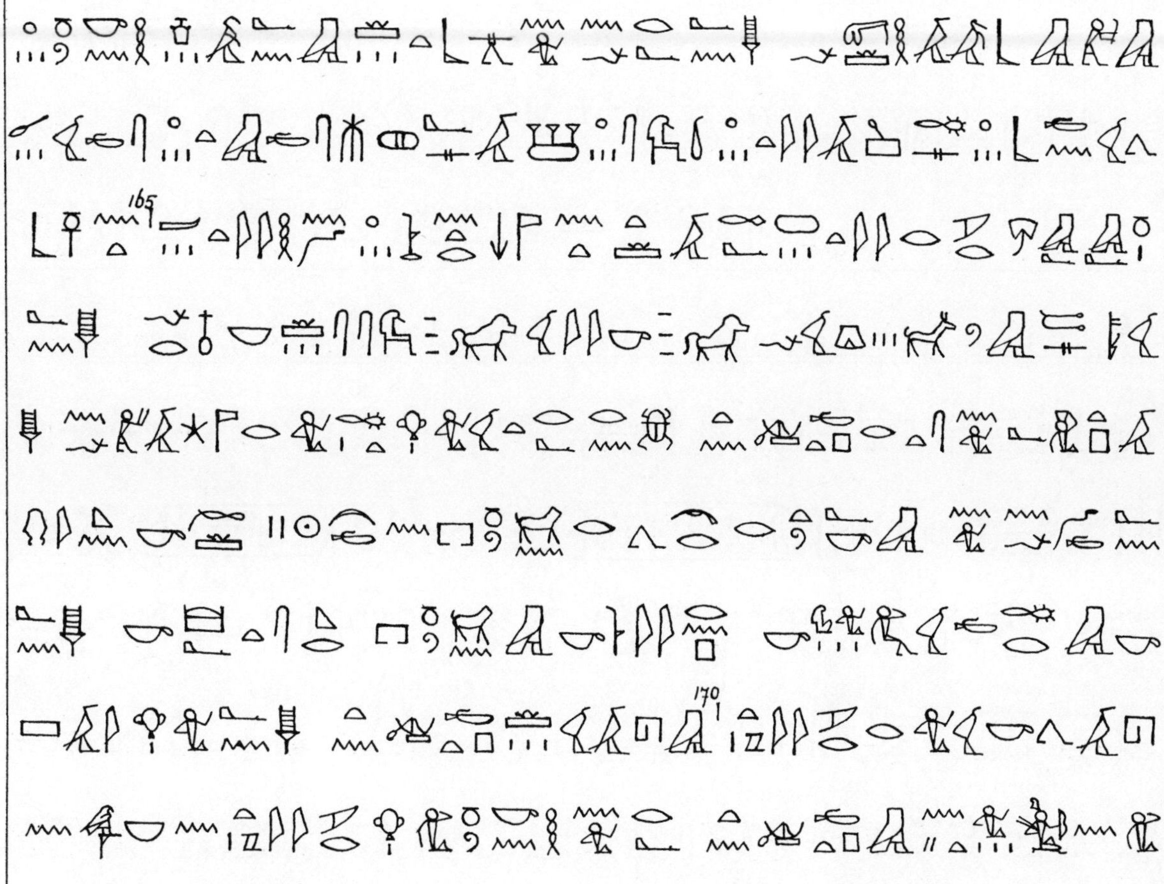

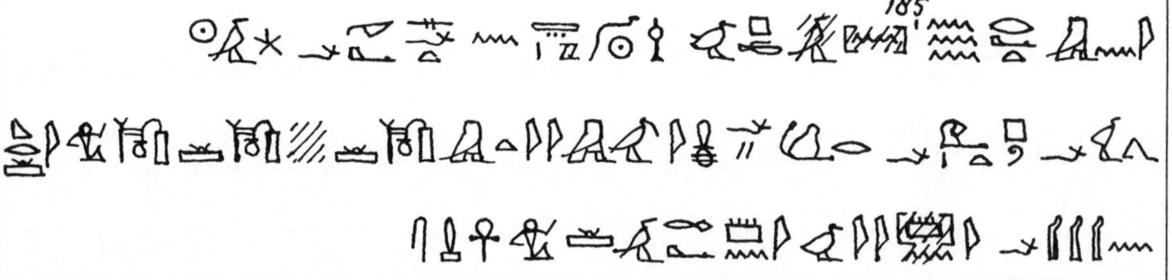

A story designed to make propaganda for the cult of Khonsu.

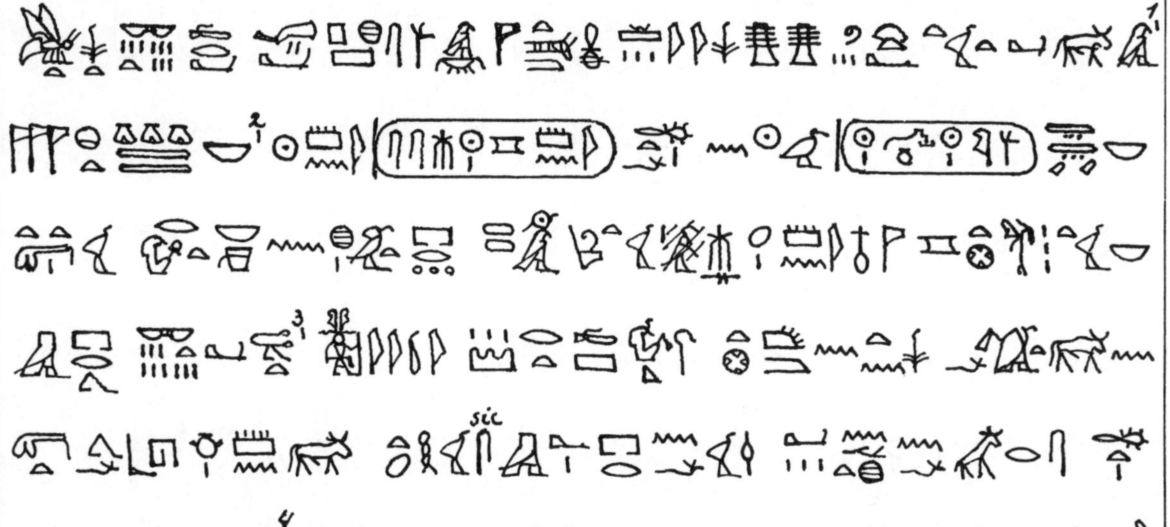

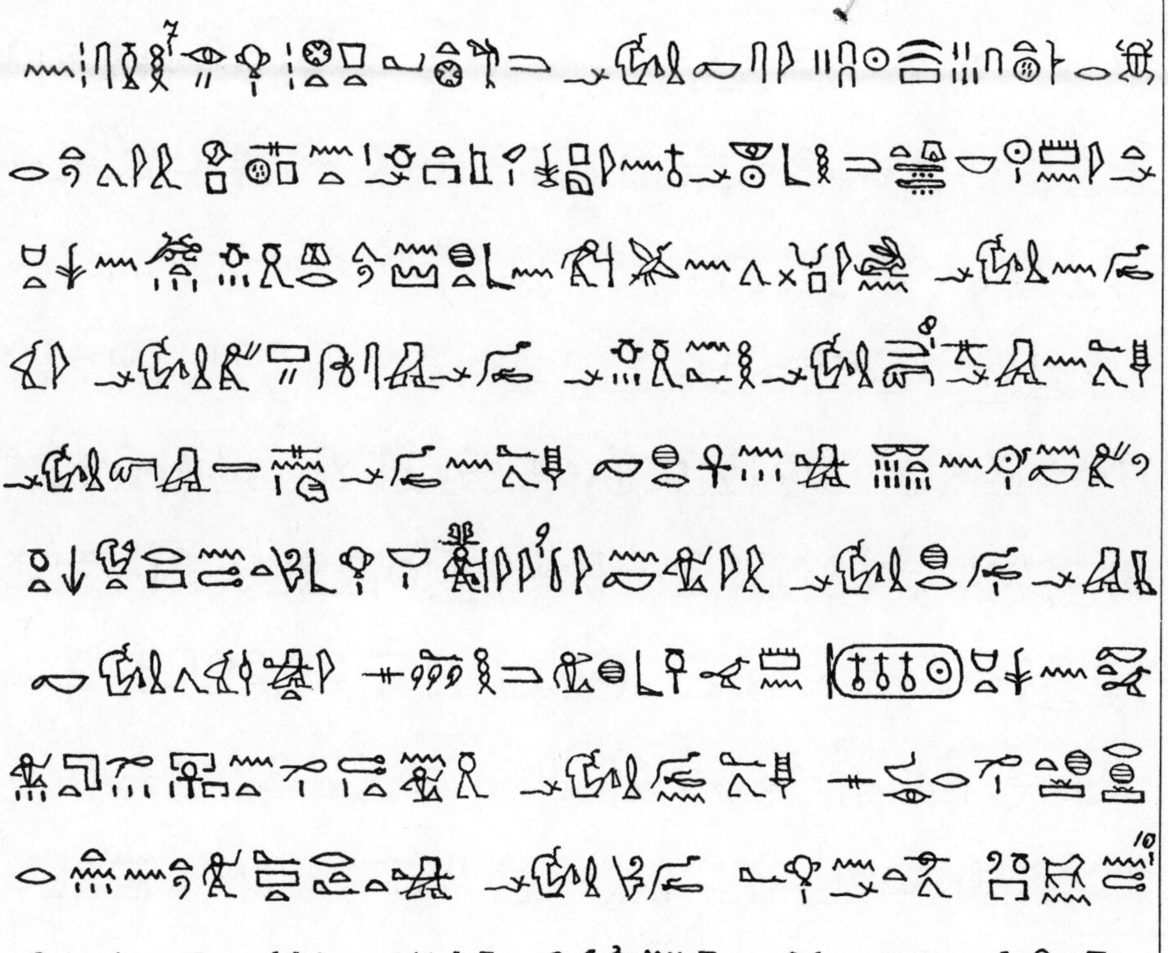

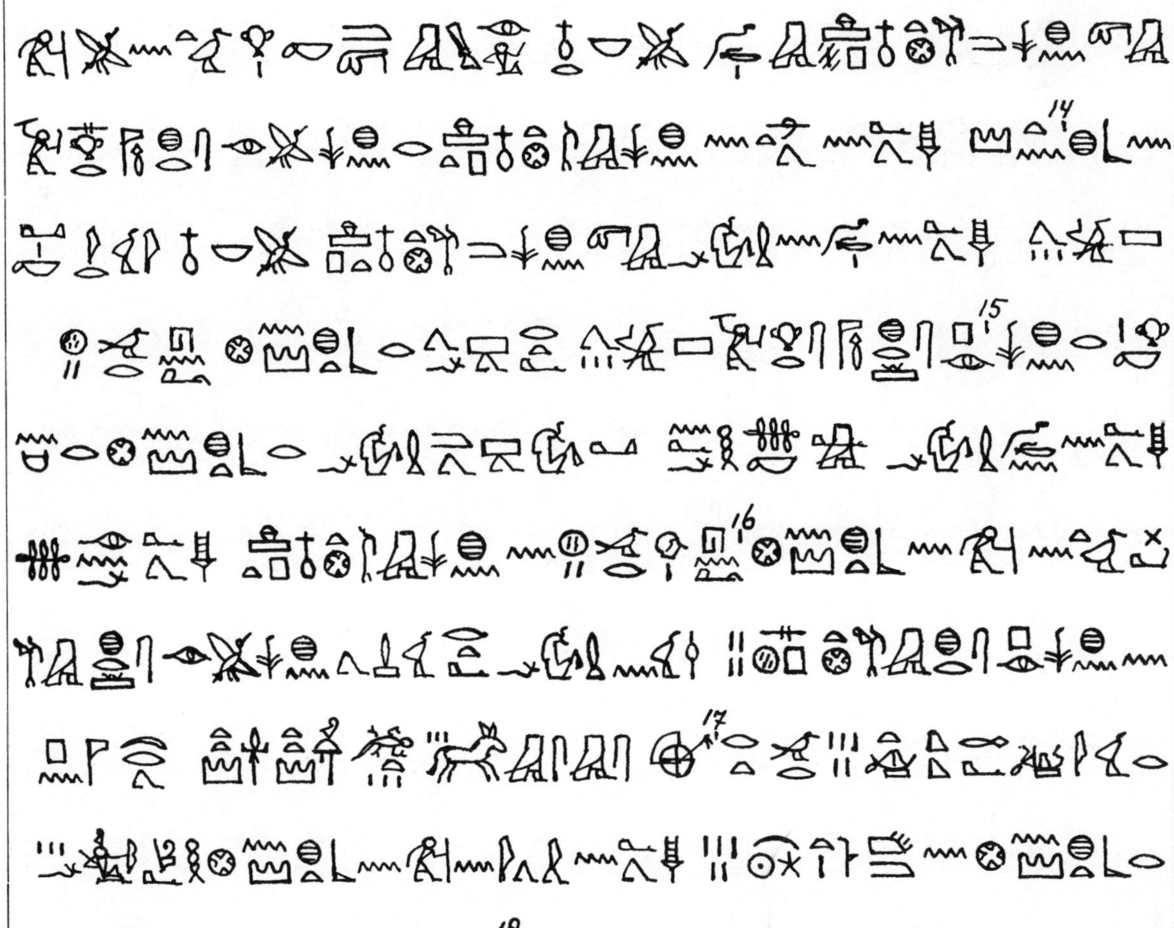

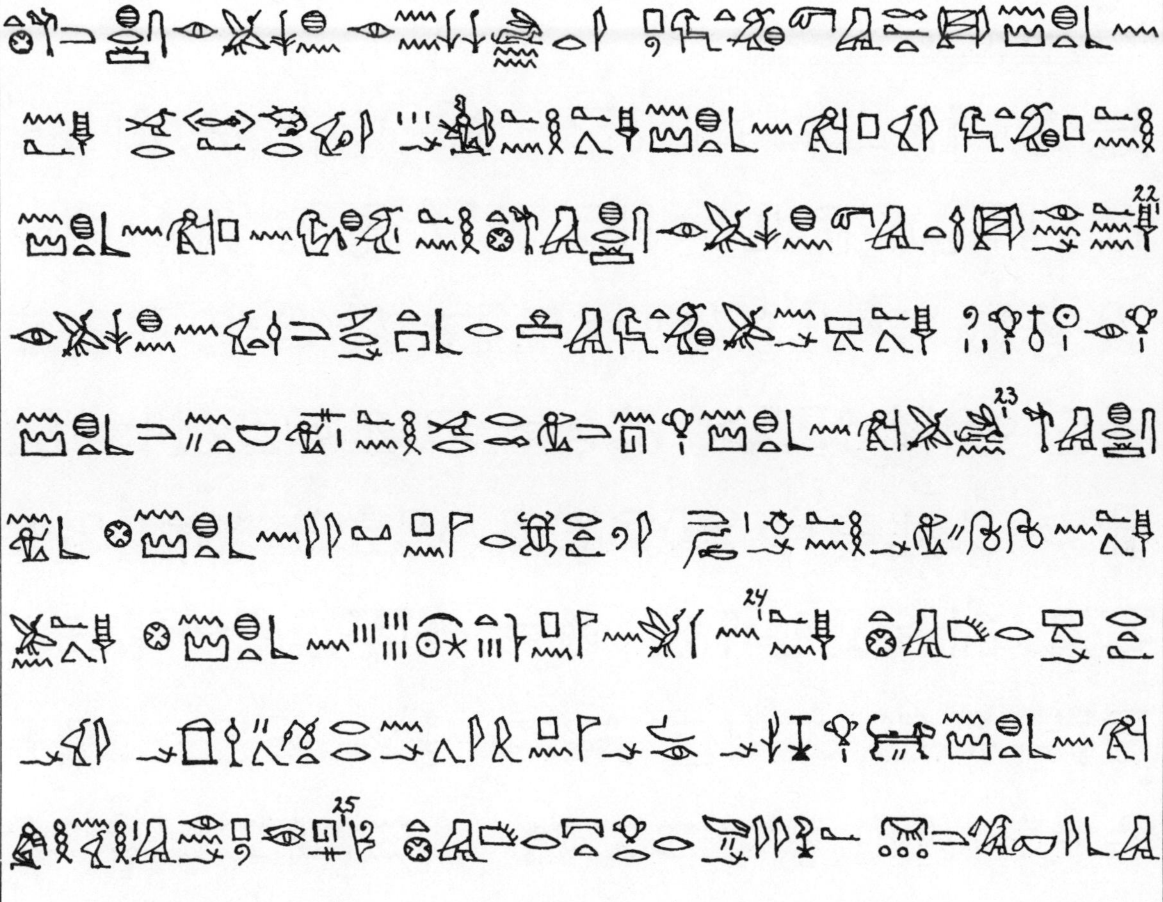

Hymn to Osiris.

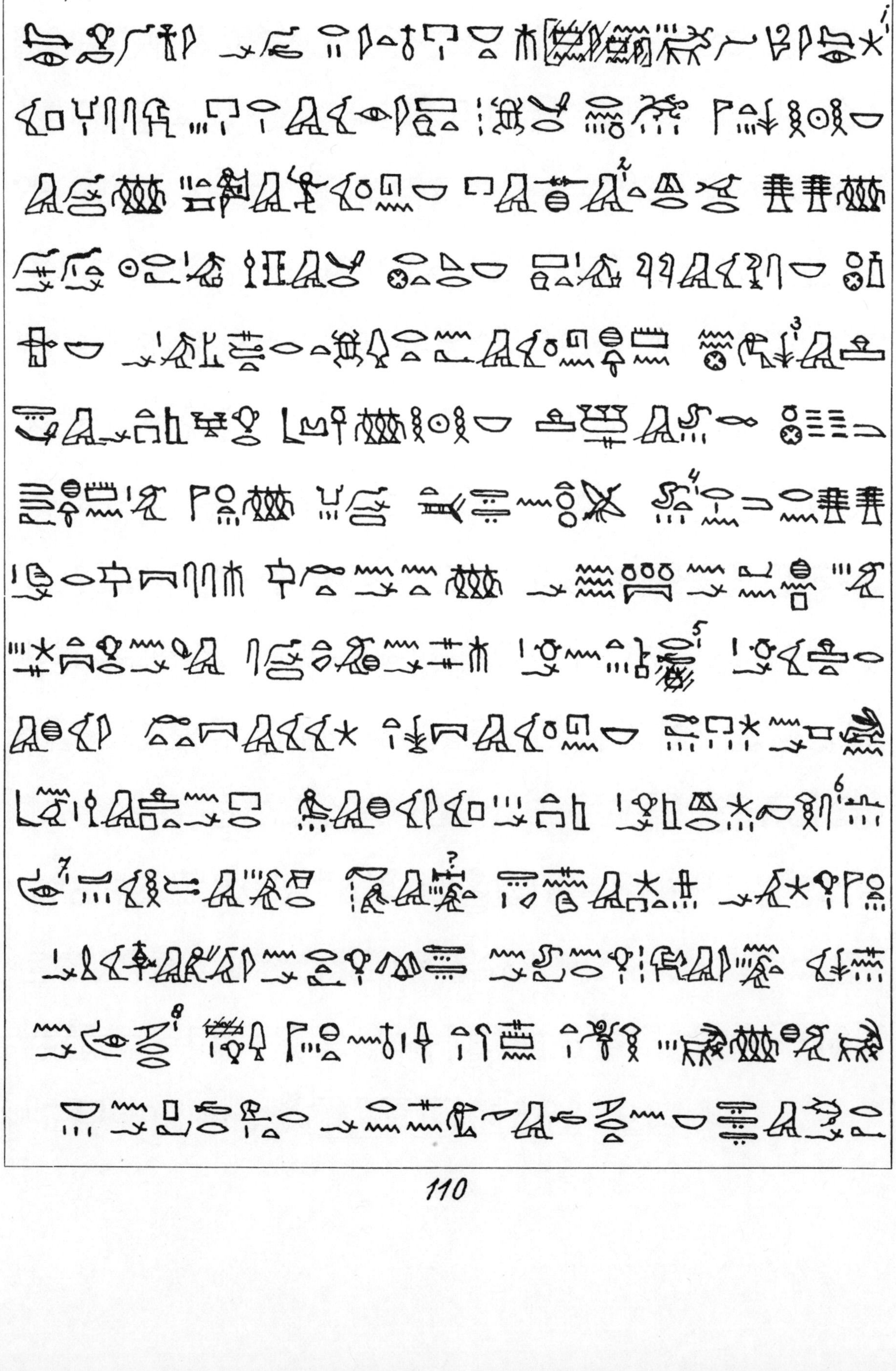

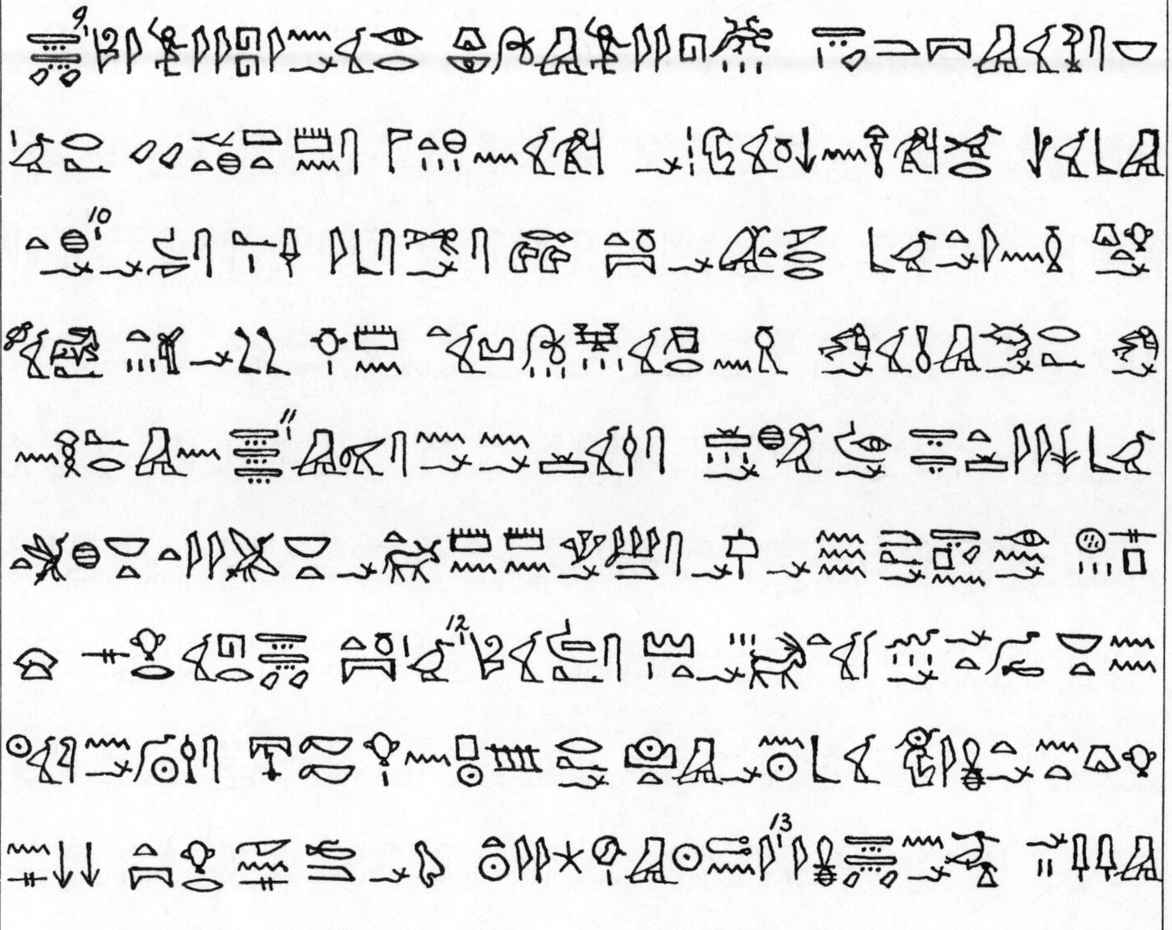

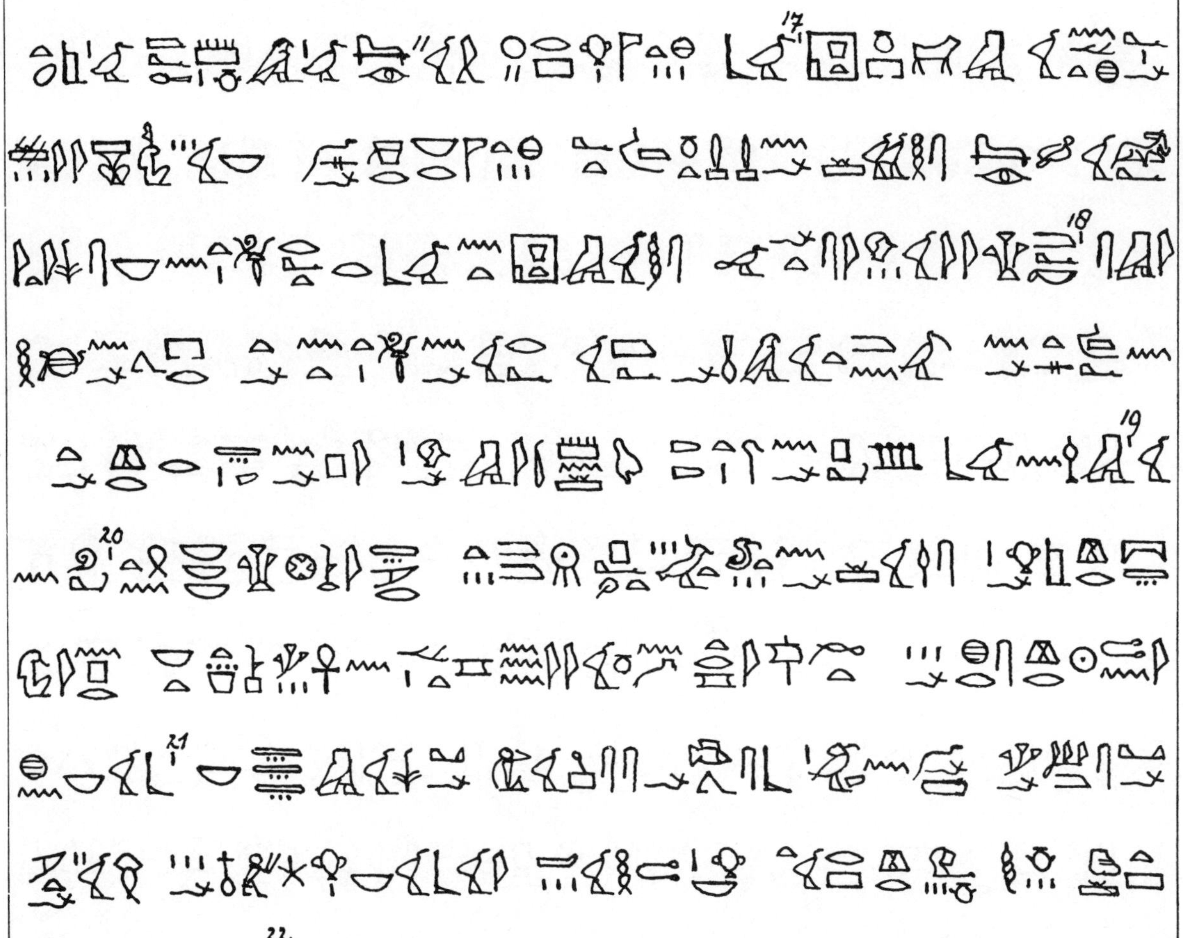

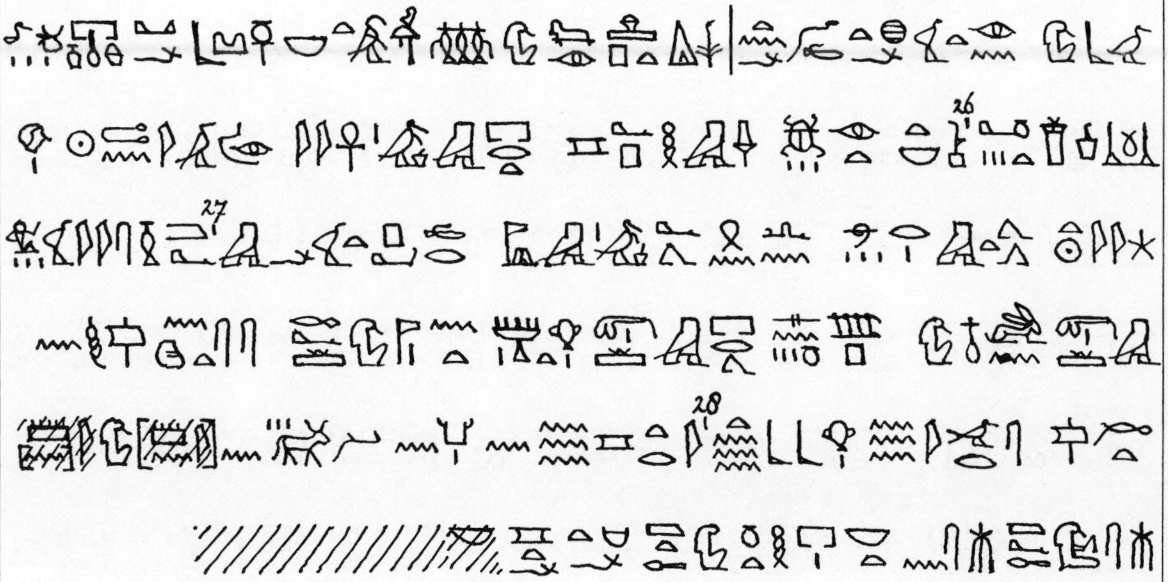

Hymn to the Sun-god.

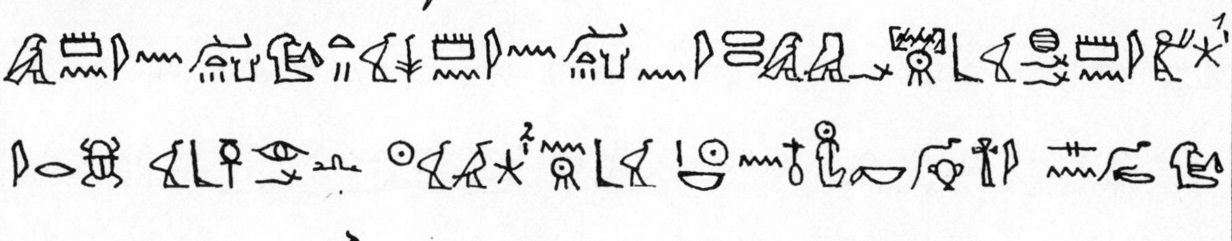

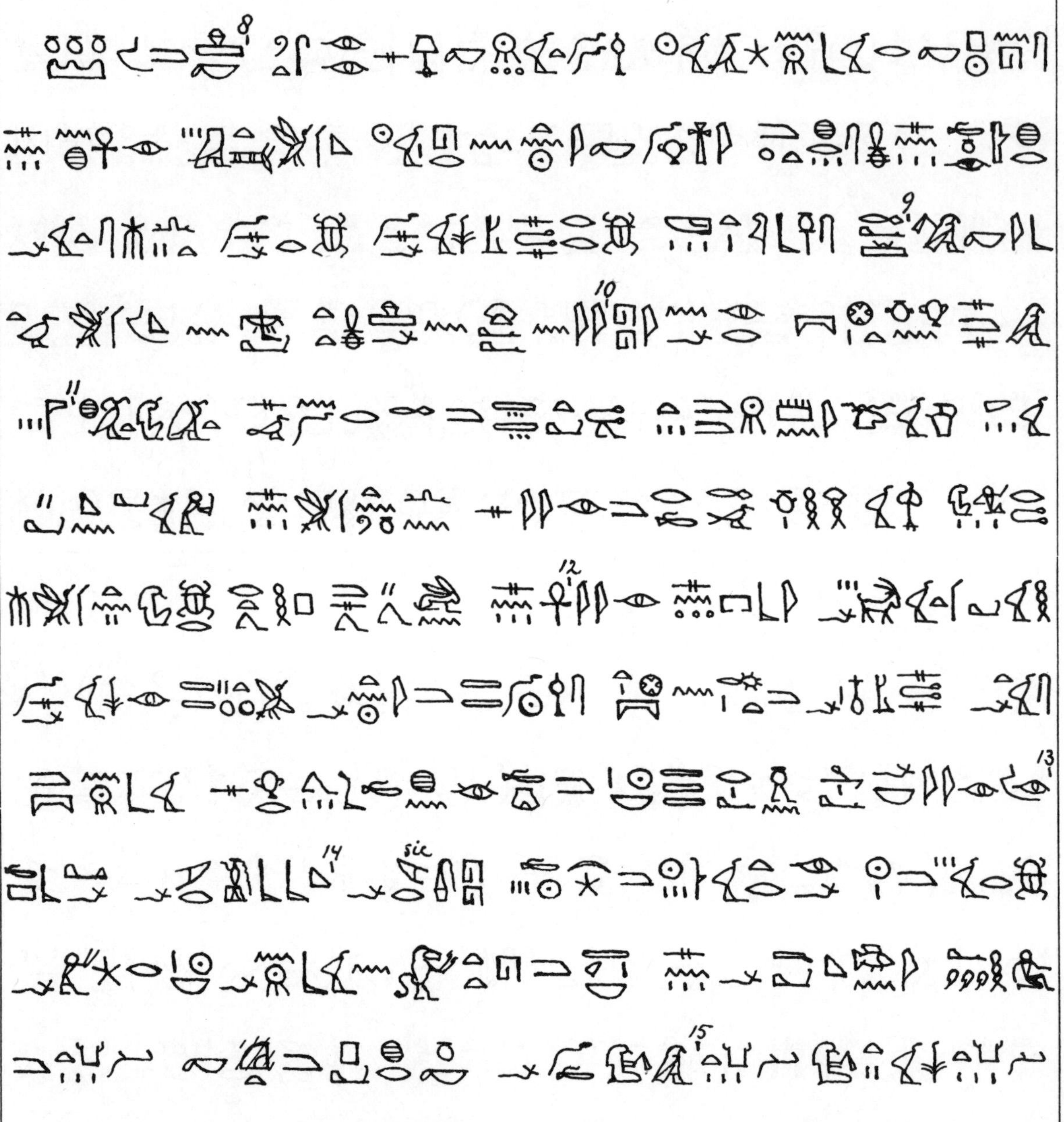

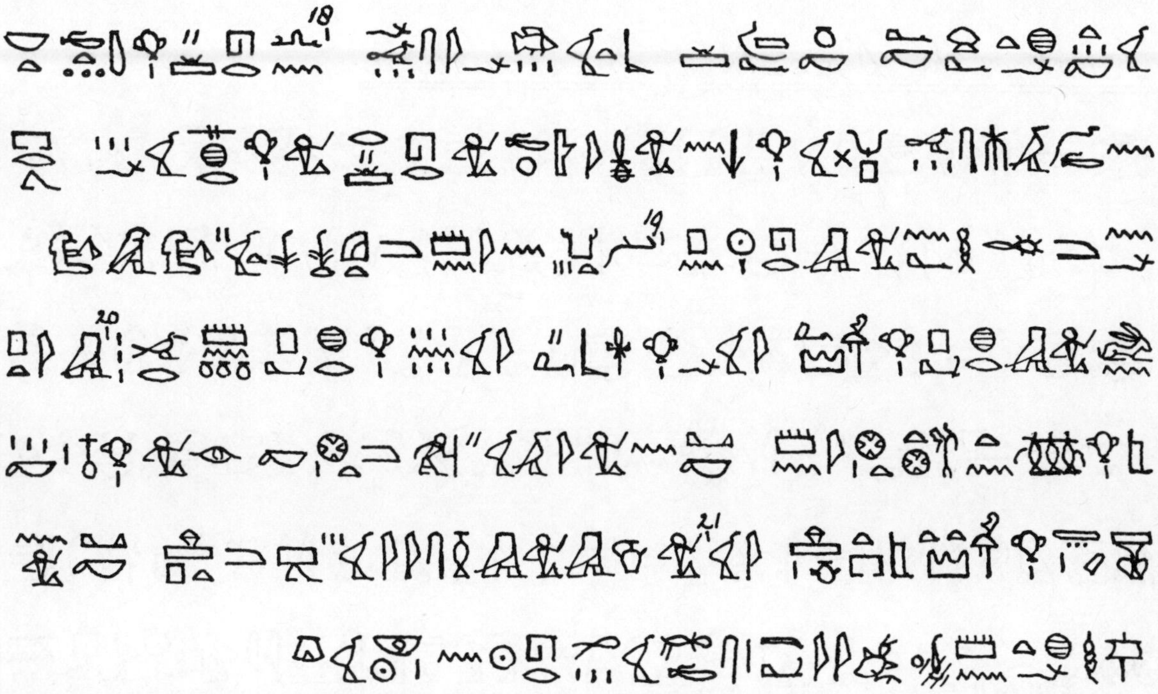

Magical spell for the protection of a baby.

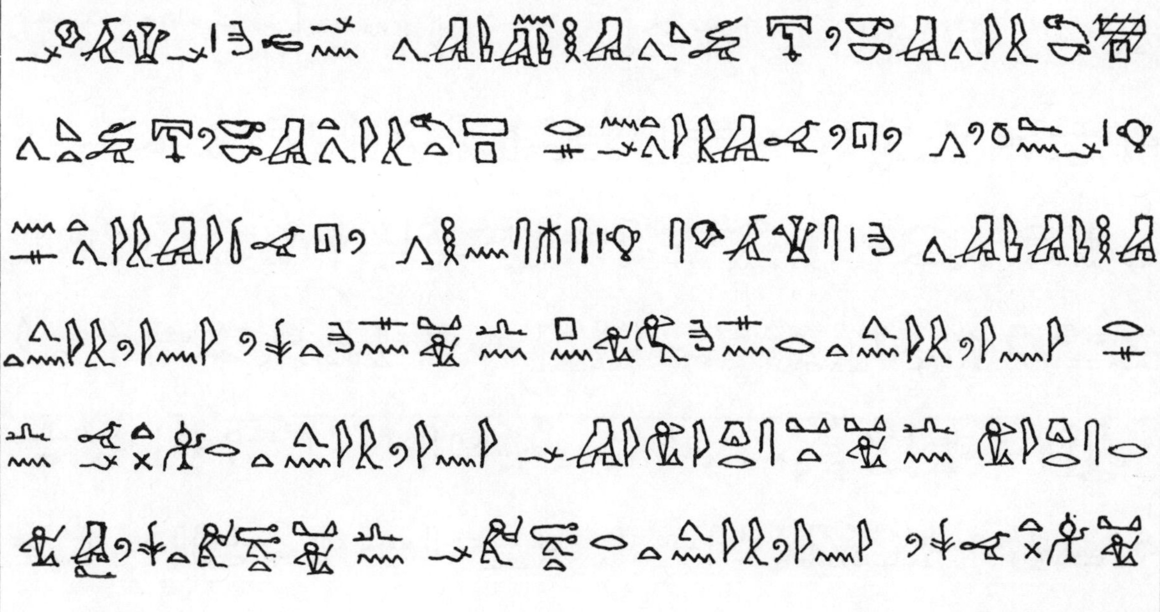

Book of the Dead 125, Introduction.

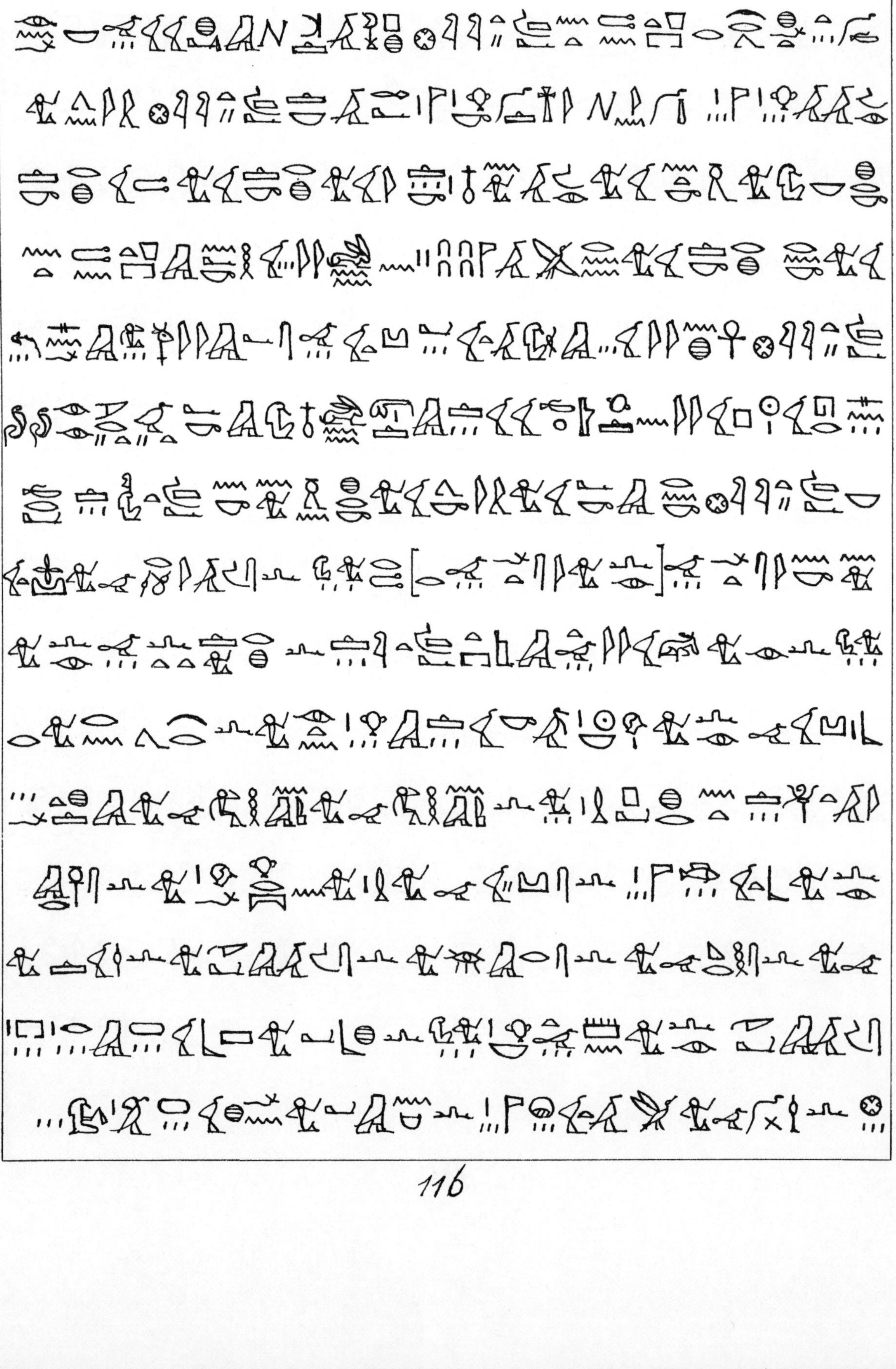

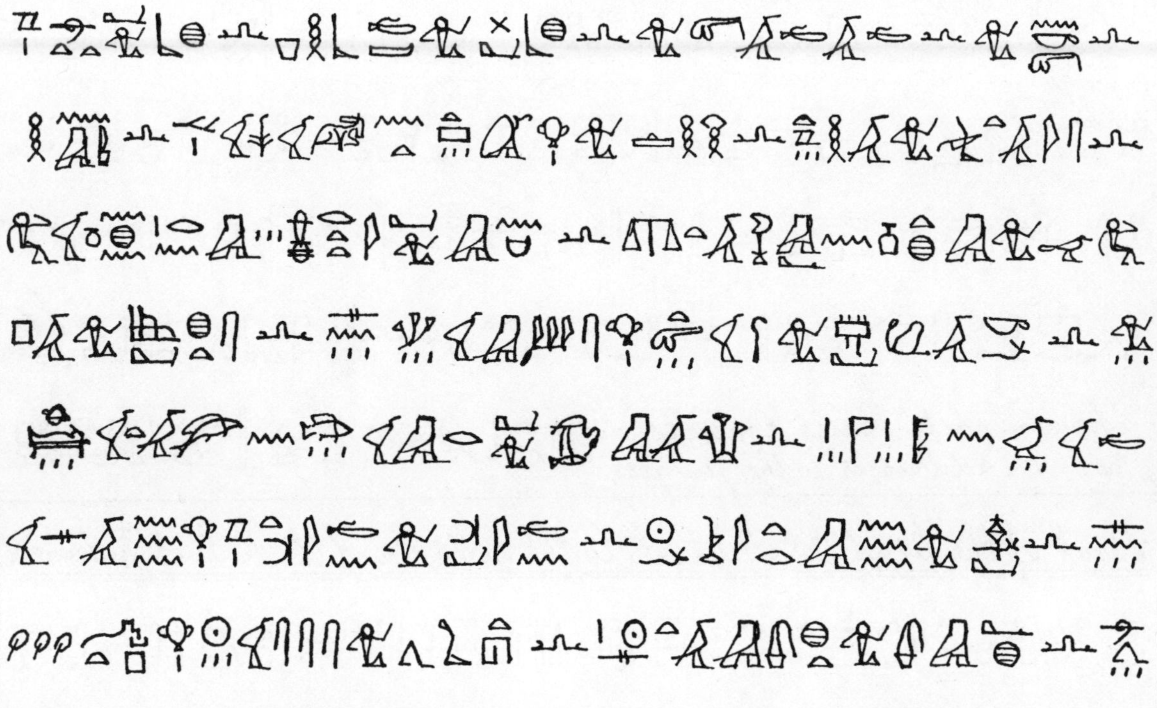

Book of the Dead 125, the Negative Confession.

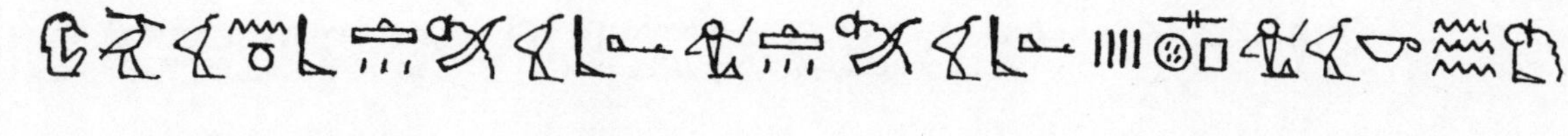

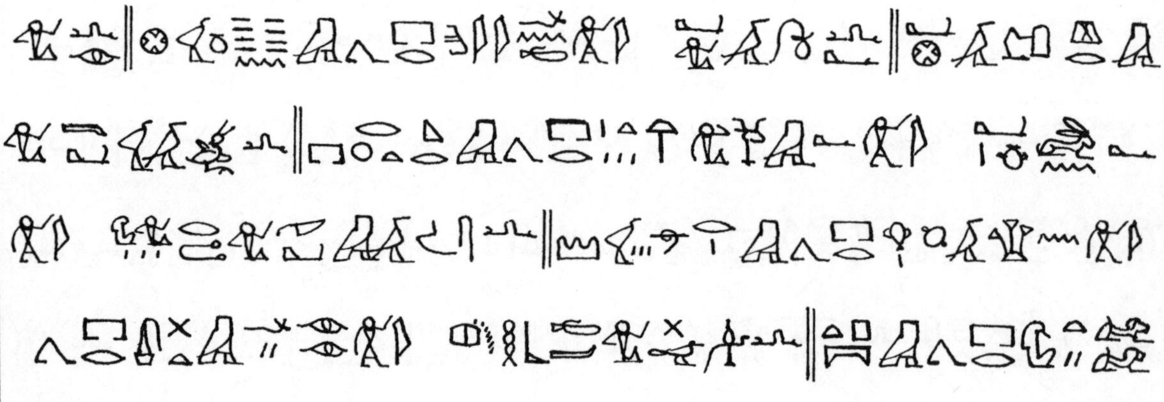

The complete series consists of 42 addresses to the Judges.

Book of the Dead 125, Address to the gods, etc. of the Hall of Judgment.

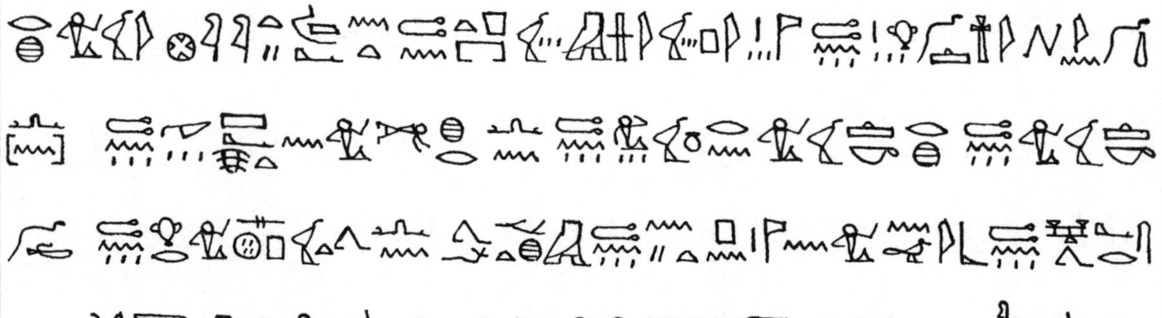

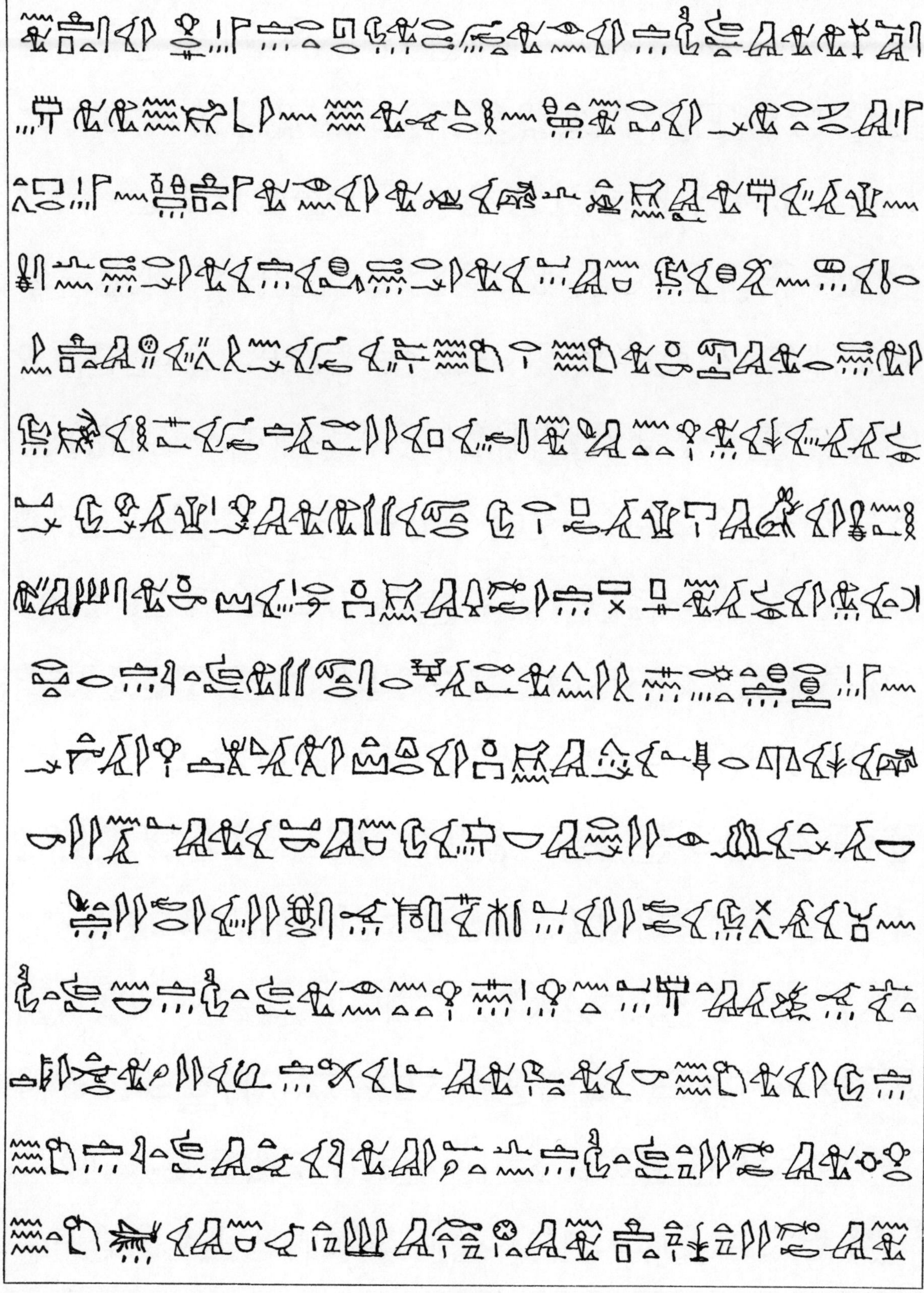

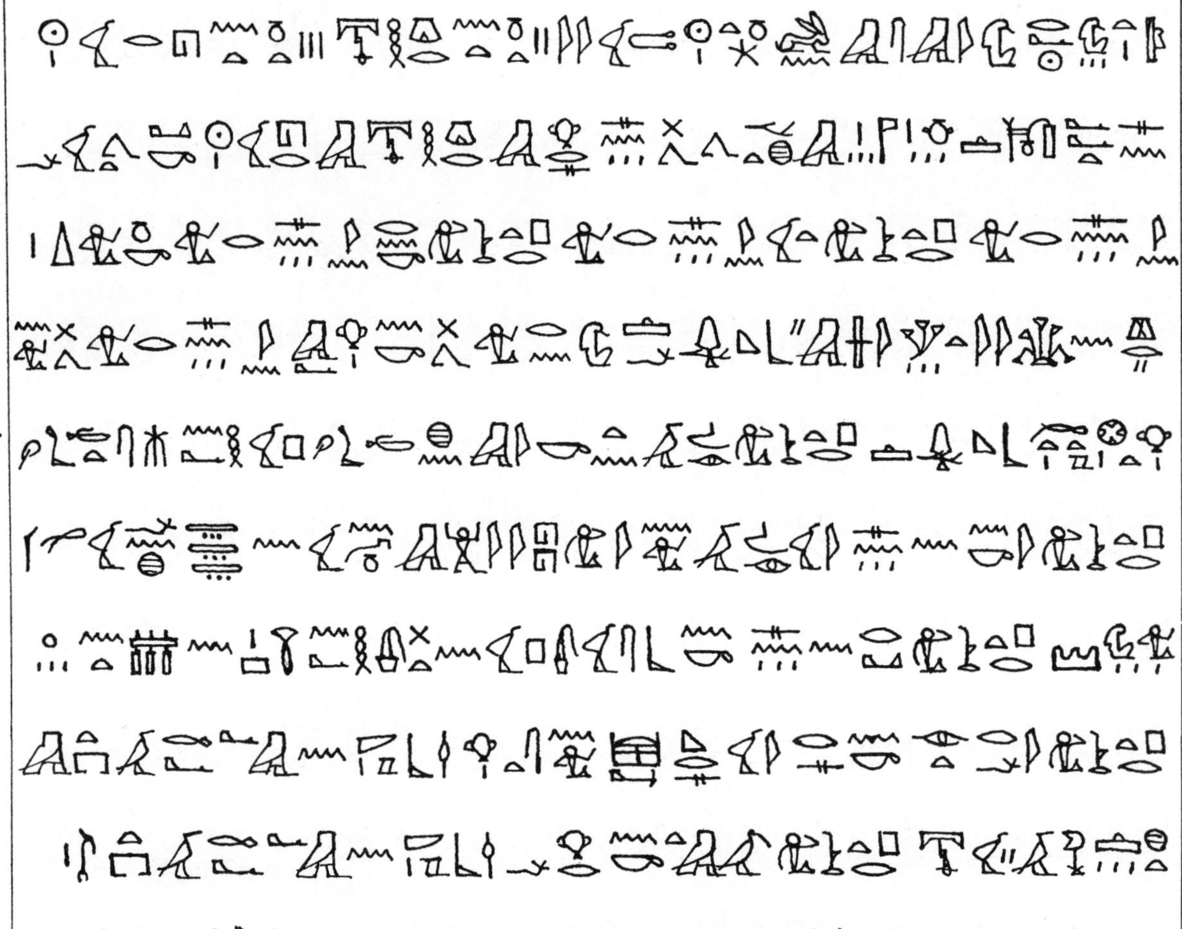

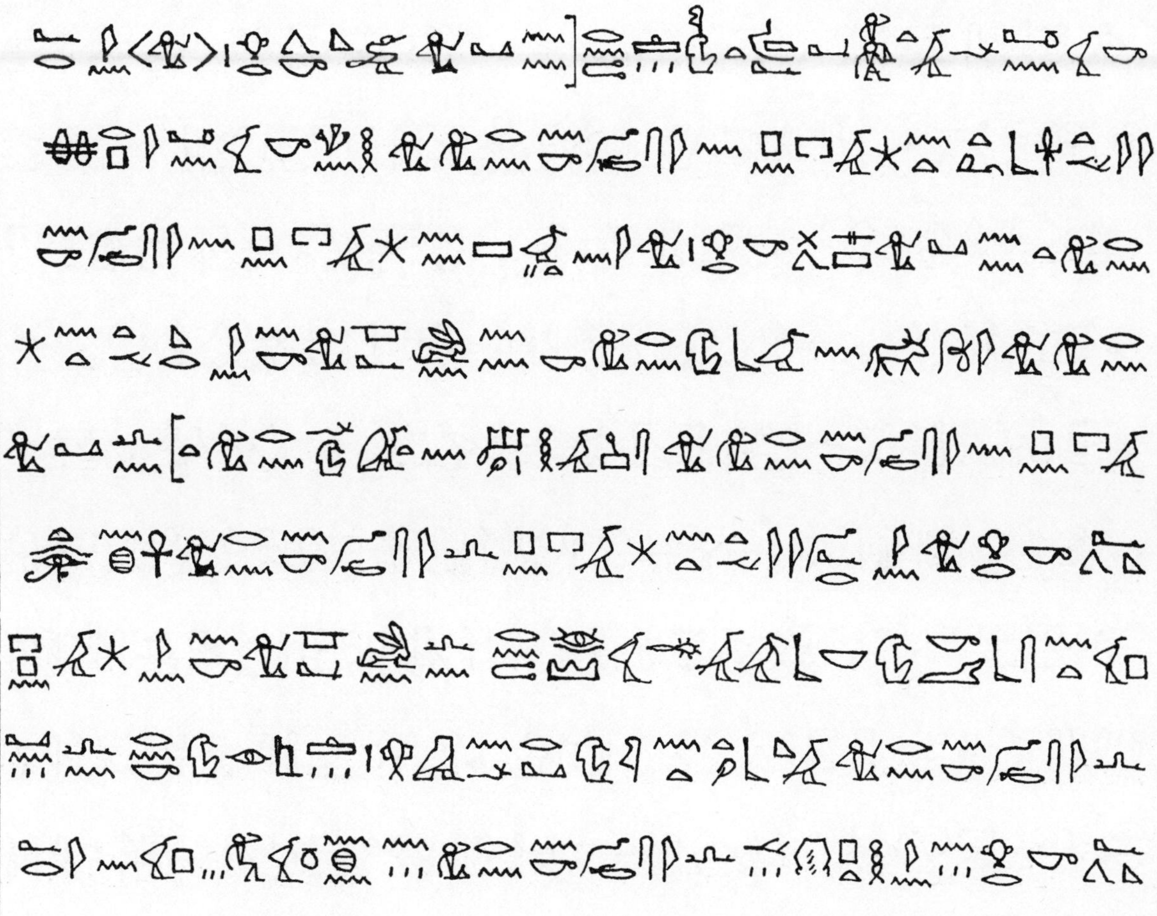

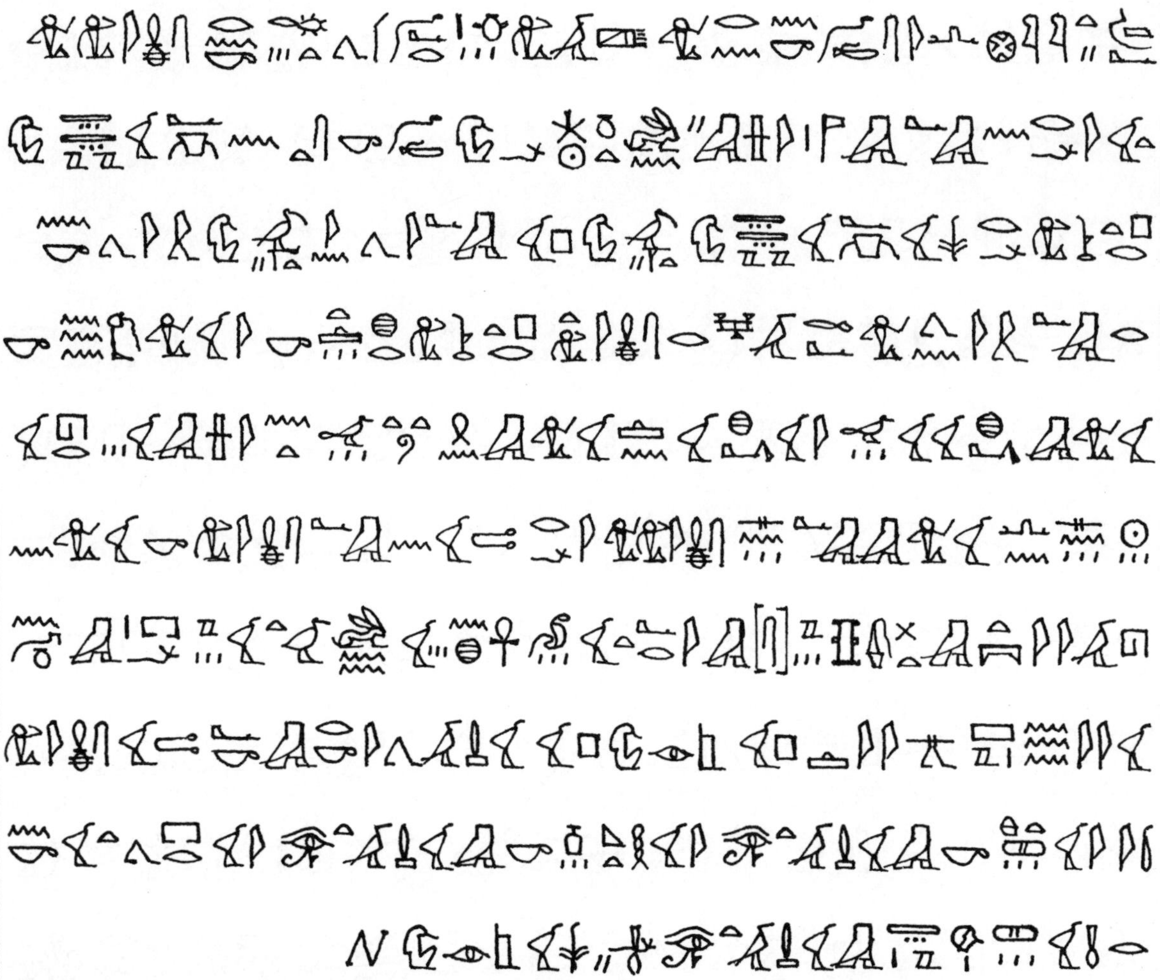

Book of the Dead 125, Rubric.

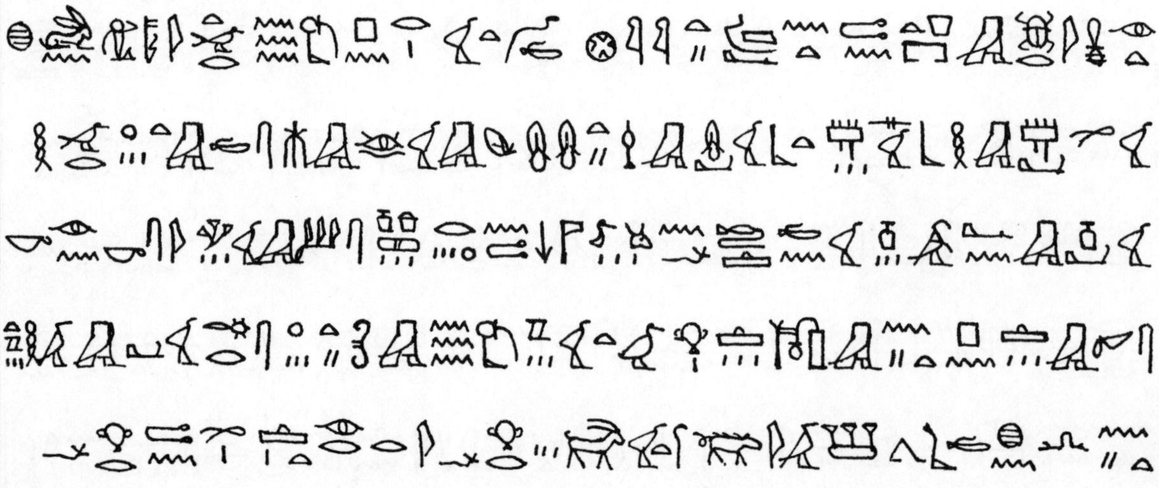

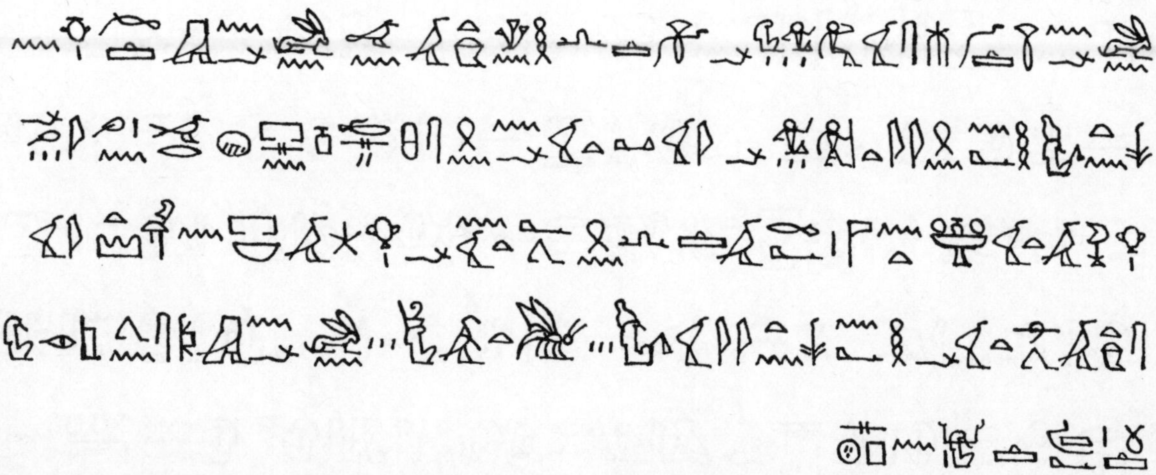

The myth of the Destruction of Mankind.

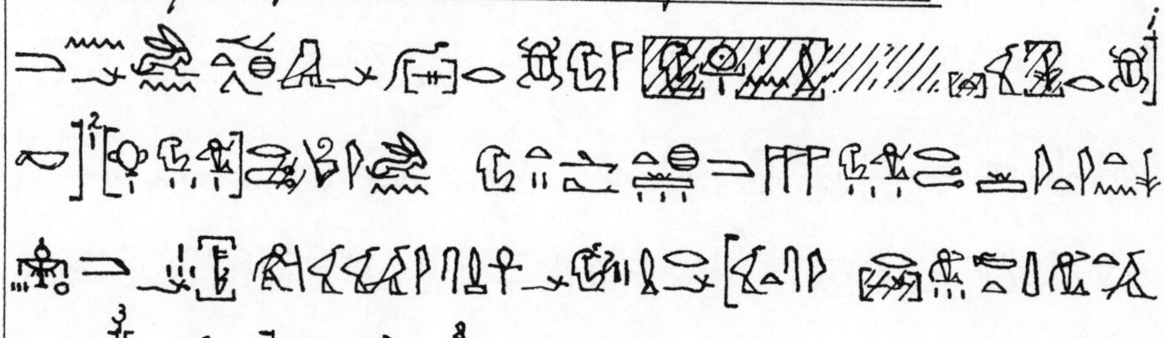

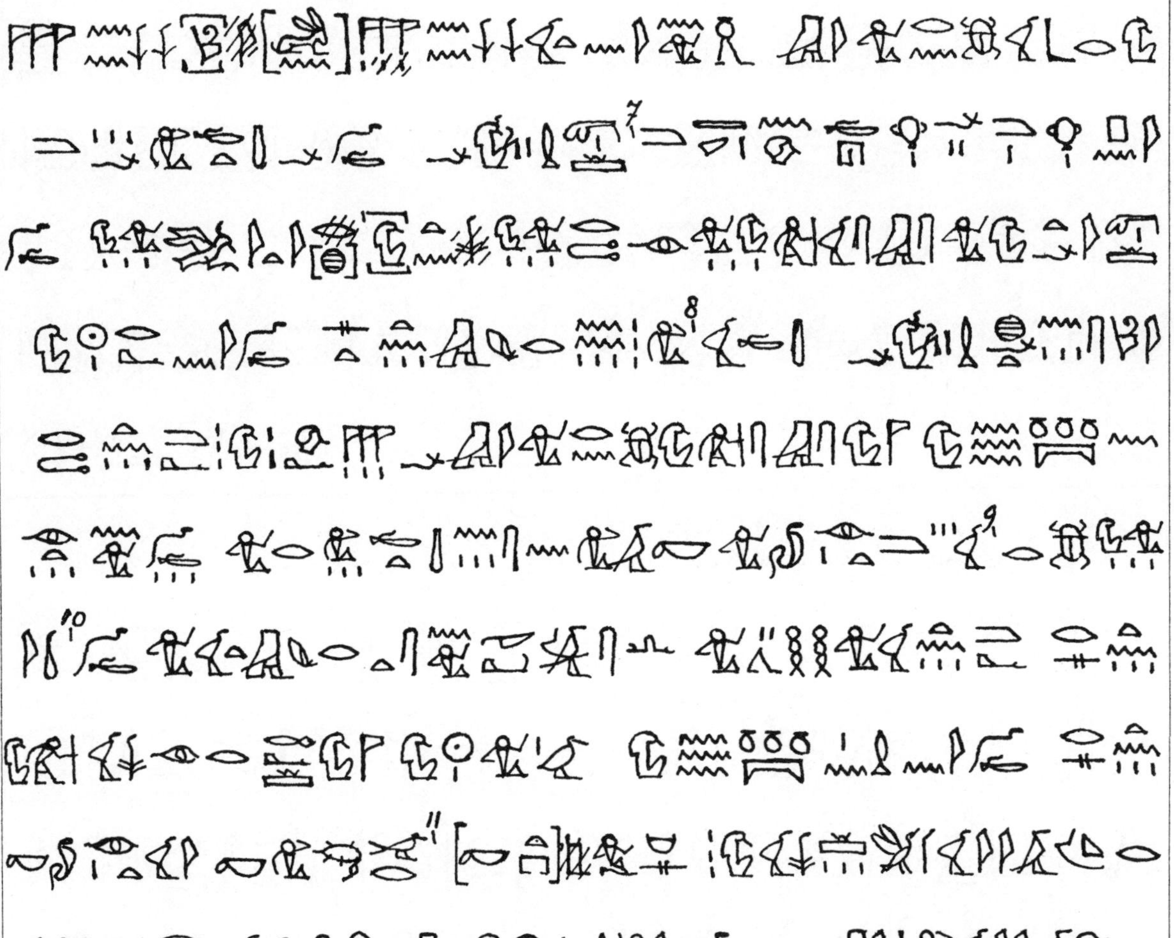

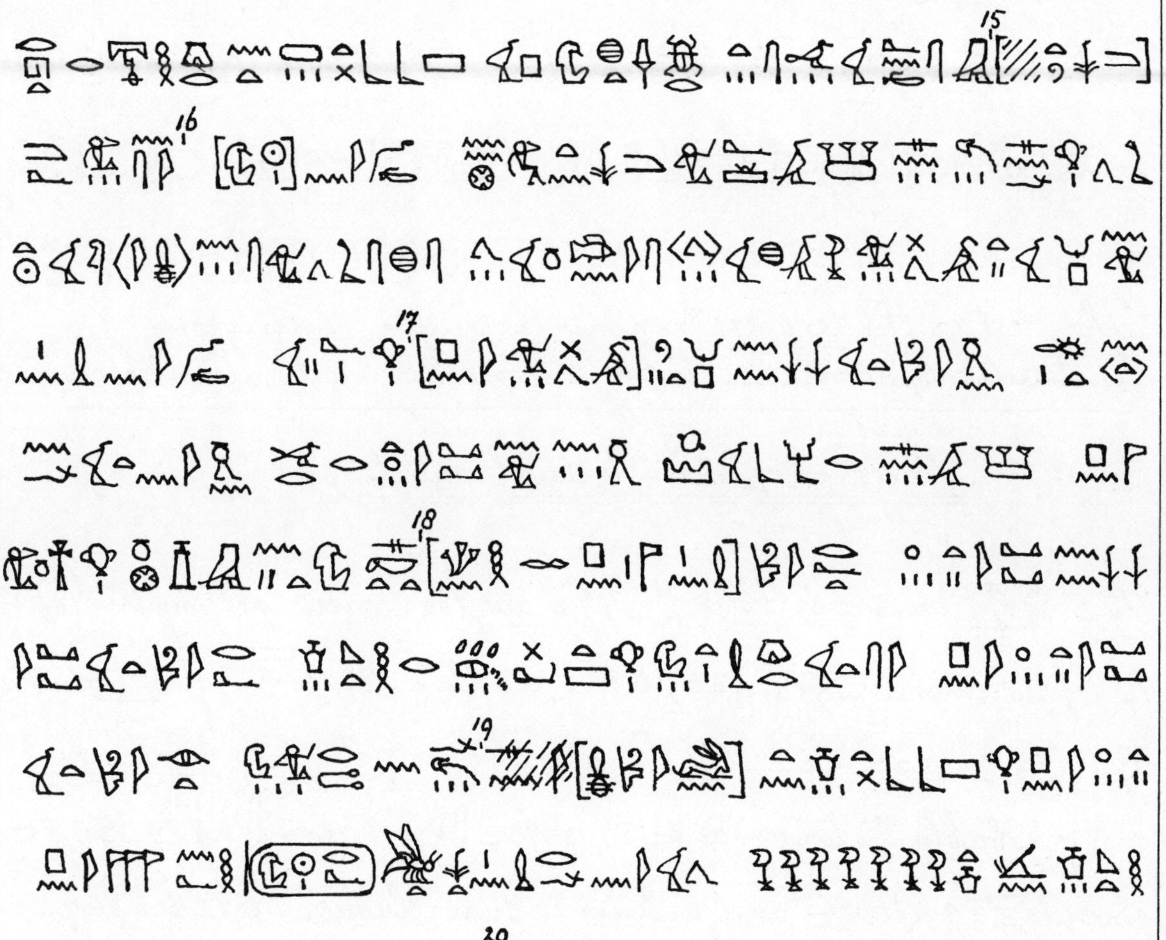

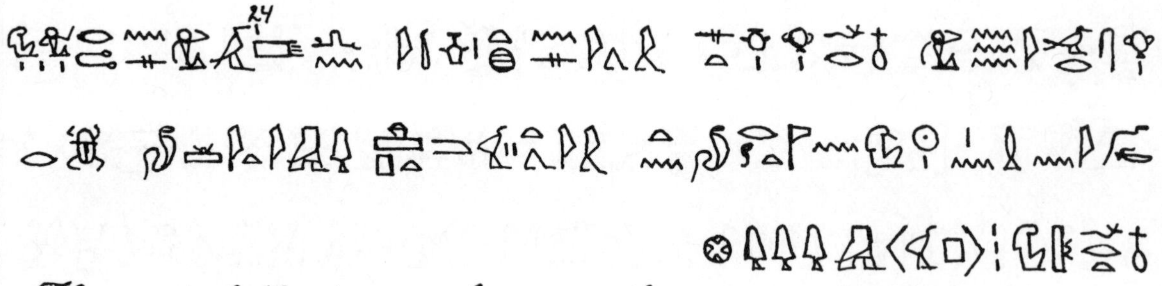

The rest of the text explaining the origin of religious institutions, names, etc. is for the greater part rather obscure.

Notes on purely textual matters.

47,5 *šfšf·t*, emend *šfšf·t*⟨[hieroglyphs]⟩ – 47,6 *gw*, the correct spelling is [hieroglyphs] 47,7 *f ḫw*, emend ⟨[hieroglyphs]⟩[hieroglyphs] – 47,8 [hieroglyphs], read [hieroglyphs] – 47,13 [hieroglyphs] for *šꜥ·t*, also 48,3 47,14 [hieroglyphs] emend [hieroglyphs] – 50,2 [hieroglyphs], also 52,6, for *grt* – 50,7 *iri·n·i n·i*?, but probably [hieroglyphs] for [hieroglyphs] as in 50,12.13 – [hieroglyphs], read [hieroglyphs] – 50,8 [hieroglyphs] emend [hieroglyphs]; [hieroglyphs] after [hieroglyphs] and in [hieroglyphs] is superfluous – 50,12 see 50,7 – 51,6 delete [hieroglyphs] of [hieroglyphs] – 51,15 read [hieroglyphs]⟨[hieroglyphs]⟩, see e.g. 46,13 – 52,6 *gt*, see 50,2 52,15 *3tp*, one [hieroglyphs] is superfluous – 53,15 emend [hieroglyphs] – 54,8 read [hieroglyphs] – 54,13 emend [hieroglyphs]⟨[hieroglyphs]⟩, see ll. 14 sqq. – 55,3 see 53,15 – 56,13 *ptri*, here and often (57,1; 58,14; 62,12) for *pri* – 56,15 *ḥrj*, correct form [hieroglyphs] – 57,6 restore [hieroglyphs] at beginning of l. 7 – 57,14 *ꜥnḫ·t*, delete one [hieroglyphs]. 58,2 *śkd·śn*, [hieroglyphs] ought to stand before the suffix – 58,5 restore [hieroglyphs] or [hieroglyphs] or [hieroglyphs] at beginning of l. 13 – 58,10 read [hieroglyphs], see 60,14 – 58,14 read [hieroglyphs] 58,15 [hieroglyphs] doubtful, perhaps [hieroglyphs] – 59,2 Amon, Amon-rē and the like obliterated by Echnaton, also 60,2.5; 61,5.8.15 – 59,4.13 read [hieroglyphs] – 59,12 *śšm·t*, delete last *š* –

60,2.5 see 59,2 – 60,9 read , see 62,2 – 60,12 after b3k·w restore or the like – 60,14 read , see 61,7; 62,10 – 60,14.15 , the ideogr. of the dom-palm was meant – 61,5.8.15 see 59,2 – 61,3 , a variant spelling of – 62,1/2 in dm3·ti is a late spelling for or – 62,2 for ? or insert (m hrj·w)? – 62,5 restore ; read ?; emend wn or – 62,8 read śdg – 62,10 restore , cf. 78,11 – 63,12 emend šfšf· ·k – 64,8 emend – 64,9 nḥ, omit ; a mistake for – 66,5 wdi, wrongly with instead of – 67,4 innj·t, normally – 67,13.14 read , cf. 69,9 – 67,14 , emend = 71,8.9 – 67,15 stands for – 68,4 , for – 68,6 emend – 68,7 (first sign of l. 30), read – 68,8 see 68,4; 70,11. 68,10 perhaps emend as in 70,10 – 68,14 read – 68,15 stands for – 69,1 read pri·t r – 69,8 emend – 69,9 , delete – 69,11 emend – 70,1 , read – 70,2 read – 70,3 correct (after ḥs·t) to – 70,3 emend – 70,12 dmd – 70,11 emend – 70,16 , an incomplete – 71,7 read – 71,11 after śdtj stands for ; is a mistake for 71,12 k3b·t; emend , see 70,3 – 72,1 , is a space-filler or does it belong to the number?; the original, vertical l. has – 72,7 h3·n·i, ought to come after – 73,4 the reading is due to Dévaud – 73 i.e. hieratic is certainly the right reading and not – 73,14 read for – 74,3 nh3·t, normally – 74,5

emend – 75,3 looks less strange in the original ; ,
emend ⟨ ⟩? – 75,4 emend – 75,13 (ı is space-filler as often in these inscriptions), read ⟨ ⟩ – 75,14 , emend ḫnmm·t – 75,16 emend ⟨ ⟩ and at end of l.6 perhaps ⟨ ⟩ – 76,1 is for 76,2 read š3k, is a mistake for – 76,4 ḥ3b – 76,5 read – 76,6 emend ⟨ ⟩ – 76,9 delete ib after w3ḥ, cf. Urk. IV 817,10.17 – 76,11 emend ⟨ ⟩, cf. 75,3 – 76,13 mistake for – 77,6 mistake for ; stands for nḥḥ – 77,8 emend ⟨ ⟩ – 77,12 read 79,13 , Late-Eg. spelling of M.-Eg – 79,14 delete in ḫntj·t – 81,1 see 79,13 – 82,13.14 words and phrases enclosed in ⟨ ⟩, these or similar words and phrases have been omitted in the Ms., passim – 85,1 emend ⟨ ⟩ ḫnmw, see 85,8.14 – 85,5 after ᶜ·wt·f insert , see 84,14 – 86,10 m mḥtj, it is, perhaps, not necessary to insert (collision of two m's) – 87,13 emend ⟨ ⟩, cf. the construction 88,2/3 (98,15), or ⟨ ⟩, 88,4.9 – 89,7 in š3sk·wt is a later addition – 89,12.14.15 im, ḥr, mnḫ inserted from Bt – 90,6 , R, Bt read – 90,10 w3t·n with repetition of before the suffix – 91,5 ⟨ ⟩ with R and 95,14 – 91,11 delete after ᶜḥᶜw – 92,11 R – 92,12 ? JEA IX 22 'sail without the mast' – 92,13 ⟨ ⟩ with R – 92,16 ⟨ ⟩ with R – 93,5 ⟨ ⟩ with R – 92,6 ⟨ etc.⟩ with R – 93,11 read – 93,16 ⟨ ⟩ with R – 94,8 ? or ? JEA IX 23 – 94,11 omit at beginning of l. (dittogr.) – 94,15 nḫt·ti, similarly 100,16, cf. 102,14 – 95,6 ⟨ ⟩ grammatically necessary – 95,13 the omission of ⟨ ⟩ in the Ms. can be defended as due to collision of two n's – 96,5 ⟨ ⟩ is necessary – 97,5 for – 97,6.7 emend – [To be continued in the commentary]